Sunset

BEST HOME PLANS

Luxury Homes

Stucco and stone façade of this grand two-story home projects
refinement and distinction. Inside, nearly all the ceilings are 10 feet high.
See plan DD-2952 on page 182.

Sunset Publishing Corporation ■ **Menlo Park, California**

SUNSET BOOKS
President and Publisher:
  Susan J. Maruyama
Director, Finance & Business
  Affairs: Gary Loebner
Director, Manufacturing & Sales
  Service: Lorinda Reichert
Director, Sales & Marketing:
  Richard A. Smeby
Editorial Director:
  Kenneth Winchester
Executive Editor:
  Bob Doyle
Assistant Editor:
  Kevin Freeland
Contributing Editor:
  Don Vandervort

**SUNSET PUBLISHING
CORPORATION**
Chairman: Jim Nelson
President/Chief Executive
  Officer: Robin Wolaner
Chief Financial Officer:
  James E. Mitchell
Publisher:
  Stephen J. Seabolt
Circulation Director:
  Robert I. Gursha
Editor, Sunset Magazine:
  William R. Marken

Photographers: Mark Englund/
HomeStyles: 4, 5; Philip Harvey:
10 top, back cover; Stephen Marley:
11 top left and right; Russ Widstrand:
10 bottom; Tom Wyatt: 11 bottom.

Cover: Pictured is plan HDS-99154
on page 140. Cover design by
Naganuma Design & Direction.
Photography by Mark Englund/
HomeStyles.

First printing April 1995
Copyright © 1995, Sunset Publishing
Corporation, Menlo Park, CA 94025.
First edition. All rights reserved, including
the right of reproduction in whole or in part
in any form.

ISBN 0-376-01138-6. Library of Congress
Catalog Card Number: 94-069960.
Printed in the United States.

For more information on Sunset's *Best Home
Plans Luxury Homes* or any other Sunset
book, call (800) 227-7346. For special sales,
bulk orders, and premium sales information,
call Sunset Custom Publishing Services at
(415) 324-5577.

A Dream Come True

Planning and building a house is one of life's most creative and rewarding challenges. Whether you're seriously considering building a new home or you're just dreaming about it, this book offers a wealth of inspiration and information to help you get started.

On the following pages, you'll learn how to plan and manage a home-building project—and how to ensure its success. Then you'll discover more than 200 proven home plans, designed for families just like yours by architects and professional designers. Peruse the pages and study the floor plans; you're sure to find a home that's just right for you. When you're ready to order blueprints, you can simply call or mail in your order, and you'll receive the plans within days.

Enjoy the adventure!

Dramatic rooflines and generous bay windows flanking a formal entry give this handsome home a stately presence. The plan features a formal dining room, an island kitchen, and a 10-foot-high living room. See plan DD-2513 on page 124.

Contents

In the Lap of Luxury   4

The Art of Building   6

Recruiting Your Home Team   8

Personalizing Stock Plans   10

What the Plans Include   12

Before You Order   14

Blueprint Order Form   15

Home Plans 16–224

Luxury Homes Under 2,500 Square Feet   16

Luxury Homes Over 2,500 Square Feet   120

In the Lap of Luxury

Achieving the home you and your family have always wanted is surely a dream come true. If that dream is within your reach, you'll appreciate the home plans presented here. These proven designs, created by some of America's foremost architects and designers, reflect style and elegance. Classic façades, island kitchens, stunning foyers, formal dining rooms, and luxurious master baths are just a few of the amenities you'll find. Moreover, these homes offer plenty of space for entertaining and family living. They're designed to be built with quality materials and distinctive detailing for durability and lasting beauty.

The two keys to success in building are capable project management and good design. The next few pages will walk you through some of the most important aspects of project management: you'll find an overview of the building process, directions for selecting the right plan and getting the most from it, and methods for successfully working with a builder and other professionals.

The balance of the book presents professionally designed stock plans. Once you find a plan that will work for you—perhaps with a few modifications made later to personalize it for your family—you can order construction blueprints for a fraction of the cost of a custom design, a savings of many thousands of dollars (see pages 12–15 for information on how to order).

Space abounds in this two-story beauty endowed with simple, classic lines. The main floor features a huge sunken living room. In addition to three large bedrooms upstairs, there's a luxurious master suite with a sitting area and a skylighted bath. See plan AX-87105 on page 191.

Handsome exterior detailing previews an interior that's both elegant and well conceived. Behind the central entry lie the family living and entertaining spaces. The master suite is on one side, a three-bedroom wing on the other. See plan HDS-99-171 on page 138.

Colonial-style home with contemporary comforts stands proud, its stature expressed by artful symmetry and two-story columns. Both the master suite and the vast living room access a rear porch and deck. See plan E-2800 on page 141.

Porte cochere greets guests at the entry of this stunning home, designed for entertaining. A sunken wet bar off the living room extends into the pool area. The master suite views the pool through a curved window wall. See plan HDS-99-154 on page 140.

The Art of Building

As you embark on your home-building project, think of it as a trip—clearly not a vacation but rather an interesting, adventurous, at times difficult expedition. Meticulous planning will make your journey not only far more enjoyable but also much more successful. By careful planning, you can avoid—or at least minimize—some of the pitfalls along the way.

Start with realistic expectations of the road ahead. To do this, you'll want to gain an understanding of the basic house-building process, settle on a design that will work for you and your family, and make sure your project is actually doable. By taking those initial steps, you can gain a clear idea of how much time, money, and energy you'll need to invest to make your dream come true.

The Building Process

Your role in planning and managing a house-building project can be divided into two parts: prebuilding preparation and construction management.

■ **Prebuilding preparation.** This is where you should focus most of your attention. In the hands of a qualified contractor whose expertise you can rely on, the actual building process should go fairly smoothly. But during most of the prebuilding stage, you're generally on your own. Your job will be to launch the project and develop a talented team that can help you bring your new home to fruition.

When you work with stock plans, the prebuilding process usually goes as follows:

First, you research the general area where you want to live, selecting one or more possible home sites (unless you already own a suitable lot). Then you choose a basic house design, with the idea that it may require some modification. Finally, you analyze the site, the design, and your budget to determine if the project is actually attainable.

If you decide that it is, you purchase the land and order blue-prints. If you want to modify them, you consult an architect, designer, or contractor. Once the plans are finalized, you request bids from contractors and arrange any necessary construction financing.

After selecting a builder and signing a contract, you (or your contractor) then file the plans with the building department. When the plans are approved, often several weeks—or even months—later, you're ready to begin construction.

■ **Construction management.** Unless you intend to act as your own contractor, your role during the building process is mostly one of quality control and time management. Even so, it's important to know the sequence of events and something about construction methods so you can discuss progress with your builder and prepare for any important decisions you may need to make along the way.

Decision-making is critical. Once construction begins, the builder must usually plunge ahead, keeping his carpenters and subcontractors progressing steadily. If you haven't made a key decision—which model bathtub or sink to install, for example—it can bring construction to a frustrating and expensive halt.

Usually, you'll make such decisions before the onset of building, but, inevitably, some issue or another will arise during construction. Being knowledgeable about the building process will help you anticipate and circumvent potential logjams.

Selecting a House Plan

Searching for the right plan can be a fun, interactive family experience—one of the most exciting parts of a house-building project. Gather the family around as you peruse the home plans in this book. Study the size, location, and configuration of each room; traffic patterns both inside the house and to the outdoors; exterior style; and how you'll use the available space. Discuss the pros and cons of the various plans.

Browse through pictures of homes in magazines to stimulate ideas. Clip the photos you like so you can think about your favorite options. When you visit the homes of friends, note special features that appeal to you. Also, look carefully at the homes in your neighborhood, noting their style and how they fit the site.

Mark those plans that most closely suit your ideals. Then, to narrow down your choices, critique each plan, using the following information as a guide.

■ **Overall size and budget.** How large a house do you want? Will the house you're considering fit your family's requirements? Look at the overall square footage and room sizes. If you have a hard time visualizing room sizes, measure some of the rooms in your present home and compare.

It's often better for the house to be a little too big than a little too small, but remember that every extra square foot will cost more money to build and maintain.

■ **Number and type of rooms.** Beyond thinking about the number of bedrooms and baths you want, consider your family's life-style and how you use space. Do you want both a family room and a living room? Do you need a formal dining space? Will you require some extra rooms, or "swing spaces," that can serve multiple purposes, such as a home office–guest room combination?

■ **Room placement and traffic patterns.** What are your preferences for locations of formal living areas, master bedroom, and children's rooms? Do you prefer a kitchen that's open to family areas or one that's private and out of the way? How much do you use exterior spaces and how should they relate to the interior?

Once you make those determinations, look carefully at the floor plan of the house you're considering to see if it meets your needs and if the traffic flow will be convenient for your family.

■ **Architectural style.** Have you always wanted to live in a Victorian farmhouse? Now is your chance to create a house that matches your idea of "home" (taking into account, of course, styles in your neighborhood). But don't let your preference for one particular architectural style dictate your home's floor plan. If the floor plan doesn't work for your family, keep looking.

■ **Site considerations.** Most people choose a site before selecting a plan—or at least they've zeroed in on the basic type of land where they'll situate their house. It sounds elementary, but choose a house that will fit the site.

When figuring the "footprint" of a house, you must know about any restrictions that will affect your home's height or proximity to the property lines. Call the local building department (look under city or county listings in the phone book) and get a very clear description of any restrictions, such as setbacks, height limits, and lot coverage, that will affect what you can build on the site (see "Working with City Hall," at right).

When you visit potential sites, note trees, rock outcroppings, slopes, views, winds, sun, neighboring homes, and other factors. All will impact on how your house works on a particular site.

Once you've narrowed down the choice of sites, consult an architect or building designer (see page 8) to help you evaluate how some potential houses will work on the sites you have in mind.

Is Your Project Doable?

Before you purchase land, make sure your project is doable. Although it's too early at this stage to pinpoint costs, making a few phone calls will help you determine whether your project is realistic. You'll be able to learn if you can afford to build the house, how long it will take, and what obstacles may stand in your way.

To get a ballpark estimate of cost, multiply a house's total square footage (of livable space) by the local average cost per square foot for new construction. (To obtain local averages, call a contractor, an architect, a realtor, or the local chapter of the National Association of Home Builders.) Some contractors may even be willing to give you a preliminary bid. Once you know approximate costs, speak to your lender to explore financing.

Working with City Hall

For any building project, even a minor one, it's essential to be familiar with building codes and other restrictions that can affect your project.

■ **Building codes,** generally implemented by the city or county building department, set the standards for safe, lasting construction. Codes specify minimum construction techniques and materials for foundations, framing, electrical wiring, plumbing, insulation, and all other aspects of a building. Although codes are adopted and enforced locally, most regional codes conform to the standards set by the national Uniform Building Code, Standard Building Code, or Basic Building Code. In some cases, local codes set more restrictive standards than national ones.

■ **Building permits** are required for home-building projects nearly everywhere. If you work with a contractor, the builder's firm should handle all necessary permits.

More than one permit may be needed; for example, one will cover the foundation, another the electrical wiring, and still another the heating equipment installation. Each will probably involve a fee and require inspections by building officials before work can proceed. (Inspections benefit *you*, as they ensure that the job is being done satisfactorily.) Permit fees are generally a percentage (1 to 1.5 percent) of the project's estimated value, often calculated on square footage.

It's important to file for the necessary permits. Failure to do so can result in fines or legal action against you. You can even be forced to undo the work performed. At the very least, your negligence may come back to haunt you later when you're ready to sell your house.

■ **Zoning ordinances,** particular to your community, restrict setbacks (how near to property lines you may build), your house's allowable height, lot coverage factors (how much of your property you can cover with structures), and other factors that impact design and building. If your plans don't conform to zoning ordinances, you can try to obtain a variance, an exception to the rules. But this legal work can be expensive and time-consuming. Even if you prove that your project won't negatively affect your neighbors, the building department can still refuse to grant the variance.

■ **Deeds and covenants** attach to the lot. Deeds set out property lines and easements; covenants may establish architectural standards in a neighborhood. Since both can seriously impact your project, make sure you have complete information on any deeds or covenants before you turn over a spadeful of soil.

It's a good idea to discuss your project with several contractors (see page 8). They may be aware of problems in your area that could limit your options—bedrock that makes digging basements difficult, for example. These conversations are actually the first step in developing a list of contractors from which you'll choose the one who will build your home.

Recruiting Your Home Team

A home-building project will inter-ject you and your family into the building business, an area that may be unfamiliar territory. Among the people you'll be working with are architects, designers, landscapers, contractors, and subcontractors.

Design Help

A qualified architect or designer can help you modify and personal-ize your home plan, taking into account your family's needs and budget and the house's style. In fact, you may want to consider consulting such a person while you're selecting a plan to help you articulate your needs.

Design professionals are capable of handling any or all aspects of the design process. For example, they can review your house plans, suggest options, and then provide rough sketches of the options on tracing paper. Many architects will even secure needed permits and negotiate with contractors or sub-contractors, as well as oversee the quality of the work.

Of course, you don't necessarily need an architect or designer to implement minor changes in a plan; although most contractors aren't trained in design, some can help you with modifications.

An open-ended, hourly-fee arrangement that you work out with your architect or designer allows for flexibility, but it often turns out to be more costly than working on a flat-fee basis. On a flat fee, you agree to pay a specific amount of money for a certain amount of work.

To find architects and designers, contact such trade associations as the American Institute of Architects (AIA), American Institute of Build-ing Designers (AIBD), American Society of Landscape Architects (ASLA), and American Society of Interior Designers (ASID). Although many professionals choose not to belong to trade associations, those who do have met the standards of their respective associations. For phone numbers of local branches, check the Yellow Pages.

■ **Architects** are licensed by the state and have degrees. They're trained in all facets of building design and construction. Although some can handle interior design and structural engineering, others hire specialists for those tasks.

■ **Building designers** are generally unlicensed but may be accredited by the American Institute of Building Designers. Their back-grounds are varied: some may be unlicensed architects in apprentice-ship; others are interior designers or contractors with design skills.

■ **Draftspersons** offer an economi-cal route to making simple changes on your drawings. Like building designers, these people may be unlicensed architect apprentices, engineers, or members of related trades. Most are accomplished at drawing up plans.

■ **Interior designers,** as their job title suggests, design interiors. They work with you to choose room fin-ishes, furnishings, appliances, and decorative elements. Part of their expertise is in arranging furnishings to create a workable space plan. Some interior designers are em-ployed by architectural firms; others work independently. Financial arrangements vary, depending on the designer's preference.

Related professionals are kitchen and bathroom designers, who con-centrate on fixtures, cabinetry, appliances, materials, and space planning for the kitchen and bath.

■ **Landscape architects, design-ers, and contractors** design out-door areas. Landscape architects are state-licensed to practice landscape design. A landscape designer usual-ly has a landscape architect's educa-tion and training but does not have a state license. Licensed landscape contractors specialize in garden construction, though some also have design skills and experience.

■ **Soils specialists and structural engineers** may be needed for proj-ects where unstable soils or uncom-mon wind loads or seismic forces must be taken into account. Any

structural changes to a house re-quire the expertise of a structural engineer to verify that the house won't fall down.

Services of these specialists can be expensive, but they're impera-tive in certain conditions to ensure a safe, sturdy structure. Your build-ing department will probably let you know if their services are re-quired.

General Contractors

To build your house, hire a licensed general contractor. Most states re-quire a contractor to be licensed and insured for worker's compensa-tion in order to contract a building project and hire other subcontrac-tors. State licensing ensures that contractors have met minimum training standards and have a spec-ified level of experience. Licensing does not guarantee, however, that they're good at what they do.

When contractors hire subcon-tractors, they're responsible for overseeing the quality of work and materials of the subcontractors and for paying them.

■ **Finding a contractor.** How do you find a good contractor? Start by getting referrals from people you know who have built or remodeled their home. Nothing beats a personal recommendation. The best contractors are usually busily moving from one satisfied client to another prospect, adver-tised only by word of mouth.

You can also ask local real estate brokers and lenders or even your building inspector for names of qualified builders. Experienced lumber dealers are another good source of names.

In the Yellow Pages, look under "Contractors–Building, General"; or call the local chapter of the National Association of Home Builders.

■ **Choosing a contractor.** Once you have a list of names of pro-spective builders, call several of them. On the telephone, ask first whether they handle your type of job and can work within your schedule. If they can, arrange a meeting with each one and ask them to be prepared with references of former clients and photos of previous jobs. Better still, meet them at one of their current work sites so you can get a glimpse of the quality of their work and how organized and thorough they are.

Take your plan to the meeting and discuss it enough to request a rough estimate (some builders will comply, while others will be reluctant to offer a ballpark estimate, preferring to give you a hard bid based on complete drawings). Don't hesitate to probe for advice or suggestions that might make building your house less expensive.

Be especially aware of each contractor's personality and how well you communicate. Good chemistry between you and your builder is a key ingredient for success.

Narrow down the candidates to three or four. Ask each for a firm bid, based on the exact same set of plans and specifications. For the bids to be accurate, your plans need to be complete and the specifications as precise as possible, call-

ing out particular appliances, fixtures, floorings, roofing material, and so forth. (Some of these are specified in a stock-plan set; others are not.)

Call the contractors' references and ask about the quality of their work, their relationship with their clients, their promptness, and their readiness to follow up on problems. Visit former clients to check the contractor's work firsthand.

Be sure your final candidates are licensed, bonded, and insured for worker's compensation, public liability, and property damage. Also, try to determine how financially solvent they are (you can call their bank and credit references). Avoid contractors who are operating hand-to-mouth.

Don't automatically hire the contractor with the lowest bid if you don't think you'll get along well or if you have any doubts about the quality of the person's work. Instead, look for both the most reasonable bid and the contractor with the best credentials, references, terms, and compatibility with your family.

A word about bonds: You can request a performance bond that guarantees that your job will be finished by your contractor. If the job isn't completed, the bonding company will cover the cost of hiring another contractor to finish it. Bonds cost from 2 to 6 percent of the value of the project.

Your Building Contract

A building contract (see below) binds and protects both you and your contractor. It isn't just a legal document. It's also a list of the expectations of both parties. The best way to minimize the possibility of misunderstandings and costly changes later on is to write down every possible detail. Whether the contract is a standard form or one composed by you, have an attorney look it over before both you and the contractor sign it.

The contract should clearly specify all the work that needs to be done, including particular materials and work descriptions, the time schedule, and method of payment. It should be keyed to the working drawings.

A Sample Building Contract

Project and participants. Give a general description of the project, its address, and the names and addresses of both you and the builder.

Construction materials. Identify all construction materials by brand name, quality markings (species, grades, etc.), and model numbers where applicable. Avoid the clause "or equal," which allows the builder to substitute other materials for your choices. For materials you can't specify now, set down a budget figure.

Time schedule. Include both start and completion dates and specify that work will be "continuous." Although a contractor cannot be responsible for delays caused by strikes and material shortages, your builder should assume responsibility for completing the project within a reasonable period of time.

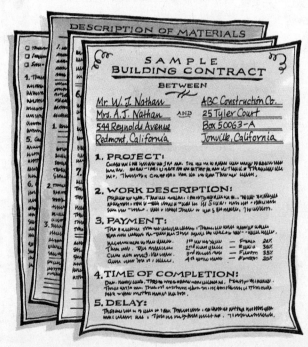

Work to be performed. State all work you expect the contractor to perform, from initial grading to finished painting.

Method and schedule of payment. Specify how and when payments are to be made. Typical agreements specify installment payments as particular phases of work are completed. Final payment is withheld until the job receives its final inspection and is cleared of all liens.

Waiver of liens. Protect yourself with a waiver of liens signed by the general contractor, the subcontractors, and all major suppliers. That way, subcontractors who are not paid for materials or services cannot place a lien on your property.

Personalizing Stock Plans

The beauty of buying stock plans for your new home is that they offer tested, well-conceived design at an affordable price. And stock plans dramatically reduce the time it takes to design a house, since the plans are ready when you are.

Because they were not created specifically for your family, stock plans may not reflect your personal taste. But it's not difficult to make revisions in stock plans that will turn your home into an expression of your family's personality. You'll surely want to add personal touches and choose your own finishes.

Ideally, the modifications you implement will be fairly minor. The more extensive the changes, the more expensive the plans. Major changes take valuable design time, and those that affect a house's structure may require a structural engineer's approval.

If you anticipate wholesale changes, such as moving a number of bearing walls or changing the roofline significantly, you may be better off selecting another plan. On the other hand, reconfiguring or changing the sizes of some rooms can probably be handled fairly easily.

Some structural changes may even be necessary to comply with local codes. Your area may have specific requirements for snow loads, energy codes, seismic or wind resistance, and so forth. Those types of modifications are likely to require the services of an architect or structural engineer.

Plan Modifications

Before you pencil in any changes, live with your plans for a while. Study them carefully—at your building site, if possible. Try to picture the finished house: how rooms will interrelate, where the sun will enter and at what angle, what the view will be from each window. Think about traffic patterns, access to rooms, room sizes, window and door locations, natural light, and kitchen and bathroom layouts.

Typical changes might involve adding windows or skylights to bring in natural light or capture a view. Or you may want to widen a hallway or doorway for roomier access, extend a room, eliminate doors, or change window and door sizes. Perhaps you'd like to shorten a room, stealing the gained space for a large closet. Look closely at the kitchen; it's not difficult to reconfigure the layout if it makes the space more convenient for you.

Above all, take your time—this is your home and it should reflect your taste and needs. Make your changes now, during the planning stage. Once construction begins, it will take crowbars, hammers, saws, new materials, and, most significantly, time to alter the plans. Because changes are not part of your building contract, you can count on them being expensive extras once construction begins.

Specifying Finishes

One way to personalize a house without changing its structure is to substitute your favorite finishes for those specified on the plan.

Would you prefer a stuccoed exterior rather than the wood siding shown on the plan? In most cases, this is a relatively easy change. Do you like the look of a wood shingle roof rather than the composition shingles shown on the plan? This, too, is easy. Perhaps you would like to change the windows from sliders to casements, or upgrade to high-efficiency glazing. No problem. Many of those kinds of changes can be worked out with your contractor.

Inside, you may want hardwood where vinyl flooring is shown. In fact, you can—and should—choose types, colors, and styles of floorings, wall coverings, tile, plumbing fixtures, door hardware, cabinetry, appliances, lighting fixtures, and other interior details, for it's these materials that will personalize your home. For help in making selections, consult an architect or interior designer (see page 8).

Each material you select should be spelled out clearly and precisely in your building contract.

Finishing touches can transform a house built from stock plans into an expression of your family's taste and style. Clockwise, from far left: Colorful tilework and custom cabinetry enliven a bathroom (Design: Osburn Design); highly organized closet system maximizes storage space (Architect: David Jeremiah Hurley); low-level deck expands living space to outdoor areas (Landscape architects: The Runa Group, Inc.); built-ins convert the corner of a guest room into a home office (Design: Lynn Williams of The French Connection); French country cabinetry lends style and old-world charm to a kitchen (Design: Garry Bishop/Showcase Kitchens).

What the Plans Include

Complete construction blueprints are available for every house shown in this book. Clear and concise, these detailed blueprints are designed by licensed architects or members of the American Institute of Building Designers (AIBD). Each plan is designed to meet standards set down by nationally recognized building codes (the Uniform Building Code, Standard Building Code, or Basic Building Code) at the time and for the area where they were drawn.

Remember, however, that every state, county, and municipality has its own codes, zoning requirements, ordinances, and building regulations. Modifications may be necessary to comply with such local requirements as snow loads, energy codes, seismic zones, and flood areas.

Although blueprint sets vary depending on the size and complexity of the house and on the individual designer's style, each set may include the elements described below and shown at right.

■ **Exterior elevations** show the front, rear, and sides of the house, including exterior materials, details, and measurements.

■ **Foundation plans** include drawings for a full, partial, or daylight basement, crawlspace, pole, pier, or slab foundation. All necessary notations and dimensions are included. (Foundation options will vary for each plan. If the plan you choose doesn't have the type of foundation you desire, a generic conversion diagram is available.)

■ **Detailed floor plans** show the placement of interior walls and the dimensions of rooms, doors, windows, stairways, and similar elements for each level of the house.

■ **Cross sections** show details of the house as though it were cut in slices from the roof to the foundation. The cross sections give the home's construction, insulation, flooring, and roofing details.

■ **Interior elevations** show the specific details of cabinets (kitchen, bathroom, and utility room), fireplaces, built-in units, and other special interior features.

■ **Roof details** give the layout of rafters, dormers, gables, and other roof elements, including clerestory windows and skylights. These details may be shown on the elevation sheet or on a separate diagram.

■ **Schematic electrical layouts** show the suggested locations for switches, fixtures, and outlets. These details may be shown on the floor plan or on a separate diagram.

■ **General specifications** provide instructions and information regarding excavation and grading, masonry and concrete work, carpentry and woodwork, thermal and moisture protection, drywall, tile, flooring, glazing, and caulking and sealants.

Other Helpful Building Aids

In addition to the construction information on every set of plans, you can buy the following guides.

■ **Reproducible blueprints** are helpful if you'll be making changes to the stock plan you've chosen. These blueprints are original line drawings produced on erasable, reproducible paper for the purpose of modification. When alterations are complete, working copies can be made.

■ **Itemized materials list** details the quantity, type, and size of materials needed to build your home. (This list is extremely helpful in obtaining an accurate construction bid. It's not intended for use to order materials.)

■ **Mirror-reverse plans** are useful if you want to build your home in the reverse of the plan that's shown. Because the lettering and dimensions read backwards, be sure to buy at least one regular-reading set of blueprints.

■ **Description of materials** gives the type and quality of materials suggested for the home. This form may be required for obtaining FHA or VA financing.

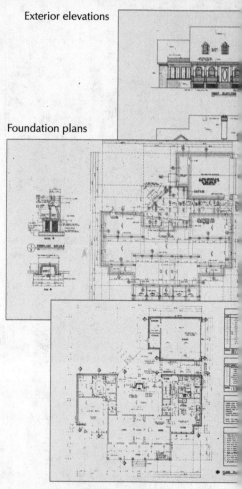

Exterior elevations

Foundation plans

Detailed floor plans

■ **How-to diagrams** for plumbing, wiring, solar heating, framing and foundation conversions show how to plumb, wire, install a solar heating system, convert plans with 2 by 4 exterior walls to 2 by 6 construction (or vice versa), and adapt a plan for a basement, crawlspace, or slab foundation. These diagrams are not specific to any one plan.

NOTE: Due to regional variations, local availability of materials, local codes, methods of installation, and individual preferences, detailed heating, plumbing, and electrical specifications are not included on plans. The duct work, venting, and other details will vary, depending on the heating and cooling system you use and the type of energy that operates it. These details and specifications are easily obtained from your builder or local supplier.

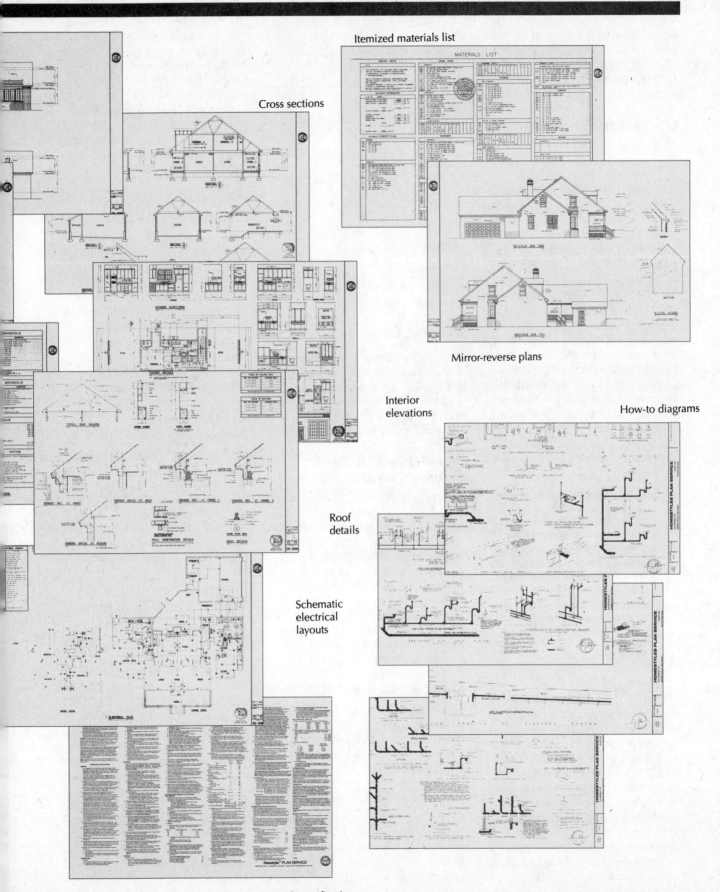

Itemized materials list

Cross sections

Mirror-reverse plans

Interior elevations

How-to diagrams

Roof details

Schematic electrical layouts

General specifications

Before You Order

Once you've chosen the one or two house plans that work best for you, you're ready to order blueprints. Before filling in the form on the facing page, note the information that follows.

How Many Blueprints Will You Need?

A single set of blueprints will allow you to study a home design in detail. You'll need more for obtaining bids and permits, as well as some to use as reference at the building site. If you'll be modifying your home plan, order a reproducible set (see page 12).

Figure you'll need at least one set each for yourself, your builder, the building department, and your lender. In addition, some subcontractors—foundation, plumber, electrician, and HVAC—may also need at least partial sets. If they do, ask them to return the sets when they're finished. The chart below can help you calculate how many sets you're likely to need.

Blueprint Checklist

____ Owner's set(s)

____ Builder usually requires at least three sets: one for legal documentation, one for inspections, and a minimum of one set for subcontractors.

____ Building department requires at least one set. Check with your local department before ordering.

____ Lending institution usually needs one set for a conventional mortgage, three sets for FHA or VA loans.

____ TOTAL SETS NEEDED

Blueprint Prices

The cost of having an architect design a new custom home typically runs from 5 to 15 percent of the building cost, or from $5,000 to $15,000 for a $100,000 home. A single set of blueprints for the plans in this book ranges from $295 to $505, depending on the house's size. Working with these drawings, you can save enough on design fees to add a deck, a swimming pool, or a luxurious kitchen.

Pricing is based on "total finished living space." Garages, porches, decks, and unfinished basements are not included.

Price Code (Size)	1 Set	4 Sets	7 Sets	Reproducible Set
A (under 1,500 sq. ft.)	$295	$345	$380	$455
B (1,500-1,999 sq. ft.)	$330	$380	$415	$490
C (2,000-2,499 sq. ft.)	$365	$415	$450	$525
D (2,500-2,999 sq. ft.)	$400	$450	$485	$560
E (3,000-3,499 sq. ft.)	$435	$485	$520	$595
F (3,500-3,999 sq. ft.)	$470	$520	$555	$630
G (4,000 sq. ft. and up)	$505	$555	$590	$665

Building Costs

Building costs vary widely, depending on a number of factors, including local material and labor costs and the finishing materials you select. For help estimating costs, see "Is Your Project Doable?" on page 7.

Foundation Options & Exterior Construction

Depending on your site and climate, your home will be built with a slab, pier, pole, crawlspace, or basement foundation. Exterior walls will be framed with either 2 by 4s or 2 by 6s, determined by structural and insulation standards in your area. Most contractors can easily adapt a home to meet the foundation and/or wall requirements for your area. Or ask for a conversion how-to diagram (see page 12).

Service & Blueprint Delivery

Service representatives are available to answer questions and assist you in placing your order. Every effort is made to process and ship orders within 48 hours.

Returns & Exchanges

Each set of blueprints is specially printed and shipped to you in response to your specific order; consequently, requests for refunds cannot be honored. However, if the prints you order cannot be used, you may exchange them for another plan from any Sunset home plan book. For an exchange, you must return all sets of plans within 30 days. A nonrefundable service charge will be assessed for all exchanges; for more information, call the toll-free number on the facing page. Note: Reproducible sets cannot be exchanged.

Compliance with Local Codes & Regulations

Because of climatic, geographic, and political variations, building codes and regulations vary from one area to another. These plans are authorized for your use expressly conditioned on your obligation and agreement to comply strictly with all local building codes, ordinances, regulations, and requirements, including permits and inspections at time of construction.

Architectural & Engineering Seals

With increased concern about energy costs and safety, many cities and states now require that an architect or engineer review and "seal" a blueprint prior to construction. To find out whether this is a requirement in your area, contact your local building department.

License Agreement, Copy Restrictions & Copyright

When you purchase your blueprints, you are granted the right to use those documents to construct a single unit. All the plans in this publication are protected under the Federal Copyright Act, Title XVII of the United States Code and Chapter 37 of the Code of Federal Regulations. Each designer retains title and ownership of the original documents. The blueprints licensed to you cannot be used by or resold to any other person, copied, or reproduced by any means. The copying restrictions do not apply to reproducible blueprints. When you buy a reproducible set, you may modify and reproduce it for your own use.

Blueprint Order Form

Complete this order form in just three easy steps. Then mail in your order or, for faster service, call toll-free.

1. Blueprints & Accessories

BLUEPRINT CHART

Price Code	1 Set	4 Sets	7 Sets	Reproducible Set*
A	$295	$345	$380	$455
B	$330	$380	$415	$490
C	$365	$415	$450	$525
D	$400	$450	$485	$560
E	$435	$485	$520	$595
F	$470	$520	$555	$630
G	$505	$555	$590	$665

Prices subject to change

*A reproducible set is produced on erasable paper for the purpose of modification. It is only available for plans with prefixes A, AG, AGH, AH, AHP, APS, AX, B, C, CPS, DCL, DD, DW, E, EOF, FB, GL, GML, GSA, H, HDG, HDS, HFL, J, K, KLF, LMB, LRD, M, NW, OH, PH, PI, S, SDG, THD, U, UDG, V.

Mirror-Reverse Sets: $40 surcharge. From the total number of sets you ordered above, choose the number you want to be reversed. *Note: All writing on mirror-reverse plans is backwards. Order at least one regular-reading set.*

Itemized Materials List: One set $40; each additional set $10. Details the quantity, type, and size of materials needed to build your home.

Description of Materials: Sold in a set of two for $40 (for use in obtaining FHA or VA financing).

Typical How-To Diagrams: One set $15; two sets $25; three sets $35; four sets $40. General guides on plumbing, wiring, and solar heating, plus information on how to convert from one foundation or exterior framing to another. *Note: These diagrams are not specific to any one plan.*

2. Sales Tax & Shipping

Determine your subtotal and add appropriate local state sales tax, plus shipping and handling (see chart below).

SHIPPING & HANDLING

	1–3 Sets	4–6 Sets	7 or More Sets	Reproducible Set
U.S. Regular (4–6 working days)	$15.00	$17.50	$20.00	$15.00
U.S. Express (2–3 working days)	$27.50	$30.00	$32.50	$27.50
Canada Regular (2–3 weeks)	$15.00	$17.50	$20.00	$15.00
Canada Express (4–6 working days)	$27.50	$32.50	$37.50	$27.50
Overseas/Airmail (7–10 working days)	$52.50	$62.50	$72.50	$52.50

3. Customer Information

Choose the method of payment you prefer. Include check, money order, or credit card information, complete name and address portion, and mail to:

Sunset/HomeStyles Plan Service
P.O. Box 50670
Minneapolis, MN 55405

FOR FASTER SERVICE
CALL 1-800-547-5570

SS11

COMPLETE THIS FORM

Plan Number _____ Price Code _____

Foundation _____
(Review your plan carefully for foundation options—basement, pole, pier, crawlspace, or slab. Many plans offer several options; others offer only one.)

Number of Sets: $_____
- [ ] One Set   (See chart at left)
- [ ] Four Sets
- [ ] Seven Sets
- [ ] One Reproducible Set

Additional Sets _____ $_____
                              ($40 each)

Mirror-Reverse Sets _____ $_____
                                   ($40 surcharge)

Itemized Materials List $_____
Only available for plans with prefixes AH, AHP, APS*, AX*, B*, C, CAR, CDG*, CPS, DD*, DW, E, FB, GSA, H, HDG, HFL, I*, J, K, LMB*, LRD, N, NW*, P, PH, R, S, THD, U, UDG, VL. *Not available on all plans. Please call before ordering.

Description of Materials $_____
Only available for plans with prefixes AHP, C, DW, H, HFL, J, K, LMB, P, PH, VL.

Typical How-To Diagrams $_____
- [ ] Plumbing [ ] Wiring [ ] Solar Heating [ ] Foundation & Framing Conversion

SUBTOTAL $_____

SALES TAX $_____

SHIPPING & HANDLING $_____

GRAND TOTAL $_____

- [ ] Check/money order enclosed (in U.S. funds)
- [ ] VISA   [ ] MasterCard   [ ] AmEx   [ ] Discover

Credit Card # _____ Exp. Date _____

Signature _____

Name _____

Address _____

City _____ State ____ Country _____

Zip _____ Daytime Phone (____) _____

- [ ] Please check if you are a contractor.

Mail form to: Sunset/HomeStyles Plan Service
                    P.O. Box 50670
                    Minneapolis, MN 55405

Or fax to: (612) 338-1626

FOR FASTER SERVICE
CALL 1-800-547-5570

SS11

Vaulted Ceilings Expand Interior

- A dignified exterior and a gracious, spacious interior combine to make this an outstanding plan for today's families.
- A step down from the vaulted entry, the living room offers a 12-ft.-high vaulted ceiling brightened by an arch-top boxed window and a nice fireplace.
- The vaulted dining room ceiling rises to more than 15 ft., and sliding glass doors open to a unique central atrium.
- The island kitchen shares a snack bar with the bayed nook and provides easy service to the dining room.
- The spacious family room boasts a sloped ceiling that peaks at 18 ft. and a woodstove that warms the entire area.
- The master suite is first-class all the way, with a spacious sleeping room and an opulent bath, which features a walk-in closet, a sunken garden tub, a separate shower and a skylighted dressing area with a dual-sink vanity.
- Two secondary bedrooms have window seats and share another full bath.

Plans P-7697-4A & -4D

Bedrooms: 3	Baths: 2
Living Area:	
Main floor (crawlspace version)	2,003 sq. ft.
Main floor (basement version)	2,030 sq. ft.
Total Living Area:	**2,003/2,030 sq. ft.**
Daylight basement	2,015 sq. ft.
Garage	647 sq. ft.
Exterior Wall Framing:	2x6
Foundation Options:	**Plan #**
Daylight basement	P-7697-4D
Crawlspace	P-7697-4A

(All plans can be built with your choice of foundation and framing. A generic conversion diagram is available. See order form.)

BLUEPRINT PRICE CODE:	C

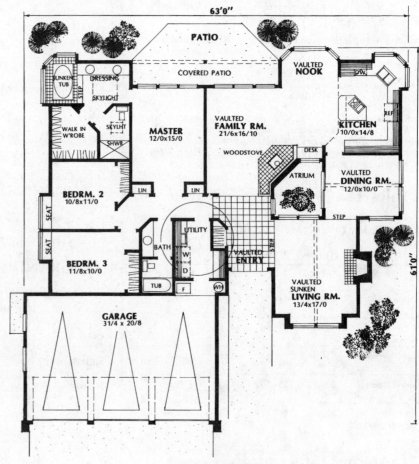

MAIN FLOOR

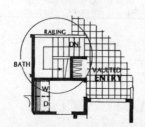

BASEMENT STAIRWAY LOCATION

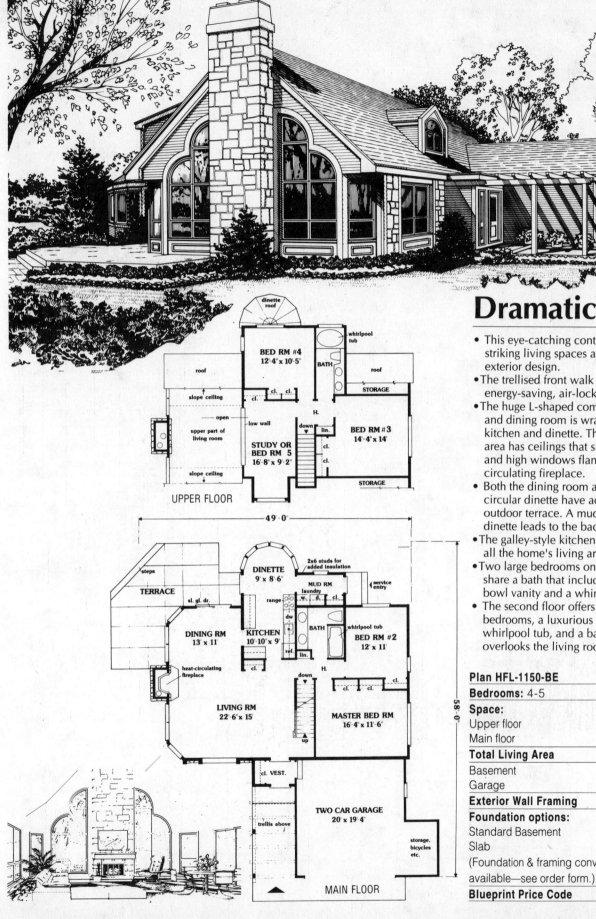

Dramatic Living

- This eye-catching contemporary features striking living spaces and a dramatic exterior design.
- The trellised front walk leads to an energy-saving, air-lock entry vestibule.
- The huge L-shaped combination living and dining room is wrapped around the kitchen and dinette. The living/dining area has ceilings that slope up to16 ft. and high windows flanking a heat-circulating fireplace.
- Both the dining room and the semi-circular dinette have access to a large outdoor terrace. A mud room off the dinette leads to the backyard.
- The galley-style kitchen is convenient to all the home's living areas.
- Two large bedrooms on the first floor share a bath that includes a double-bowl vanity and a whirlpool tub.
- The second floor offers two more bedrooms, a luxurious bath with an oval whirlpool tub, and a balcony study that overlooks the living room.

Plan HFL-1150-BE

Bedrooms: 4-5	Baths: 2
Space:	
Upper floor	656 sq. ft.
Main floor	1,345 sq. ft.
Total Living Area	**2,001 sq. ft.**
Basement	1,359 sq. ft.
Garage	467 sq. ft.
Exterior Wall Framing	2x6

Foundation options:
Standard Basement
Slab
(Foundation & framing conversion diagram available—see order form.)

Blueprint Price Code	C

European Charm

- This distinguished European home offers today's most luxurious features.
- In the formal living and dining rooms, 15-ft. vaulted ceilings add elegance.
- The informal areas are oriented to the rear of the home, entered through French doors in the foyer. The family room features a 12-ft. tray ceiling, a fireplace with an adjoining media center and a view of a backyard deck.

- The open kitchen and breakfast area is bright and cheerful, with a window wall and French-door deck access.
- Double doors lead into the luxurious master suite, which showcases a 14-ft. vaulted ceiling and a see-through fireplace that is shared with the spa bath. The splashy bath includes a dual-sink vanity, a separate shower and a wardrobe closet and dressing area.
- Two more bedrooms, one with private deck access, and a full bath are located on the opposite side of the home.
- Unless otherwise mentioned, 9-ft. ceilings enhance every room.

Plan APS-2006	
Bedrooms: 3	**Baths:** 2
Living Area:	
Main floor	2,006 sq. ft.
Total Living Area:	**2,006 sq. ft.**
Standard basement	2,006 sq. ft.
Garage	448 sq. ft.
Exterior Wall Framing:	2x4

Foundation Options:

Standard basement
Slab
(All plans can be built with your choice of foundation and framing. A generic conversion diagram is available. See order form.)

BLUEPRINT PRICE CODE:	C

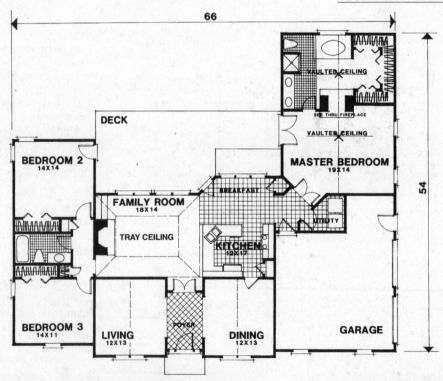

MAIN FLOOR

Ever-Popular Floor Plan

- Open living spaces that are well integrated with outdoor areas give this plan its popularity.
- The covered porch ushers guests into a roomy entry that separates the formal entertaining areas.
- Double doors open to the huge family room, which boasts a 13-ft. vaulted ceiling accented by rustic beams, a raised-hearth fireplace and built-in book-shelves. Glass doors lead to a covered porch and an adjoining patio, creating a perfect poolside setting.
- A bayed eating area is open to the family room, separated only by a decorative half-wall, and features a large china hutch and great views. The adjacent kitchen has an angled sink for easy service to the family room and the eating area. The utility room and the garage are close by.
- The master suite is secluded to the rear of the home, with a private bath and access to the patio. The two remaining bedrooms share a dual-access bath.

Plan E-2000	
Bedrooms: 3	**Baths:** 2
Living Area:	
Main floor	2,009 sq. ft.
Total Living Area:	**2,009 sq. ft.**
Garage and storage	550 sq. ft.
Exterior Wall Framing:	2x4

Foundation Options:

Crawlspace

Slab

(All plans can be built with your choice of foundation and framing. A generic conversion diagram is available. See order form.)

BLUEPRINT PRICE CODE:	C

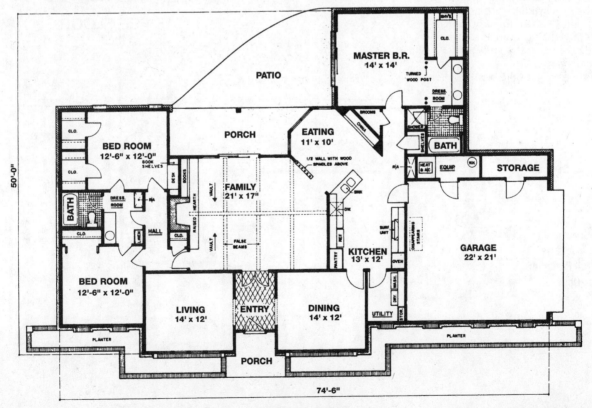

MAIN FLOOR

Updated Colonial

- This home offers Colonial styling on the outside, with an updated, ultra-modern floor plan inside.
- Guests are welcomed into a formal gallery that leads to all of the main-floor living areas. The large living room and the formal dining room flank the gallery. Optional folding doors open the living room to the family room.
- The family room features an inviting fireplace as its hub and sliding-door access to a backyard terrace.
- The kitchen is located for easy service to the formal dining room as well as the bayed dinette. A mudroom/laundry room and a powder room are nearby.
- Upstairs, the master suite boasts a private bath and a wall of closets. Three unique secondary bedrooms share a hall bath, which has a dual-sink vanity.

Plan K-274-M

Bedrooms: 4	Baths: 2½
Living Area:	
Upper floor	990 sq. ft.
Main floor	1,025 sq. ft.
Total Living Area:	**2,015 sq. ft.**
Standard basement	983 sq. ft.
Garage and storage	520 sq. ft.
Exterior Wall Framing:	2x4 or 2x6

Foundation Options:

Standard basement

Slab

(All plans can be built with your choice of foundation and framing. A generic conversion diagram is available. See order form.)

BLUEPRINT PRICE CODE:	C

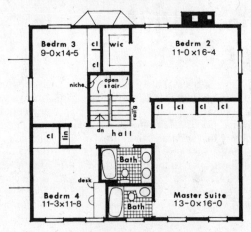

UPPER FLOOR

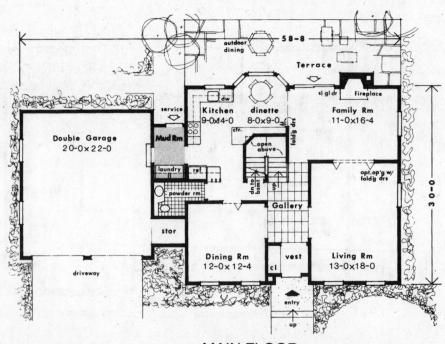

MAIN FLOOR

Plan K-274-M

PRICES AND DETAILS ON PAGES 12-15

French Garden Design

- A creative, angular design gives this traditional French garden home an exciting, open and airy floor plan.
- Guests enter through a covered, columned porch that opens into the large, angled living and dining rooms.
- High 12-ft. ceilings highlight the living and dining area, which also features corner windows, a wet bar, a cozy fireplace and access to a huge covered backyard porch.
- The angled walk-through kitchen, also with a 12-ft.-high ceiling, offers plenty of work space and an adjoining informal eating nook that faces a delightful private courtyard. The nearby utility area has extra freezer space, a walk-in pantry and garage access.
- The home's bedrooms are housed in two separate wings. One wing boasts a luxurious master suite, which features a large walk-in closet, an angled tub and a separate shower.
- Two large bedrooms in the other wing share a hall bath. Each bedroom has a walk-in closet.

Plan E-2004

Bedrooms: 3	Baths: 2
Living Area:	
Main floor	2,023 sq. ft.
Total Living Area:	**2,023 sq. ft.**
Garage	484 sq. ft.
Storage	87 sq. ft.
Exterior Wall Framing:	2x6

Foundation Options:

Crawlspace

Slab

(All plans can be built with your choice of foundation and framing. A generic conversion diagram is available. See order form.)

BLUEPRINT PRICE CODE: C

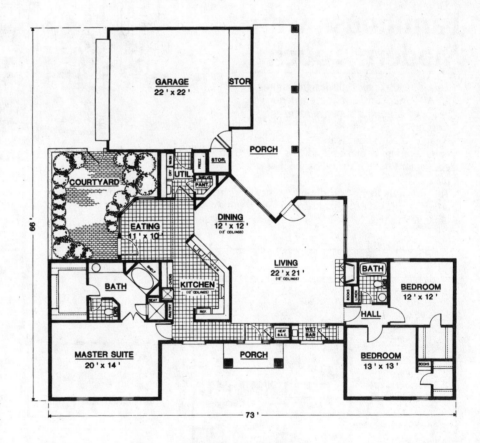

MAIN FLOOR

Farmhouse with Modern Touch

- This classic center-hall design features an All-American Farmhouse exterior wrapped around a super-modern interior.
- A large family room features a built-in entertainment center and adjoins a convenient dinette for quick family meals.
- The spacious living and dining rooms adjoin to provide abundant space for large gatherings.
- An inviting porch leads into a roomy foyer which highlights a curved staircase.
- The second floor features a deluxe master suite and three secondary bedrooms.

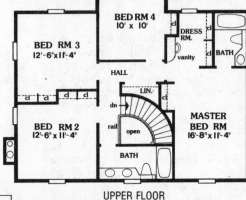

VIEW INTO LIVING ROOM FROM FOYER.

UPPER FLOOR

BED RM 4
10' x 10'

DRESS. RM.

BATH

BED RM 3
12'-6"x11'-4"

HALL

BED RM 2
12'-6" x 11'-4"

LIN.

dn

rail

open

vanity

MASTER BED RM
16'-8" x 11'-4"

BATH

UPPER FLOOR

MAIN FLOOR

60'-0"

35'-6"

TERRACE

sliding glass doors

s.   dw.

range

KITCHEN
10'-8" x 10'

ref.

LAV.

DINING RM
12'-6" x 11'-6"

DINETTE
8'-8" x 8'-8"

sliding glass doors

service entry

MUD RM

cl

LAUNDRY
d.   w.

TWO CAR GARAGE
21'-4" x 19'-8"

heat-circulating fireplace

dn

railing

open

FAMILY RM
16' x 12'-2"(avg.)

entertainment center

LIVING RM
19'-8"x 12'-6"

FOYER

up

cl

high ceiling

PORCH

MAIN FLOOR

Plan HFL-1040-MB

Bedrooms: 4	Baths: 2½
Space:	
Upper floor	936 sq. ft.
Main floor	1,094 sq. ft.
Total Living Area	**2,030 sq. ft.**
Basement	1,022 sq. ft.
Garage	420 sq. ft.
Exterior Wall Framing	2x6

Foundation options:
Standard Basement
Slab
(Foundation & framing conversion diagram available—see order form.)

Blueprint Price Code	C

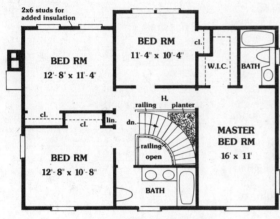

2x6 studs for
added insulation

BED RM
12'-8" x 11'-4"

BED RM
11'-4" x 10'-4"

cl.

W.I.C.

BATH

cl.

cl.

lin.

BED RM
12'-8" x 10'-8"

H.

railing

planter

dn.

railing
open

MASTER
BED RM
16' x 11'

BATH

UPPER FLOOR

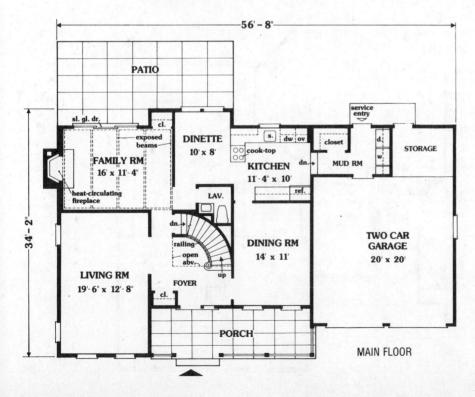

56'-8"

PATIO

sl. gl. dr.

cl.

exposed
beams

DINETTE
10' x 8'

s.

dw

ov

cook-top

service
entry

closet

d.

w.

STORAGE

34'-2"

FAMILY RM
16' x 11'-4"

KITCHEN
11'-4" x 10'

dn.

MUD RM

heat-circulating
fireplace

LAV.

ref.

dn.

railing
open
abv.

DINING RM
14' x 11'

TWO CAR
GARAGE
20' x 20'

LIVING RM
19'-6" x 12'-8"

FOYER

up

cl.

PORCH

MAIN FLOOR

Distinctive Colonial Farmhouse

- Although a casual living theme flows throughout this farmhouse, elegance is not forgotten.
- A beautiful circular stair ascends from the central foyer to the bedrooms on the upper level.
- Formal living and dining rooms flank the foyer.
- The informal family room at the rear captures an Early American style with exposed beams, wood paneling and a brick fireplace wall. Sliding glass doors provide access to the adjoining patio.
- A sunny dinette opens to an efficiently arranged kitchen with a handy laundry room near the garage entrance.
- A decorative railing and a planter adorn the second-floor balcony that overlooks the foyer below. Four generous-sized bedrooms and two baths share this level.

Plan HFL-1010-CR

Bedrooms: 4	Baths: 2 ½
Space:	
Upper floor	932 sq. ft.
Main floor	1,099 sq. ft.
Total Living Area	**2,031 sq. ft.**
Basement	998 sq. ft.
Garage and storage	476 sq. ft.
Exterior Wall Framing	2x4

Foundation options:
Standard Basement
Slab
(Foundation & framing conversion diagram available—see order form.)

Blueprint Price Code	C

Charming One-Story

- The charming facade of this home conceals an exciting angled interior with many accesses to the outdoors.
- At the center of the floor plan is a spacious family activity area that combines the Great Room, the breakfast room and the kitchen.
- The sunny sunken Great Room features a 12½-ft. cathedral ceiling and an exciting two-sided fireplace. The adjacent breakfast room offers French doors to a covered backyard patio.

- The unique angled kitchen has a bright sink, a serving bar and plenty of counter space. Across the hall are the dining room, the laundry room and access to the three-car garage.
- The secluded master bedroom boasts a 12½-ft. cathedral ceiling, a roomy walk-in closet and French doors to a private covered patio. The lavish master bath has a bright garden tub, a separate shower and a dual-sink vanity.
- The secondary bedrooms both have walk-in closets. The rear-facing bedroom has patio access through its own full bath. The parlor off the entry could serve as a fourth bedroom, a guest room or a home office.

Plan Q-2033-1A	
Bedrooms: 3+	**Baths: 3**
Living Area:	
Main floor	2,033 sq. ft.
Total Living Area:	**2,033 sq. ft.**
Garage	592 sq. ft.
Exterior Wall Framing:	2x4

Foundation Options:

Slab
(All plans can be built with your choice of foundation and framing. A generic conversion diagram is available. See order form.)

BLUEPRINT PRICE CODE:	**C**

MAIN FLOOR

Plan Q-2033-1A

Big, Bright Country Kitchen

- Decorative dormers, shuttered windows and a large covered front porch give this charming two-story home a pleasant country flavor.
- Inside, the central Great Room is warmed by a handsome fireplace. The adjoining dining room offers sliding glass doors to a backyard deck.
- The enormous country kitchen features a sunny bay-windowed eating area and a convenient island counter. The nearby laundry/utility area accesses the garage and the backyard.
- The main-floor master bedroom boasts a roomy walk-in closet and private access to a compartmentalized bath with an oversized linen closet.
- Upstairs, two bedrooms with window seats share a full bath. An easy-to-access storage area is above the garage. Another convenient storage area can be reached from the garage.

Plan C-8040

Bedrooms: 3	Baths: 2
Living Area:	
Upper floor	718 sq. ft.
Main floor	1,318 sq. ft.
Total Living Area:	**2,036 sq. ft.**
Daylight basement	1,221 sq. ft.
Garage	436 sq. ft.
Exterior Wall Framing:	2x4

Foundation Options:

Daylight basement

Crawlspace

Slab

(All plans can be built with your choice of foundation and framing. A generic conversion diagram is available. See order form.)

BLUEPRINT PRICE CODE: **C**

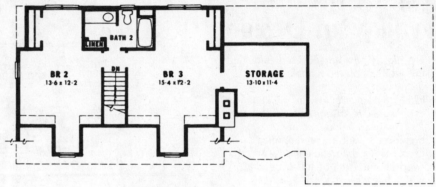

UPPER FLOOR

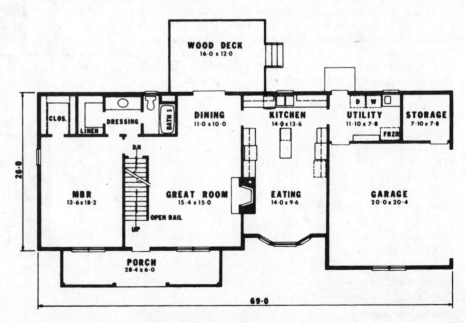

MAIN FLOOR

Well-Appointed Walk-Out Design

- The hipped roof and covered entry give this well-appointed home a look of distinction.
- Inside, the foyer leads directly into the expansive Great Room, which boasts a 13-ft. vaulted ceiling, an inviting fireplace, a built-in entertainment center and a dramatic window wall that overlooks an exciting full-width deck with a hot tub!
- A half-wall separates the Great Room from the nook, which is open to the U-shaped kitchen. The impressive kitchen includes a snack bar, a walk-in pantry and a greenhouse window.
- The isolated master suite offers a vaulted ceiling that slopes up to 9 feet. A French door opens to the deck and hot tub, while a pocket door accesses the sumptuous master bath with a spa tub under a glass-block wall.
- Two more bedrooms in the walk-out basement share another full bath. The optional expansion areas provide an additional 730 sq. ft. of space.

Plan S-41792

Bedrooms: 3	Baths: 3
Living Area:	
Main floor	1,450 sq. ft.
Partial daylight basement	590 sq. ft.
Total Living Area:	**2,040 sq. ft.**
Garage	429 sq. ft.
Unfinished expansion areas	730 sq. ft.
Exterior Wall Framing:	2x6

Foundation Options:

Partial daylight basement

(All plans can be built with your choice of foundation and framing. A generic conversion diagram is available. See order form.)

BLUEPRINT PRICE CODE: **C**

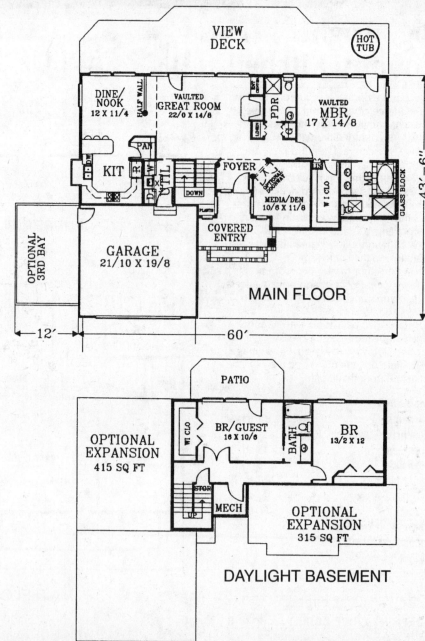

MAIN FLOOR

DAYLIGHT BASEMENT

Plan S-41792

PRICES AND DETAILS
ON PAGES 12-15

Elaborate Entry

- This home's important-looking covered entry greets guests with heavy, banded support columns, sunburst transom windows and dual sidelights.
- Once inside, the 15-ft.-high foyer is flanked by the formal living and dining rooms, which have 10½-ft. vaulted ceilings. Straight ahead and beyond decorative columns lies the spacious family room.
- Surrounded by 8-ft.-high walls, the family room features a 13-ft. vaulted ceiling, a corner fireplace and sliding doors to a rear covered patio.
- The bright and airy kitchen has a 13-ft. ceiling and serves the family room and the breakfast area, which is enhanced by a corner window and a French door.
- The master suite enjoys a 13-ft. vaulted ceiling and features double-door patio access, a large walk-in closet and a private bath with a corner platform tub and a separate shower.

Plan HDS-90-806

Bedrooms: 4	Baths: 2
Living Area:	
Main floor	2,041 sq. ft.
Total Living Area:	**2,041 sq. ft.**
Garage	452 sq. ft.

Exterior Wall Framing:

2x4 or 8-in. concrete block

Foundation Options:

Slab

(All plans can be built with your choice of foundation and framing. A generic conversion diagram is available. See order form.)

BLUEPRINT PRICE CODE:	C

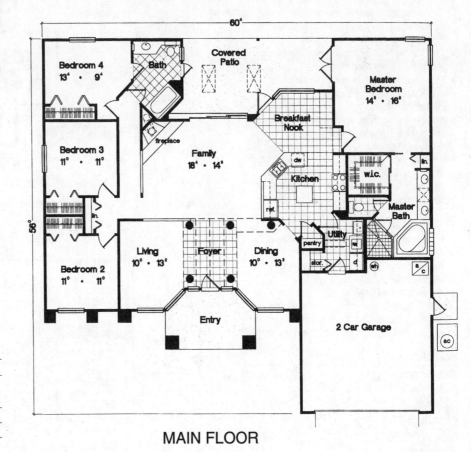

MAIN FLOOR

French Beauty

- High-pitched gables and a stucco facade accent this French beauty.
- Off the two-story-high foyer, the sunken living room features a warm fireplace, a front-facing bay window and a vaulted ceiling that soars to 14½ feet.
- The formal dining room is a quiet spot for special occasions.
- The gourmet kitchen offers an island work area, a roomy pantry, a handy planning desk and a corner sink under windows. Sliding glass doors open from the sunny breakfast nook to an inviting backyard deck.
- Three steps below the main level, the family room is visible from the nook through an open railing. The spacious family room boasts a second fireplace and easy access to a large patio.
- A bedroom, a full bath and a utility room with garage access are nearby.
- Three bedrooms are housed on the upper floor. The master bedroom includes a private bath.
- A skylighted·bath serves the two secondary bedrooms, one of which is highlighted by a 12½-ft. vaulted ceiling and a Palladian window arrangement.

Plan U-89-403

Bedrooms: 4	Baths: 3
Living Area:	
Upper floor	656 sq. ft.
Main floor	1,385 sq. ft.
Total Living Area:	**2,041 sq. ft.**
Partial basement	704 sq. ft.
Garage	466 sq. ft.
Exterior Wall Framing:	2x4

Foundation Options:

Partial basement
Crawlspace
Slab

(All plans can be built with your choice of foundation and framing. A generic conversion diagram is available. See order form.)

BLUEPRINT PRICE CODE: C

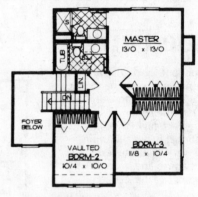

UPPER FLOOR

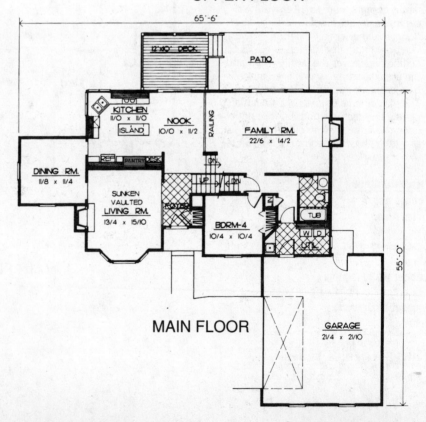

MAIN FLOOR

Arresting Angles

- This arresting design, with its towering windows and vertical angles, is filled with light and luxurious spaces.
- A bridge on the upper floor visually separates the soaring reception area from the living room, which features a cathedral ceiling. The floor-to-ceiling stone-faced fireplace is framed by glass, starting with sliding glass doors and rising to triangular-shaped windows.
- The kitchen is flanked by the casual dinette and the formal dining room. The dining room is open to the living room, and both rooms view out to a partially covered backyard terrace.
- A den overlooking a side terrace and a library/guest room with a nearby bath add to the main floor's versatility.
- The upper floor is highlighted by great views and a superb master suite. The spacious sleeping area overlooks the living room below and accesses a private deck. The luxurious master bath includes a whirlpool tub, a separate dressing area and a walk-in closet.

Plan K-653-U

Bedrooms: 3+	Baths: 3
Living Area:	
Upper floor	844 sq. ft.
Main floor	1,208 sq. ft.
Total Living Area:	**2,052 sq. ft.**
Standard basement	1,208 sq. ft.
Garage	427 sq. ft.
Exterior Wall Framing:	2x4 or 2x6

Foundation Options:

Standard basement
Slab
(All plans can be built with your choice of foundation and framing. A generic conversion diagram is available. See order form.)

BLUEPRINT PRICE CODE: C

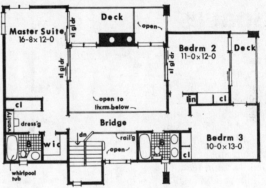

UPPER FLOOR

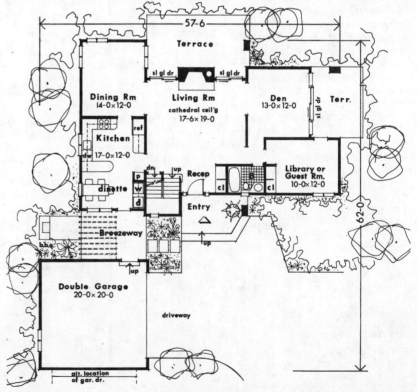

MAIN FLOOR

Great Spaces

- Open, airy casual living spaces and intimate formal areas are the hallmarks of this intriguing home.
- A two-story-high foyer introduces the the living room, where French doors open to a veranda. On the opposite side of the foyer is a spacious dining room with a delightful bay window.
- The casual areas combine at the back of the home. The family room features a two-story-high ceiling and a fireplace framed with glass, including a French door that opens to the backyard.
- A half-wall is all that separates the family room from the inviting bay-windowed nook. An angled serving counter/snack bar keeps the kitchen open to the activity areas.
- A walk-in pantry and a laundry room are nearby, just off the garage entrance.
- Upstairs, the luxurious master suite features an elegant 9-ft. tray ceiling. The master bath boasts a 12-ft. vaulted ceiling, an oval garden tub, a private toilet compartment and a walk-in closet adorned with a plant shelf.
- Two more bedrooms, a versatile loft and a hall bath complete the upper floor.

Plan FB-5056-MAGU

Bedrooms: 3+	Baths: 2½
Living Area:	
Upper floor	1,019 sq. ft.
Main floor	1,034 sq. ft.
Total Living Area:	**2,053 sq. ft.**
Daylight basement	1,034 sq. ft.
Garage	415 sq. ft.
Exterior Wall Framing:	2x4

Foundation Options:

Daylight basement

(All plans can be built with your choice of foundation and framing. A generic conversion diagram is available. See order form.)

BLUEPRINT PRICE CODE:	C

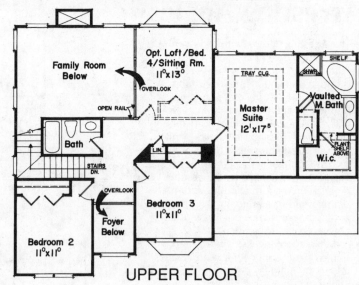

UPPER FLOOR

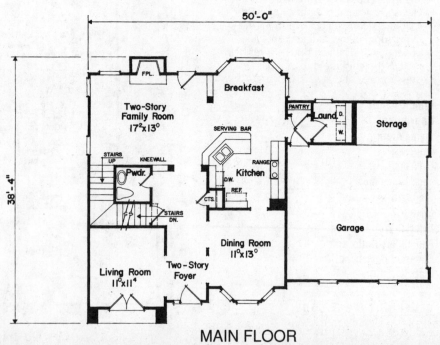

MAIN FLOOR

Modern Charmer

- This attractive plan combines country-style charm with a modern floor plan.
- The central foyer ushers guests past a study and on into the huge living room, which is highlighted by a high, flat ceiling, a corner fireplace and access to a big, covered backyard porch.
- An angled snack bar joins the living room to the bayed nook and the efficient kitchen. The formal dining room is easily reached from the kitchen and the foyer. A utility room and a half-bath are just off the garage entrance.
- The master suite, isolated for privacy, boasts a magnificent bath with a garden tub, a separate shower, double vanities and two walk-in closets.
- Two more bedrooms are located on the opposite side of the home and are separated by a hall bath.
- Ceilings in all rooms are at least 9 ft. high for added spaciousness.

REAR VIEW

Plan VL-2069

Bedrooms: 3	Baths: 2½
Living Area:	
Main floor	2,069 sq. ft.
Total Living Area:	**2,069 sq. ft.**
Garage	460 sq. ft.
Exterior Wall Framing:	2x4

Foundation Options:

Crawlspace

Slab

(All plans can be built with your choice of foundation and framing. A generic conversion diagram is available. See order form.)

BLUEPRINT PRICE CODE:	C

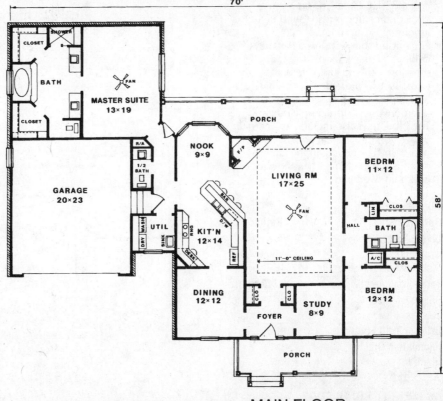

MAIN FLOOR

Fluid Floor Plan

- This updated 1½-story home features cathedral ceilings and a fluid floor plan that combine for easy family living.
- Several design options are offered, including a hutch space in the formal dining room, a 30-sq.-ft. extension off the family room, a window seat in the master bedroom, an alternate master bath layout and an alternate mudroom/entry design.
- A handsome fireplace and an 11½-ft. cathedral ceiling highlight the large family room, which opens to the dinette and the island kitchen. An 11-ft. cathedral ceiling is also found in the adjoining living room.
- The master suite features a 9-ft. tray ceiling, a large walk-in closet, a dressing area and a private bath.
- Upstairs, two more bedrooms share a hall bath. A window seat in the front bedroom offers storage space below.
- The blueprints also include an alternate upper-floor layout that adds another bedroom. The ceiling in the family room is lowered to 8 ft. to allow for a bedroom overhead.

Plan GL-2070

Bedrooms: 3	Baths: 2½
Living Area:	
Upper floor	509 sq. ft.
Main floor	1,561 sq. ft.
Total Living Area:	**2,070 sq. ft.**
Standard basement	1,561 sq. ft.
Garage	462 sq. ft.
Exterior Wall Framing:	2x6
Foundation Options:	

Standard basement
(All plans can be built with your choice of foundation and framing. A generic conversion diagram is available. See order form.)

BLUEPRINT PRICE CODE: C

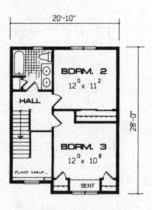

UPPER FLOOR

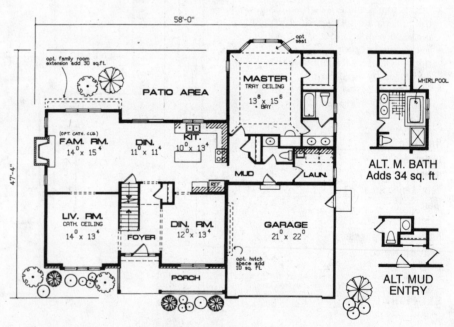

MAIN FLOOR

ALT. M. BATH
Adds 34 sq. ft.

ALT. MUD ENTRY

Luxurious Ranch

- This luxurious farmhouse is introduced by a covered front porch, which opens to a sidelighted foyer.
- A spectacular central living room with an 11-ft. ceiling and a corner fireplace lies at the center of the home. A French door accesses a wide backyard porch.
- An angled eating bar joins the living room to the kitchen and bayed nook. The formal dining room is located on the opposite end of the kitchen, overlooking the front porch.
- The lavish master suite is separated from the other bedrooms and boasts a bayed sitting area and a private bath with dual vanities and a walk-in closet.
- A study, two additional bedrooms and a second full bath are located to the right of the foyer.
- Ceilings in all rooms are at least 9 ft. high for added spaciousness.

Plan VL-2085

Bedrooms: 3+	Baths: 2½
Living Area:	
Main floor	2,085 sq. ft.
Total Living Area:	**2,085 sq. ft.**
Garage	460 sq. ft.
Exterior Wall Framing:	2x4

Foundation Options:

Crawlspace

Slab

(All plans can be built with your choice of foundation and framing. A generic conversion diagram is available. See order form.)

BLUEPRINT PRICE CODE:	C

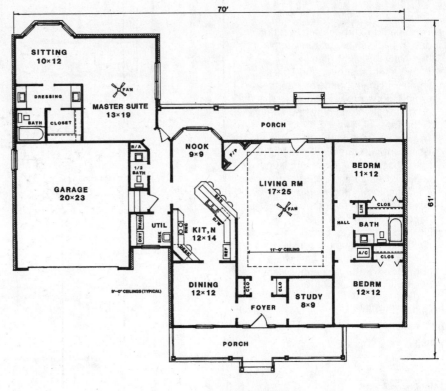

MAIN FLOOR

Distinctive Family Design

- This beautiful, time-tested traditional design packs many features into a highly livable floor plan.
- To the left of the foyer, the 16½-ft. vaulted living room flows into the dining room, providing a huge space for both formal entertaining and family gatherings.
- The big kitchen includes a handy work island and a sunny dinette, which opens to the backyard. A half-bath, laundry facilities and garage access are nearby.
- The large family room adjoins the casual dinette area and boasts a handsome fireplace.
- Upstairs, the master bedroom features two large closets and a private bath. Three additional bedrooms share another full bath. A central balcony overlooks the foyer below.

Plan A-2109-DS

Bedrooms: 4	Baths: 2½
Living Area:	
Upper floor	942 sq. ft.
Main floor	1,148 sq. ft.
Total Living Area:	**2,090 sq. ft.**
Standard basement	1,148 sq. ft.
Garage	484 sq. ft.
Exterior Wall Framing:	2x4

Foundation Options:

Standard basement

(All plans can be built with your choice of foundation and framing. A generic conversion diagram is available. See order form.)

BLUEPRINT PRICE CODE:	C

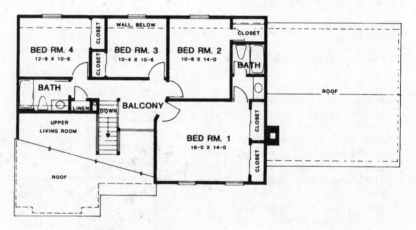

UPPER FLOOR

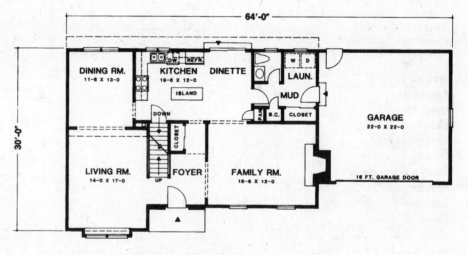

MAIN FLOOR

Plan A-2109-DS

PRICES AND DETAILS ON PAGES 12-15

Easy to Build

- The basic rectangular shape of this two-story home makes it economical to build. The well-zoned interior isolates all four bedrooms on the upper floor.
- Off the covered porch, the airy foyer reveals the open stairway and unfolds to each of the living areas.
- The formal rooms are positioned at the front of the home and overlook the porch. The large living room boasts a handsome fireplace and extends to a rear porch through sliding glass doors.
- The central family room hosts casual family activities and shows off a rustic wood-beam ceiling. This room also opens to the porch and integrates with the kitchen and the bright dinette for a big, open atmosphere.
- A half-bath, a laundry area and a handy service porch are located near the entrance from the garage.
- Two dual-sink bathrooms serve the bedrooms upstairs. The spacious master bedroom has a private bath and a big walk-in closet.

Plan HFL-1070-RQ

Bedrooms: 4	Baths: 2½
Living Area:	
Upper floor	1,013 sq. ft.
Main floor	1,082 sq. ft.
Total Living Area:	**2,095 sq. ft.**
Standard basement	889 sq. ft.
Garage and storage	481 sq. ft.
Exterior Wall Framing:	2x6

Foundation Options:

Standard basement

Slab

(All plans can be built with your choice of foundation and framing. A generic conversion diagram is available. See order form.)

BLUEPRINT PRICE CODE: C

VIEW INTO FAMILY ROOM, KITCHEN AND DINETTE

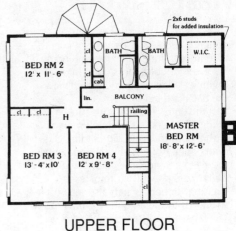

UPPER FLOOR

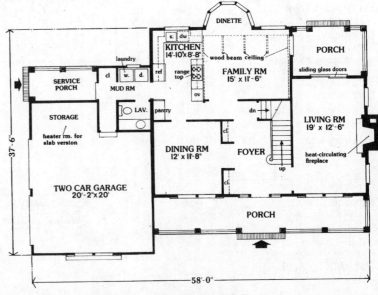

MAIN FLOOR

Deluxe
Master Bath

- Stylish decks, bay windows and a deluxe master bath are just some of the amenities found in this modern home.
- Recessed double doors open into the inviting skylighted entry, which views the backyard beyond.
- Past the entry, the spacious sunken living room offers a unique fireplace with a built-in wood bin. Sliding glass doors open from the living and dining rooms to a handsome backyard deck.
- A dramatic skywall illuminates the exciting kitchen, which also features a snack bar to the adjoining dining room.
- The fantastic master suite boasts a private backyard deck, in addition to a lavish bath that showcases a step-up spa tub, a designer shower, a dual-sink vanity and a roomy walk-in closet.
- Another full bath is convenient to the two secondary bedrooms, each with a window seat in a split bay.

Plans P-6600-4A & -4D

Bedrooms: 3	Baths: 2
Living Area:	
Main floor (crawlspace version)	2,050 sq. ft.
Main floor (basement version)	2,110 sq. ft.
Total Living Area:	**2,050/2,110 sq. ft.**
Daylight basement	2,080 sq. ft.
Garage	794 sq. ft.
Exterior Wall Framing:	2x6
Foundation Options:	**Plan #**
Daylight basement	P-6600-4D
Crawlspace	P-6600-4A

(All plans can be built with your choice of foundation and framing. A generic conversion diagram is available. See order form.)

BLUEPRINT PRICE CODE:	C

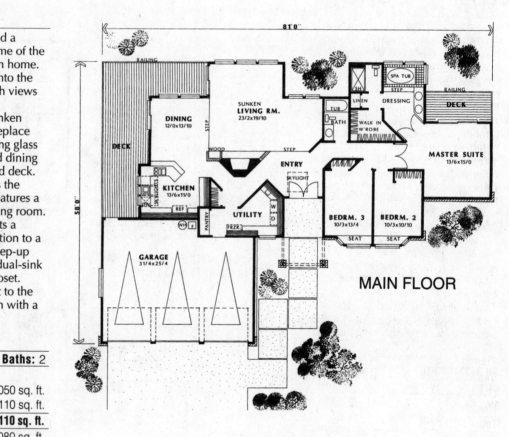

MAIN FLOOR

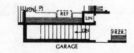

BASEMENT STAIRWAY LOCATION

Wonderful Windows

- This one-story's striking stucco and stone facade is enhanced with wonderful windows and great gables.
- A beautiful bay augments the living room/den, which can be closed off.
- A wall of windows lets sunbeams brighten the exquisite formal dining room, which is open but defined by decorative columns.
- The oversized family room offers a nice fireplace and a handy serving bar.
- The walk-through kitchen boasts a large pantry and a corner sink.
- A lovely window seat is found in one of the two secondary bedrooms.
- The magnificent master suite features a symmetrical tray ceiling that sets off a round-top window.
- Large walk-in closets flank the entry to the master bath, which offers a garden tub and two vanities. One of the vanities has knee space for a sit-down makeup area.

Plan FB-5009-CHAD

Bedrooms: 3	Baths: 2
Living Area:	
Main floor	2,115 sq. ft.
Total Living Area:	**2,115 sq. ft.**
Daylight basement	2,115 sq. ft.
Garage	517 sq. ft.
Storage	18 sq. ft.
Exterior Wall Framing:	2x4

Foundation Options:

Daylight basement
Slab
(Typical foundation & framing conversion diagram available—see order form.)

BLUEPRINT PRICE CODE: C

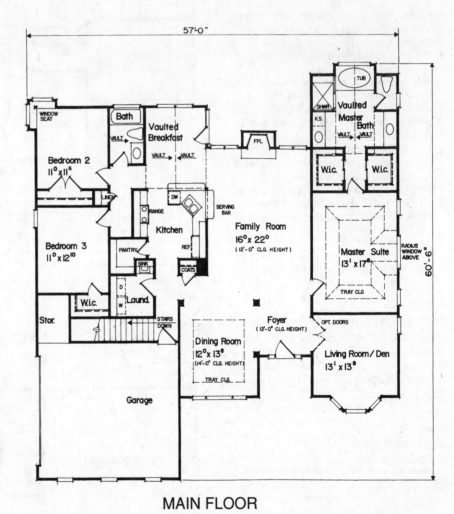

MAIN FLOOR

Comfortable Country Home

- A central gable and a wide, welcoming front porch with columns give this design comfortable country charm.
- The large living room is open to the dining room, which features a tray ceiling and views to the backyard.
- The kitchen offers an oversized island counter with a snack bar. The adjoining breakfast area has a sliding glass door to the backyard and a half-wall that separates it from the family room. This inviting room includes a fireplace and a bay window with a cozy seat.
- Upstairs, the master suite boasts three windows, including a lovely arched window, that overlook the front yard. The private bath offers a whirlpool tub and a separate shower.
- Three more bedrooms, a second full bath and a multipurpose den make this a great family-sized home.

Plan OH-165

Bedrooms: 4+	Baths: 2½
Living Area:	
Upper floor	1,121 sq. ft.
Main floor	1,000 sq. ft.
Total Living Area:	**2,121 sq. ft.**
Standard basement	1,000 sq. ft.
Garage	400 sq. ft.
Exterior Wall Framing:	2x4

Foundation Options:

Standard basement

(All plans can be built with your choice of foundation and framing. A generic conversion diagram is available. See order form.)

BLUEPRINT PRICE CODE: C

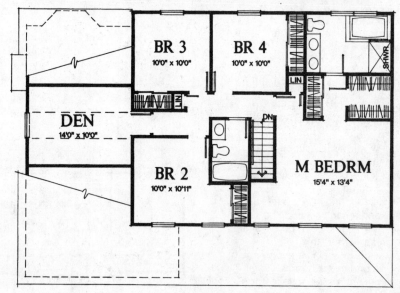

UPPER FLOOR

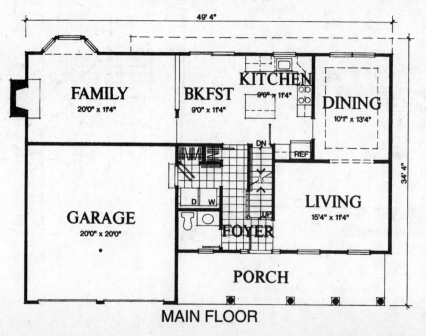

MAIN FLOOR

Plan OH-165
PRICES AND DETAILS ON PAGES 12-15

Visual Surprises

- The exterior of this home is accented with a dramatic roof cavity, while the inside uses angles to enhance the efficiency and variety of the floor plan.
- The double-door entry opens to a reception area, which unfolds to the spacious living room. A 16½-ft. sloped ceiling and an angled fireplace add drama to the living room and the adjoining bayed dining room, where sliding doors access a backyard terrace.
- The efficient kitchen easily serves both the formal dining room and the cheerful dinette, which offers sweeping outdoor views. A fireplace in the adjoining family room warms the entire area. A second terrace is accessible via sliding glass doors.
- The oversized laundry room could be finished as a nice hobby room.
- A skylighted stairway leads up to the sleeping areas. The master suite is fully equipped with a private bath, a separate dressing area, a walk-in closet and an exciting sun deck alcoved above the garage. Three additional bedrooms share another full bath.

Plan K-540-L

Bedrooms: 4	Baths: 2½
Living Area:	
Upper floor	884 sq. ft.
Main floor	1,238 sq. ft.
Total Living Area:	**2,122 sq. ft.**
Standard basement	1,106 sq. ft.
Garage	400 sq. ft.
Storage	122 sq. ft.
Exterior Wall Framing:	2x4 or 2x6
Foundation Options:	
Standard basement	
Slab	

(All plans can be built with your choice of foundation and framing. A generic conversion diagram is available. See order form.)

BLUEPRINT PRICE CODE: C

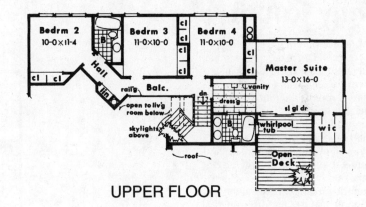

UPPER FLOOR

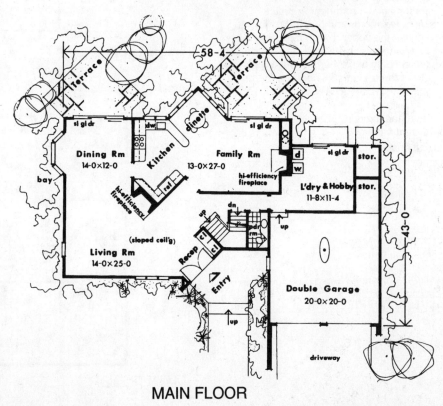

MAIN FLOOR

Dramatic Family Room

- An impressive porch and simple, balanced rooflines make this warm and friendly farmhouse a classic beauty.
- The two-story foyer and formal living and dining rooms maintain the feeling of generous hospitality.
- The large and open country kitchen, with its big, bright breakfast area, pantry, wall oven and pass-through to the family room, is the perfect host for informal family gatherings.
- The step-down family room at the back of the home features a 15-ft. cathedral ceiling and a prominent fireplace.
- Three bedrooms and two full baths occupy the upper floor. The spacious and luxurious master suite has a big private bath and inherits a huge walk-in closet through the efficient use of the space above the garage.

Plan OH-163

Bedrooms: 3	Baths: 2½
Living Area:	
Upper floor	852 sq. ft.
Main floor	1,270 sq. ft.
Total Living Area:	**2,122 sq. ft.**
Partial basement	934 sq. ft.
Garage	576 sq. ft.
Exterior Wall Framing:	2x4

Foundation Options:

Partial basement
(All plans can be built with your choice of foundation and framing. A generic conversion diagram is available. See order form.)

BLUEPRINT PRICE CODE:	**C**

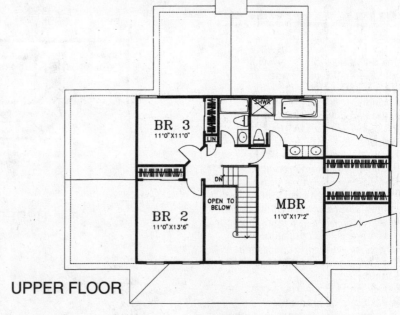

UPPER FLOOR

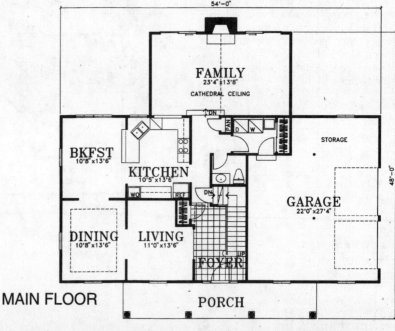

MAIN FLOOR

Alluring Two-Story

- This dramatic contemporary is adorned with staggered rooflines that overlap and outline large expanses of glass.
- Flanking the two-story-high foyer are the formal dining room and the sunken living room, which is expanded by an airy 16-ft. cathedral ceiling.
- The adjoining sunken family room boasts a fireplace and sliding glass doors to a backyard patio.
- A step up, the bright breakfast area enjoys an eating bar that extends from the efficient U-shaped kitchen. A half-bath and laundry facilities are convenient.
- The second level features a spacious master bedroom with a 12-ft. sloped ceiling, dual closets and a private bath. Two secondary bedrooms, another full bath and an optional expansion room above the garage are also included.

Plan AX-8596-A

Bedrooms: 3+	Baths: 2½
Living Area:	
Upper floor	738 sq. ft.
Main floor	1,160 sq. ft.
Bonus room	226 sq. ft.
Total Living Area:	**2,124 sq. ft.**
Standard basement	1,160 sq. ft.
Garage	465 sq. ft.
Exterior Wall Framing:	2x4

Foundation Options:

Standard basement

(All plans can be built with your choice of foundation and framing. A generic conversion diagram is available. See order form.)

BLUEPRINT PRICE CODE: C

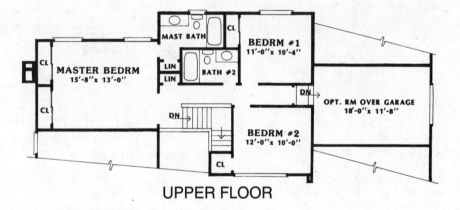

UPPER FLOOR

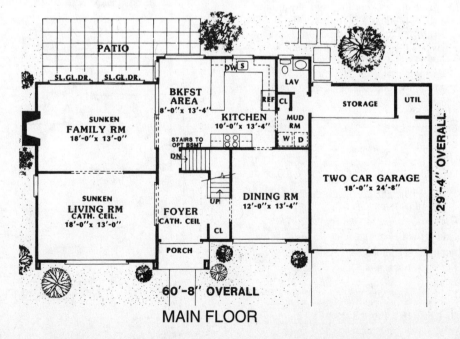

MAIN FLOOR

Classic Country Beauty

- This distinctive home boasts a classic facade, highlighted by triple dormers and an expansive covered front porch.
- An airy central gallery introduces the interior. The living room flows into the adjacent formal dining room, which features a 10-ft., 4-in. cathedral ceiling and sliding French doors to a covered back porch.
- The kitchen includes an island work counter and a sunny dinette nestled within a semi-circular glass wall.
- A wood-burning fireplace with a slate hearth accents the spacious family room. French doors lead to a lovely backyard terrace.
- Upstairs, the master suite has a 10-ft., 4-in. cathedral ceiling, two closets and a skylighted bath with dual sinks, a whirlpool tub and a separate shower.
- Two of the three remaining bedrooms offer 11-ft.-high sloped ceilings and dormers that are large enough to accommodate built-in desks.

Plan K-695-T

Bedrooms: 4	Baths: 2½
Living Area:	
Upper floor	1,030 sq. ft.
Main floor	1,100 sq. ft.
Total Living Area:	**2,130 sq. ft.**
Standard basement	1,100 sq. ft.
Garage	450 sq. ft.
Exterior Wall Framing:	2x4 or 2x6

Foundation Options:

Standard basement
Slab
(All plans can be built with your choice of foundation and framing. A generic conversion diagram is available. See order form.)

BLUEPRINT PRICE CODE:	C

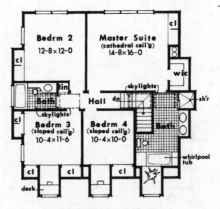

UPPER FLOOR

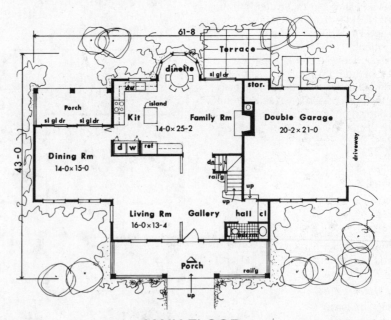

VIEW INTO FAMILY ROOM

MAIN FLOOR

Plan K-695-T

PRICES AND DETAILS ON PAGES 12-15

Upstairs Suite Creates Adult Retreat

● This multi-level design is ideal for a gently sloping site with a view to the rear.

● Upstairs master suite is a sumptuous "adult retreat" complete with magnificent bath, vaulted ceiling, walk-in closet, private deck and balcony loft.

● Living room includes wood stove area and large windows to the rear. Wood bin can be loaded from outside.

● Main floor also features roomy kitchen and large utility area.

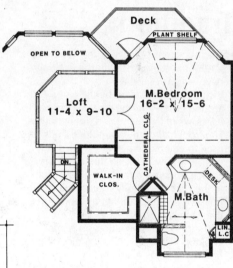

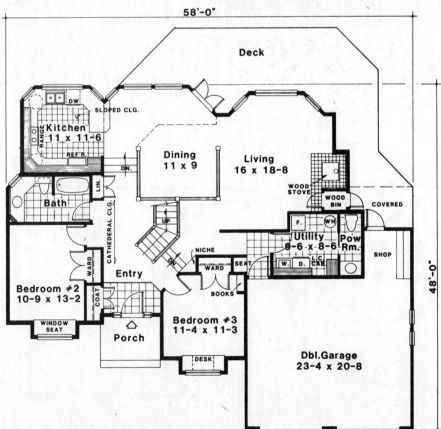

Plan NW-544-S

Bedrooms: 3	**Baths:** 2½

Space:

Upper floor:	638 sq. ft.
Main floor:	1,500 sq. ft.

Total living area:	2,138 sq. ft.
Garage:	545 sq. ft.

Exterior Wall Framing:	2x6

Foundation options:
  Crawlspace only.
(Foundation & framing conversion diagram available — see order form.)

Blueprint Price Code:	C

Today's Tradition

- This two-story country home combines traditional standards with the exciting new designs of today.
- Visitors are welcomed by the wrap-around porch and the symmetrical bay windows of the living and dining rooms.
- The front half of the main floor lends itself to entertaining as the angled entry creates a flow between the formal areas.
- French doors lead from the living room to the spacious family room, which boasts a beamed ceiling, a warm fireplace and porch access.
- The super kitchen features an island cooktop with a snack bar. A nice-sized laundry room is nearby.
- The spacious upper level hosts a master suite with two walk-in closets and a large bath with a dual-sink vanity, a tub and a separate shower. Three more bedrooms share another full bath.

Plan AGH-2143

Bedrooms: 4	Baths: 2½
Living Area:	
Upper floor	1,047 sq. ft.
Main floor	1,096 sq. ft.
Total Living Area:	**2,143 sq. ft.**
Daylight basement	1,096 sq. ft.
Garage	852 sq. ft.
Exterior Wall Framing:	2x6

Foundation Options:

Daylight basement

(All plans can be built with your choice of foundation and framing. A generic conversion diagram is available. See order form.)

BLUEPRINT PRICE CODE:	**C**

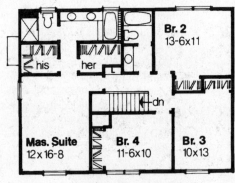

UPPER FLOOR

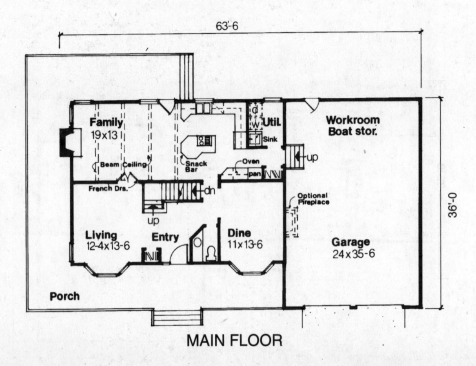

MAIN FLOOR

Plan AGH-2143

PRICES AND DETAILS
ON PAGES 12-15

Colonial for Today

- Designed for a growing family, this handsome traditional home offers four bedrooms plus a den and three complete baths. The Colonial exterior is updated by a covered front entry porch with a fanlight window above.
- The dramatic tiled foyer is two stories high and provides direct access to all of the home's living areas. The spacious living room has an inviting brick fireplace and sliding pocket doors to the adjoining dining room.
- Overlooking the backyard, the huge combination kitchen/family room is the

home's hidden charm. The kitchen features a peninsula breakfast bar with seating for six. The family room has a window wall with sliding glass doors that open to an enticing terrace. A built-in entertainment center and bookshelves line another wall.
- The adjacent mudroom is just off the garage entrance and includes a pantry closet. A full bath and a large den complete the first floor.
- The second floor is highlighted by a beautiful balcony that is open to the foyer below. The luxurious master suite is brightened by a skylight and boasts two closets, including an oversized walk-in closet. The master bath has a whirlpool tub and a dual-sink vanity.

Plan AHP-7050	
Bedrooms: 4+	**Baths:** 3
Living Area:	
Upper floor	998 sq. ft.
Main floor	1,153 sq. ft.
Total Living Area:	**2,151 sq. ft.**
Standard basement	1,067 sq. ft.
Garage	439 sq. ft.
Exterior Wall Framing:	2x6
Foundation Options:	
Standard basement	
Crawlspace	
Slab	

(All plans can be built with your choice of foundation and framing. A generic conversion diagram is available. See order form.)

BLUEPRINT PRICE CODE:	C

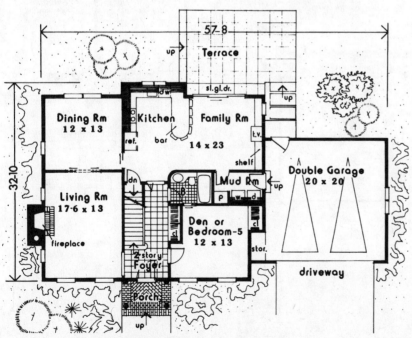

MAIN FLOOR

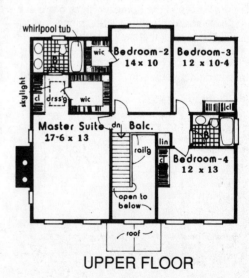

UPPER FLOOR

Vertical Dimension

- This exotic four-bedroom home is drenched in elegance and durability.
- Soaring columns, high windows and volume ceilings add a vertical dimension to the home's sprawling single-level room arrangement.
- The grand foyer reveals the formal living areas. The dining room is introduced by columns and the living room opens to a nice covered porch. All three areas have 12-ft.-high ceilings.
- The kitchen flows into a sunny breakfast nook that accesses the back porch. These areas have 12-ft. ceilings as well.
- High plant shelves surround the inviting family room, which boasts a fireplace and a 12-ft. barrel-vaulted ceiling.
- The master suite is secluded to the right of the foyer. The sleeping area features a 12-ft.-high ceiling and access to the porch. The master bath includes a huge walk-in closet and a corner step-up tub.
- At the back of the home are three more bedrooms, each with a 10-ft ceiling. The bedrooms share a full bath that can be accessed from the backyard–a nice feature if you have a pool or are entertaining outdoors.

Plan HDS-90-815

Bedrooms: 4	Baths: 2
Living Area:	
Main floor	2,153 sq. ft.
Total Living Area:	**2,153 sq. ft.**
Garage	434 sq. ft.
Exterior Wall Framing:	2x4

Foundation Options:

Slab
(All plans can be built with your choice of foundation and framing. A generic conversion diagram is available. See order form.)

BLUEPRINT PRICE CODE: C

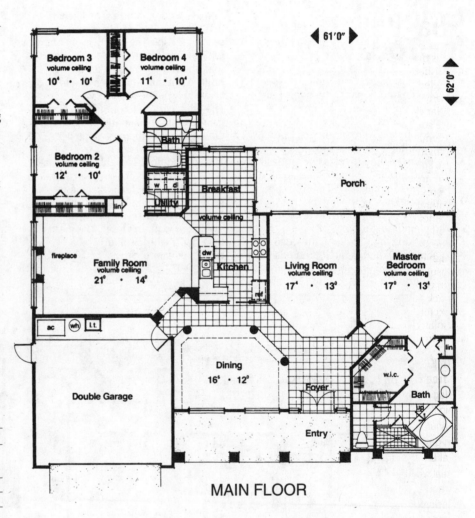

MAIN FLOOR

TO ORDER THIS BLUEPRINT, CALL TOLL-FREE 1-800-547-5570   Plan HDS-90-815   PRICES AND DETAILS ON PAGES 12-15

Solar Home Soaks Up Sun

- This dramatic passive-solar home is finished in eye-catching vertical and angled wood siding, and is adaptable to many sites and conditions.
- Solar energy is soaked up and stored in the sun garden's thermal wall and the thermal floors of the south-facing activity areas and the master suite. In the summer, overhanging eaves keep out unwanted heat, and high, operable clerestory windows give the home natural ventilation.
- Cathedral ceilings in the family, dining and living rooms keep an open air flow.
- The sheltered entry, air-lock vestibule, high-efficiency fireplace and heavy insulation are other economies.
- An expansive terrace extends along the back of the home and wraps around an exciting solarium.
- Isolated in a private wing are three bedrooms and two baths.

Plan K-395-T

Bedrooms: 3	Baths: 2½
Living Area:	
Main floor	1,921 sq. ft.
Solarium	128 sq. ft.
Sun garden	104 sq. ft.
Total Living Area:	**2,153 sq. ft.**
Partial basement	807 sq. ft.
Garage	476 sq. ft.
Exterior Wall Framing:	2x4 or 2x6

Foundation Options:

Partial basement
Slab
(All plans can be built with your choice of foundation and framing. A generic conversion diagram is available. See order form.)

BLUEPRINT PRICE CODE:	C

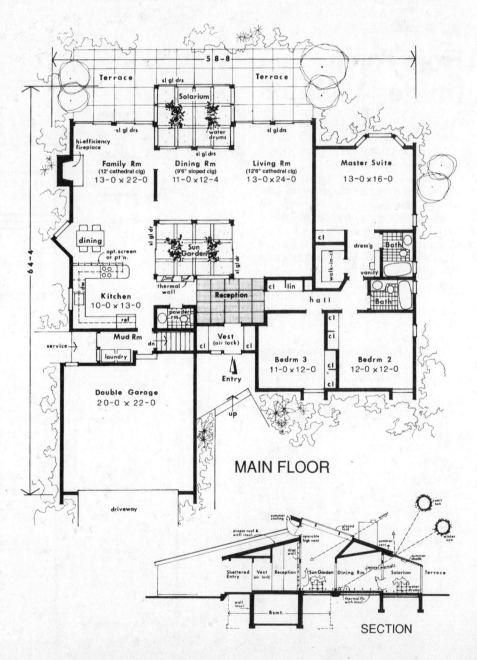

MAIN FLOOR

SECTION

Front Porch Invites Visitors

- This neat and well-proportioned design exudes warmth and charm, with an inviting front porch and a decorative sunburst in the gable.
- The broad foyer flows between the formal areas for special occasions. The living room and expansive family room join together, creating additional space for larger gatherings.
- The bright and airy kitchen, dinette and family room intermingle for great casual family living.
- Upstairs, the roomy master suite is complemented by a private bath available in two configurations. The alternate master bath adds 70 sq. ft. to the home.
- Two additional bedrooms share another full bath and a sunny library that overlooks the foyer.

Plan GL-2161

Bedrooms: 3	Baths: 2½
Living Area:	
Upper floor	991 sq. ft.
Main floor	1,170 sq. ft.
Total Living Area:	**2,161 sq. ft.**
Standard basement	1,170 sq. ft.
Garage	462 sq. ft.
Exterior Wall Framing:	2x6
Foundation Options:	

Standard basement
(All plans can be built with your choice of foundation and framing. A generic conversion diagram is available. See order form.)

BLUEPRINT PRICE CODE:	**C**

ALTERNATE BATH

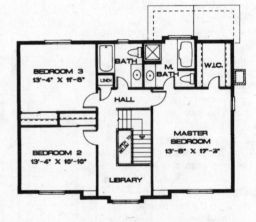

UPPER FLOOR

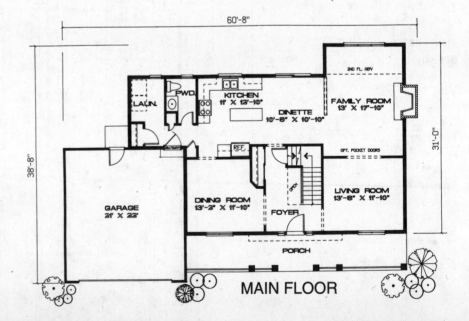

MAIN FLOOR

Plan GL-2161

PRICES AND DETAILS ON PAGES 12-15

State-of-the-Art Floor Plan

- This design's state-of-the-art floor plan begins with a two-story-high foyer that introduces a stunning open staircase and a bright Great Room.
- The Great Room is expanded by a 17-ft. vaulted ceiling and a window wall with French doors that open to a rear deck.
- Short sections of half-walls separate the Great Room from the open kitchen and dining room. Natural light streams in through a greenhouse window above the sink and lots of glass facing the deck.
- The main-floor master suite has a 9-ft. coved ceiling and private access to an inviting hot tub on the deck. Walk-in closets frame the entrance to the luxurious bath, highlighted by a 10-ft. vaulted ceiling and an arched window above a raised spa tub.
- Upstairs, a balcony hall leads to two bedrooms and a continental bath, plus a den and a storage room.

Plan S-2100

Bedrooms: 3+	Baths: 2½
Living Area:	
Upper floor	660 sq. ft.
Main floor	1,440 sq. ft.
Total Living Area:	**2,100 sq. ft.**
Standard basement	1,440 sq. ft.
Garage	552 sq. ft.
Exterior Wall Framing:	2x6

Foundation Options:

Standard basement
Crawlspace
Slab
(All plans can be built with your choice of foundation and framing. A generic conversion diagram is available. See order form.)

BLUEPRINT PRICE CODE: C

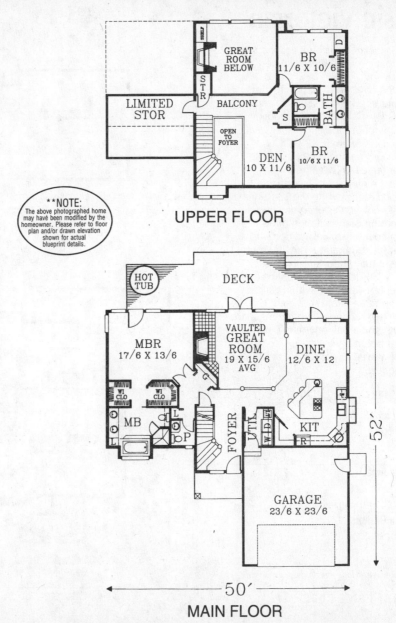

UPPER FLOOR

NOTE:
The above photographed home may have been modified by the homeowner. Please refer to floor plan and/or drawn elevation shown for actual blueprint details.

MAIN FLOOR

Classic Victorian

- This classic exterior is built around an interior that offers all the amenities desired by today's families.
- In from the covered front porch, the entry features a curved stairway and a glass-block wall to the dining room.
- A step down from the entry, the Great Room boasts a dramatic 24½-ft. cathedral ceiling and provides ample space for large family gatherings.
- The formal dining room is available for special occasions, while the 13-ft.-high breakfast nook serves everyday needs.
- The adjoining island kitchen offers plenty of counter space and opens to a handy utility room and a powder room.
- The deluxe main-floor master suite features a 14½-ft. cathedral ceiling and an opulent private bath with a garden spa tub and a separate shower.
- Upstairs, two secondary bedrooms share a full bath and a balcony overlooking the Great Room below.
- Plans for a two-car garage are available upon request.

Plan DW-2112

Bedrooms: 3	Baths: 2½
Living Area:	
Upper floor	514 sq. ft.
Main floor	1,598 sq. ft.
Total Living Area:	**2,112 sq. ft.**
Standard basement	1,598 sq. ft.
Exterior Wall Framing:	2x4

Foundation Options:

Standard basement
Crawlspace
Slab

(All plans can be built with your choice of foundation and framing. A generic conversion diagram is available. See order form.)

BLUEPRINT PRICE CODE: **C**

UPPER FLOOR

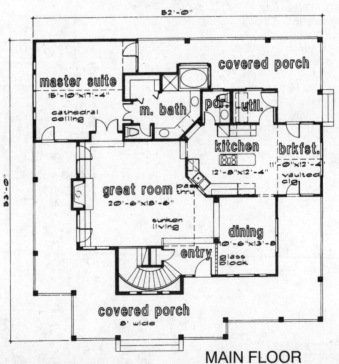

MAIN FLOOR

Open, Flowing Floor Plan

- Open, flowing rooms punctuated with wonderful windows enhance this spacious four-bedroom home.
- The two-story-high foyer is brightened by an arched window above. To the left lies the living room, which flows into the family room. An inviting fireplace and windows overlooking a rear terrace highlight the family room.
- The centrally located kitchen serves both the formal dining room and the dinette, with a view of the family room beyond. Sliding glass doors in the dinette open to a lovely terrace.
- Upstairs, the master suite features an arched window and a walk-in closet with a dressing area. The private master bath includes a dual-sink vanity, a skylighted whirlpool tub and a separate shower.
- The three remaining bedrooms share another skylighted bath.

Plan AHP-9020

Bedrooms: 4	Baths: 2½
Living Area:	
Upper floor	1,021 sq. ft.
Main floor	1,125 sq. ft.
Total Living Area:	**2,146 sq. ft.**
Standard basement	1,032 sq. ft.
Garage	480 sq. ft.
Exterior Wall Framing:	2x6

Foundation Options:

Standard basement

Crawlspace

Slab

(All plans can be built with your choice of foundation and framing. A generic conversion diagram is available. See order form.)

BLUEPRINT PRICE CODE: C

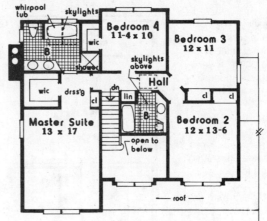

UPPER FLOOR

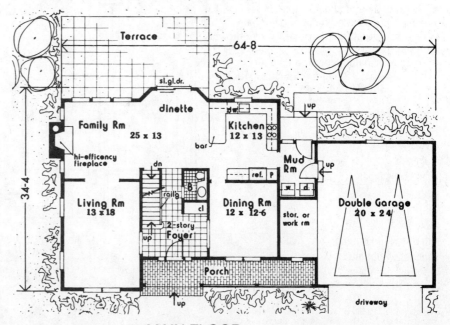

MAIN FLOOR

Spacious Country-Style

- This distinctive country-style home is highlighted by a wide front porch and multi-paned windows with shutters.
- Inside, the dining room is off the foyer and open to the living room, but is defined by elegant columns and beams above.
- The central living room boasts a 12-ft. cathedral ceiling, a fireplace and French doors to the rear patio.
- The delightful kitchen/nook area is spacious and well planned for both work and play.
- A handy utility room and a half-bath are on either side of a short hallway leading to the carport, which includes a large storage area.
- The master suite offers his-and-hers walk-in closets and an incredible bath that incorporates a plant shelf above the raised spa tub.
- The two remaining bedrooms share a hall bath that is compartmentalized to allow more than one user at a time.

Plan J-86140

Bedrooms: 3	Baths: 2½
Living Area:	
Main floor	2,177 sq. ft.
Total Living Area:	**2,177 sq. ft.**
Standard basement	2,177 sq. ft.
Carport	440 sq. ft.
Storage	120 sq. ft.
Exterior Wall Framing:	2x4

Foundation Options:

Standard basement

Crawlspace

Slab

(All plans can be built with your choice of foundation and framing. A generic conversion diagram is available. See order form.)

BLUEPRINT PRICE CODE:	C

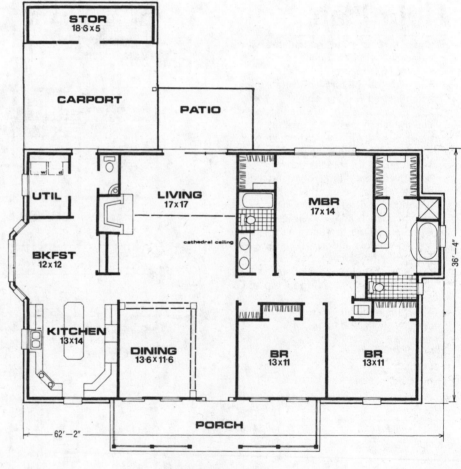

MAIN FLOOR

TO ORDER THIS BLUEPRINT, CALL TOLL-FREE 1-800-547-5570

Plan J-86140

PRICES AND DETAILS ON PAGES 12-15

Country Kitchen

- A lovely front porch, dormers and shutters give this home a country-style exterior and complement its comfortable and informal interior.
- The roomy country kitchen connects with the sunny breakfast nook and the formal dining room.
- The central portion of the home consists of a large family room with a handsome fireplace and easy access to a backyard deck.
- The main-floor master suite, particularly impressive for a home of this size, features a majestic master bath with a corner garden tub, two walk-in closets and a dual-sink vanity with knee space.
- Upstairs, you will find two more good-sized bedrooms, a double bath and a large storage area.

Plan C-8645

Bedrooms: 3	Baths: 2½
Living Area:	
Upper floor	704 sq. ft.
Main floor	1,477 sq. ft.
Total Living Area:	**2,181 sq. ft.**
Standard basement	1,400 sq. ft.
Garage and storage	561 sq. ft.
Exterior Wall Framing:	2x4

Foundation Options:

Standard basement
Crawlspace
Slab

(All plans can be built with your choice of foundation and framing. A generic conversion diagram is available. See order form.)

BLUEPRINT PRICE CODE:	C

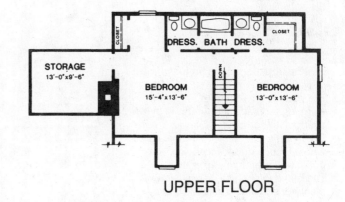

UPPER FLOOR

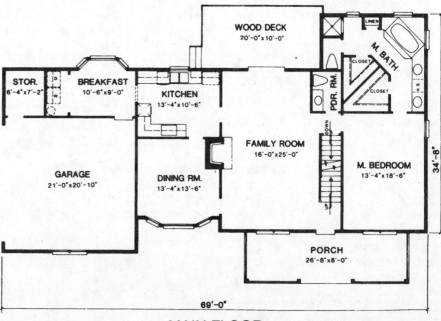

MAIN FLOOR

Versatile Sun Room

- This cozy country-style home offers an inviting front porch and an interior just as welcoming.
- The spacious living room features a warming fireplace and windows that overlook the porch.
- The living room opens to a dining area, where French doors access a covered porch and a sunny patio.
- The island kitchen has a sink view, plenty of counter space, and a handy pass-through to the adjoining sun room. The bright sun room is large enough to serve as a formal dining room, a family room or a hobby room.
- The private master suite is secluded to the rear. A garden spa tub, dual walk-in closets and separate dressing areas are nice features found in the master bath.

Plan J-90014

Bedrooms: 3	Baths: 2½
Living Area:	
Main floor	2,190 sq. ft.
Total Living Area:	**2,190 sq. ft.**
Standard basement	2,190 sq. ft.
Garage	465 sq. ft.
Storage	34 sq. ft.
Exterior Wall Framing:	2x6

Foundation Options:

Standard basement
Crawlspace
Slab

(All plans can be built with your choice of foundation and framing. A generic conversion diagram is available. See order form.)

BLUEPRINT PRICE CODE:	C

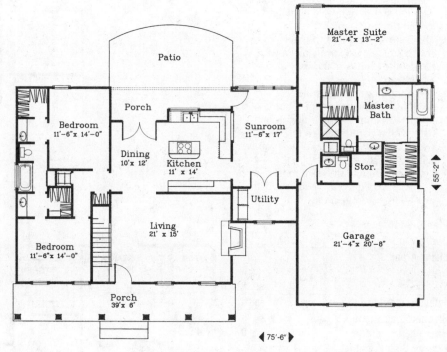

MAIN FLOOR

Plan J-90014

PRICES AND DETAILS
ON PAGES 12-15

Stunning Windows

- This one-story design is enhanced by stunning window arrangements that brighten the formal areas and beyond.
- A step down from the skylighted foyer, the living room sparkles, with a tray ceiling, a striking fireplace and a turret-like bay with high arched windows.
- The island kitchen easily services the sunny bayed dining room and includes a built-in desk, a garden sink and an eating bar to the bright, vaulted nook.
- The adjoining vaulted family room is warmed by a corner woodstove and overlooks the rear patio.
- A decorative plant shelf introduces the bedroom wing. Double doors reveal the master bedroom, which boasts a tray ceiling, a rear window wall and access to the patio. The skylighted master bath includes a raised ceiling, a step-up garden spa tub and a separate shower.
- Across the hall, a den and a second bedroom share another full bath, while the utility room offers garage access.

Plans P-7754-3A & -3D

Bedrooms: 2+	Baths: 2
Living Area:	
Main floor (crawlspace version)	2,200 sq. ft.
Main floor (basement version)	2,288 sq. ft.
Total Living Area:	**2,200/2,288 sq. ft.**
Daylight basement	2,244 sq. ft.
Garage	722 sq. ft.
Exterior Wall Framing:	**2x4**
Foundation Options:	**Plan #**
Daylight basement	P-7754-3D
Crawlspace	P-7754-3A

(All plans can be built with your choice of foundation and framing. A generic conversion diagram is available. See order form.)

BLUEPRINT PRICE CODE:	**C**

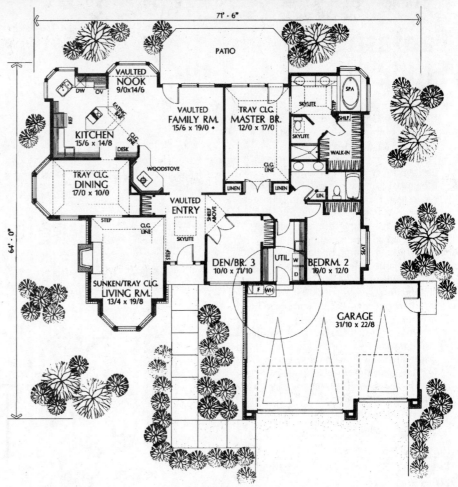

MAIN FLOOR

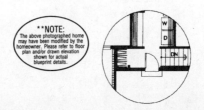

NOTE:
The above photographed home may have been modified by the homeowner. Please refer to floor plan and/or drawn elevation shown for actual blueprint details.

BASEMENT STAIRWAY LOCATION

Photo by Mark Englund

Fantastic Floor Plan!

- Featured on "Hometime," the popular PBS television program, this unique design combines a dynamic exterior with a fantastic floor plan.
- The barrel-vaulted entry leads into the vaulted foyer, which is outlined by elegant columns. To the left, the living room features a 13-ft. vaulted ceiling, a curved wall and corner windows. To the right, the formal dining room is enhanced by a tray ceiling.
- Overlooking a large backyard deck, the island kitchen includes a corner pantry and a built-in desk. The breakfast room shares a columned snack bar with the family room, which has a fireplace and a 17-ft., 8-in. vaulted ceiling.
- The master suite boasts a 15-ft. vaulted ceiling and private access to a romantic courtyard. The sunken master bath features an enticing spa tub and a separate shower, both encased by a curved glass-block wall.
- The two upstairs bedrooms have private access to a large full bath.

Plan B-88015

Bedrooms: 3	Baths: 2½
Living Area:	
Upper floor	534 sq. ft.
Main floor	1,689 sq. ft.
Total Living Area:	**2,223 sq. ft.**
Standard basement	1,689 sq. ft.
Garage	455 sq. ft.
Exterior Wall Framing:	2x4

Foundation Options:

Standard basement

(All plans can be built with your choice of foundation and framing. A generic conversion diagram is available. See order form.)

BLUEPRINT PRICE CODE:	C

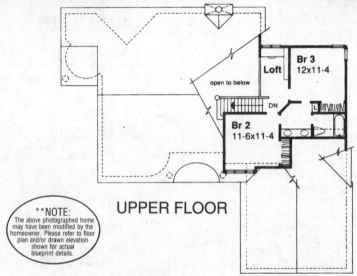

**NOTE: The above photographed home may have been modified by the homeowner. Please refer to floor plan and/or drawn elevation shown for actual blueprint details.

UPPER FLOOR

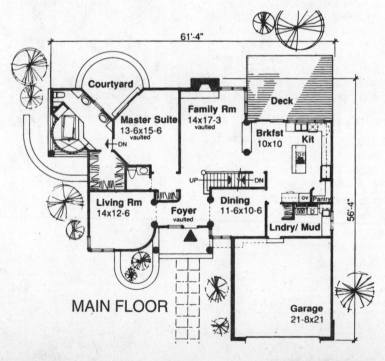

MAIN FLOOR

Plan B-88015

PRICES AND DETAILS
ON PAGES 12-15

Gracious Traditional

- This traditional home is perfect for a corner lot, with a quaint facade and an attached garage around back.
- Tall windows, elegant dormers and a covered front porch welcome guests to the front entry and into the foyer.
- Just off the foyer, the formal dining room boasts a built-in hutch and views to the front porch.
- The expansive, skylighted Great Room features a wet bar, a 16-ft. vaulted ceiling, a stunning fireplace and access to the screened back porch.
- The kitchen includes a large pantry and an eating bar to the bayed breakfast nook. A large utility room with garage access is nearby.
- The master bedroom offers a walk-in closet and a bath with a large corner tub and his-and-hers vanities.
- Two additional bedrooms have big walk-in closets, built-in desks and easy access to another full bath.
- Upstairs, a loft overlooks the Great Room and is perfect as an extra bedroom or a recreation area.

Plan C-8920

Bedrooms: 3+	**Baths:** 3

Living Area:	
Upper floor	305 sq. ft.
Main floor	1,996 sq. ft.
Total Living Area:	**2,301 sq. ft.**
Daylight basement	1,996 sq. ft.
Garage	469 sq. ft.
Exterior Wall Framing:	2x4

Foundation Options:
Daylight basement
Crawlspace
(All plans can be built with your choice of foundation and framing. A generic conversion diagram is available. See order form.)

BLUEPRINT PRICE CODE:	C

MAIN FLOOR

UPPER FLOOR

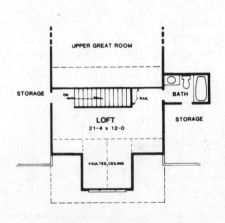

You Asked for It!

- Our most popular plan in recent years, E-3000, has now been downsized for affordability, without sacrificing character or excitement.
- Exterior appeal is created with a covered front porch with decorative columns, triple dormers and rail-topped bay windows.
- The floor plan has combined the separate living and family rooms available in E-3000 into one spacious family room with corner fireplace, which flows into the dining room through a columned gallery.
- The kitchen serves the breakfast room over an angled snack bar, and features a huge pantry.
- The stunning main-floor master suite offers a private sitting area, a walk-in closet and a dramatic, angled bath.
- There are two large bedrooms upstairs accessible via a curved staircase with bridge balcony.

Plan E-2307

Bedrooms: 3	Baths: 2½
Living Area:	
Upper floor	595 sq. ft.
Main floor	1,765 sq. ft.
Total Living Area:	**2,360 sq. ft.**
Standard basement	1,765 sq. ft.
Garage	484 sq. ft.
Storage	44 sq. ft.
Exterior Wall Framing:	2x6

Foundation Options:
Standard basement
Crawlspace
Slab
(All plans can be built with your choice of foundation and framing. A generic conversion diagram is available. See order form.)

BLUEPRINT PRICE CODE: C

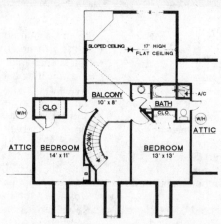

UPPER FLOOR

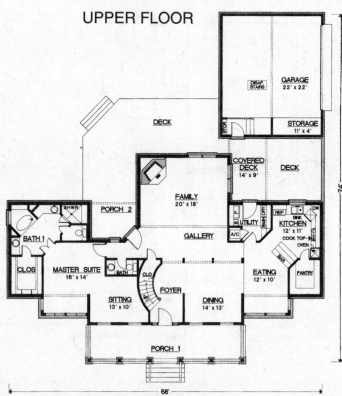

MAIN FLOOR

TO ORDER THIS BLUEPRINT, CALL TOLL-FREE 1-800-547-5570

Plan E-2307

PRICES AND DETAILS ON PAGES 12-15

High Luxury in One Story

- Beautiful arched windows lend a luxurious feeling to the exterior of this one-story home.
- Soaring 12-ft. ceilings add volume to both the wide entry area and the central living room, which boasts a large fireplace and access to a covered porch and the patio beyond.
- Double doors separate the formal dining room from the corridor-style kitchen. Features of the kitchen include a pantry and an angled eating bar. The sunny, bayed eating area is perfect for casual family meals.
- The plush master suite has amazing amenities: a walk-in closet, a skylighted, angled whirlpool tub, a separate shower and private access to the laundry/utility room and the patio.
- Three good-sized bedrooms and a full bath are situated across the home.

Plan E-2302

Bedrooms: 4	**Baths:** 2

Living Area:	
Main floor	2,396 sq. ft.
Total Living Area:	**2,396 sq. ft.**
Standard basement	2,396 sq. ft.
Garage	484 sq. ft.
Exterior Wall Framing:	2x6

Foundation Options:

Standard basement

Crawlspace

Slab

(All plans can be built with your choice of foundation and framing. A generic conversion diagram is available. See order form.)

BLUEPRINT PRICE CODE:	C

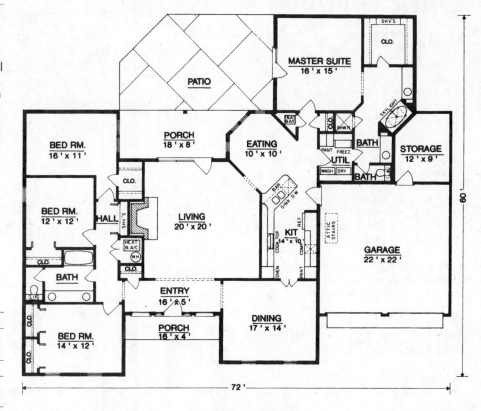

MAIN FLOOR

Photo by Mark Englund/HomeStyles

Old-Fashioned Charm

- A trio of dormers add old-fashioned charm to this modern design.
- Both the living room and the dining room offer 12-ft.-high vaulted ceilings and flow together to create a sense of even more spaciousness.
- The open kitchen/nook/family room features a sunny alcove, a walk-in pantry and a woodstove.
- A first-floor den and a walk-through utility room are other big bonuses.
- Upstairs, the master suite includes a walk-in closet and a deluxe bath with a spa tub and a separate shower and water closet.
- Two more bedrooms, each with a window seat, and a bonus room complete this stylish design.

Plan CDG-2004

Bedrooms: 3+	Baths: 2½
Living Area:	
Upper floor	928 sq. ft.
Main floor	1,317 sq. ft.
Bonus area	192 sq. ft.
Total Living Area:	**2,437 sq. ft.**
Partial daylight basement	780 sq. ft.
Garage	537 sq. ft.
Exterior Wall Framing:	2x6

Foundation Options:

Partial daylight basement

Crawlspace

(All plans can be built with your choice of foundation and framing. A generic conversion diagram is available. See order form.)

BLUEPRINT PRICE CODE:	**C**

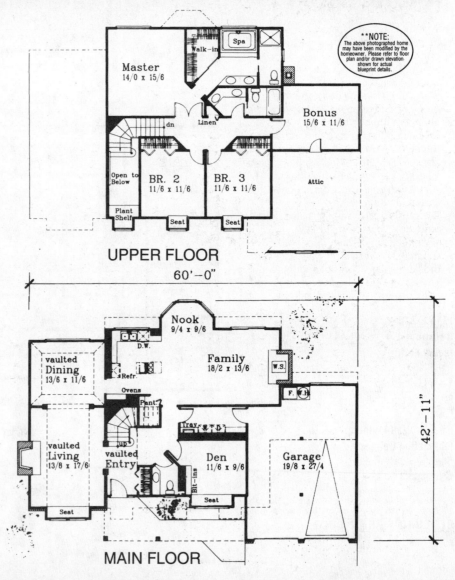

UPPER FLOOR

MAIN FLOOR

Photo by Karlis Grants

Dramatic Interior Spaces

- This home's design utilizes unique shapes and angles to create a dramatic and dynamic interior.
- Skylights brighten the impressive two-story entry from high above, as it flows to the formal living areas.
- The sunken Great Room features a massive stone-hearthed fireplace with flanking windows, plus a 19-ft. vaulted ceiling. Sliding glass doors open the formal dining room to a backyard patio.
- The spacious kitchen features an oversized island, plenty of counter space and a sunny breakfast nook.
- A den or third bedroom shares a full bath with another secondary bedroom to complete the main floor.
- An incredible bayed master suite takes up the entire upper floor of the home. The skylighted master bath features a bright walk-in closet, a dual-sink vanity, a sunken tub and a separate shower.

Plans P-6580-3A & -3D

Bedrooms: 2+	Baths: 2
Living Area:	
Upper floor	705 sq. ft.
Main floor	1,738 sq. ft.
Total Living Area:	**2,443 sq. ft.**
Daylight basement	1,738 sq. ft.
Garage	512 sq. ft.
Exterior Wall Framing:	2x4
Foundation Options:	**Plan #**
Daylight basement	P-6580-3D
Crawlspace	P-6580-3A

(All plans can be built with your choice of foundation and framing. A generic conversion diagram is available. See order form.)

BLUEPRINT PRICE CODE:	C

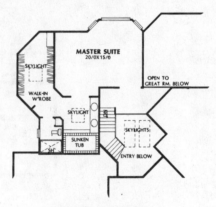

UPPER FLOOR

NOTE:
The above photographed home may have been modified by the homeowner. Please refer to floor plan and/or drawn elevation shown for actual blueprint details.

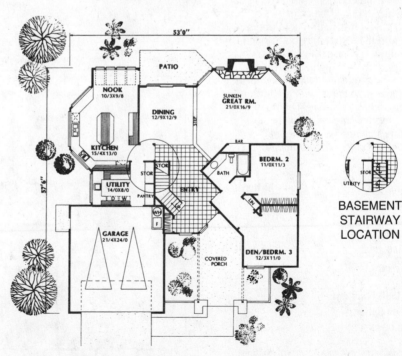

MAIN FLOOR

BASEMENT STAIRWAY LOCATION

Panoramic Porch

- A gracious, ornately rounded front porch and a two-story turreted bay lend Victorian charm to this home.
- A two-story foyer with round-top transom windows and a plant ledge above greets guests at the entry.
- The living room enjoys a 13-ft.-high ceiling and a panoramic view overlooking the front porch and yard.
- The formal dining room and den each feature a bay window for added style.
- The sunny kitchen incorporates an angled island cooktop with a eating bar to the bayed breakfast room.
- A step down, the family room offers a corner fireplace that may be enjoyed throughout the casual living spaces.
- The upper floor is highlighted by a stunning master suite, which flaunts an octagonal sitting area with a 10-ft. tray ceiling and turreted bay. The master bath offers a corner spa tub and a separate shower. Two additional bedrooms share another full bath.

Plan AX-90307

Bedrooms: 3+	Baths: 3
Living Area:	
Upper floor	956 sq. ft.
Main floor	1,499 sq. ft.
Total Living Area:	**2,455 sq. ft.**
Standard basement	1,499 sq. ft.
Garage	410 sq. ft.
Exterior Wall Framing:	2x4

Foundation Options:

Standard basement

Slab

(All plans can be built with your choice of foundation and framing. A generic conversion diagram is available. See order form.)

BLUEPRINT PRICE CODE:	C

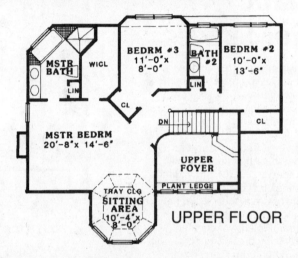

UPPER FLOOR

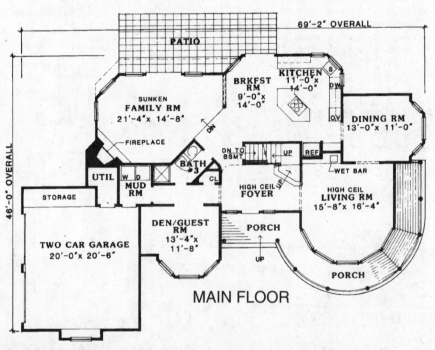

MAIN FLOOR

Photo by Kershner Communications

All-American Country Home

- The covered wraparound porch of this popular all-American home creates an old-fashioned country appeal.
- Off the entryway is the generous-sized living room, which offers a fireplace and French doors that open to the porch.
- The large adjoining dining room further expands the entertaining area.
- The country kitchen has a handy island and flows into the cozy family room, which is enhanced by exposed beams. A handsome fireplace warms the entire informal area, while windows overlook the porch.
- The quiet upper floor hosts four good-sized bedrooms and two baths. The master suite includes a walk-in closet, a dressing area and a private bath with a sit-down shower.
- This home is available with or without a basement and with or without a garage.

PLANS H-3711-1 & -1A WITH GARAGE

NOTE: The above photographed home may have been modified by the homeowner. Please refer to floor plan and/or drawn elevation shown for actual blueprint details.

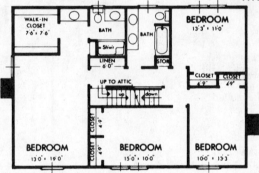

PLANS H-3711-2 & -2A WITHOUT GARAGE

Plans H-3711-1, -1A, -2 & -2A

Bedrooms: 4	Baths: 2½
Living Area:	
Upper floor	1,176 sq. ft.
Main floor	1,288 sq. ft.
Total Living Area:	**2,464 sq. ft.**
Standard basement	1,176 sq. ft.
Garage	505 sq. ft.
Exterior Wall Framing:	2x6
Foundation Options:	**Plan #**
Basement with garage	H-3711-1
Basement without garage	H-3711-2
Crawlspace with garage	H-3711-1A
Crawlspace without garage	H-3711-2A

(All plans can be built with your choice of foundation and framing. A generic conversion diagram is available. See order form.)

BLUEPRINT PRICE CODE: C

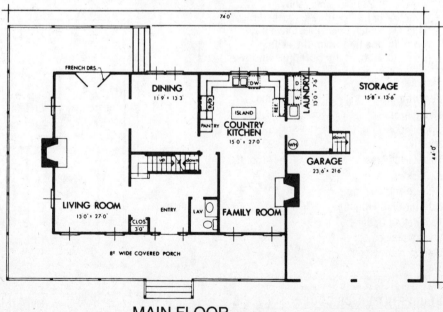

UPPER FLOOR

MAIN FLOOR

Large-Scale Living

- Eye-catching windows and an appealing wraparound porch highlight the exterior of this outstanding home.
- Inside, high ceilings and large-scale living spaces prevail, beginning with the foyer, which has an 18-ft. ceiling.
- The spacious living room flows into the formal dining room, which opens to the porch and to an optional rear deck.
- The island kitchen extends to a bright breakfast room with deck access. The family room offers an 18-ft. vaulted ceiling and a corner fireplace.
- Unless otherwise noted, every main-floor room boasts a 9-ft. ceiling.
- Upstairs, the lush master bedroom boasts an 11-ft. vaulted ceiling and two walk-in closets. The skylighted master bath features a spa tub, a separate shower and a dual-sink vanity.
- Three more bedrooms are reached by a balcony, which overlooks the family room. In one bedroom, the ceiling jumps to 10 ft. at the beautiful window.

Plan AX-93309

Bedrooms: 4	Baths: 2½
Living Area:	
Upper floor	1,180 sq. ft.
Main floor	1,290 sq. ft.
Total Living Area:	**2,470 sq. ft.**
Basement	1,290 sq. ft.
Garage and storage	421 sq. ft.
Exterior Wall Framing:	2x4

Foundation Options:

Daylight basement

Standard basement

Slab

(All plans can be built with your choice of foundation and framing. A generic conversion diagram is available. See order form.)

BLUEPRINT PRICE CODE: C

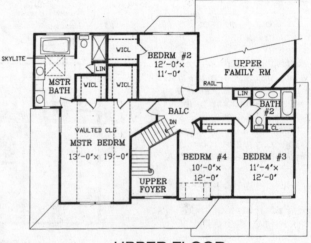

UPPER FLOOR

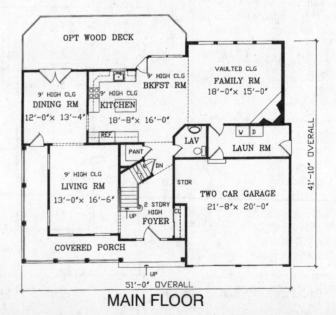

MAIN FLOOR

   Plan AX-93309   **PRICES AND DETAILS** ON PAGES 12-15

Down-Home Country Flavor!

- Open living areas, decorative dormers and a spacious wraparound porch give this charming home its country feel.
- The main entrance opens into an enormous living room, which boasts a handsome fireplace flanked by bright windows and built-in cabinets.
- The adjoining dining room is brightened by windows on three sides. A rear French door opens to the porch.
- The modern kitchen serves the dining room over an eating bar. A half-bath and a laundry/utility area with access to the garage and porch are nearby.
- The removed master bedroom includes a roomy walk-in closet and a private bath with a corner shower and a dual-sink vanity with knee space.
- All main-floor rooms have 9-ft. ceilings.
- Two upper-floor bedrooms share a hallway bath, which is enhanced by one of three dormer windows.

Plan J-90013

Bedrooms: 3	Baths: 2½
Living Area:	
Upper floor	823 sq. ft.
Main floor	1,339 sq. ft.
Total Living Area:	**2,162 sq. ft.**
Standard basement	1,339 sq. ft.
Garage	413 sq. ft.
Storage	106 sq. ft.
Exterior Wall Framing:	2x4

Foundation Options:

Standard basement
Crawlspace
Slab

(All plans can be built with your choice of foundation and framing. A generic conversion diagram is available. See order form.)

BLUEPRINT PRICE CODE:	C

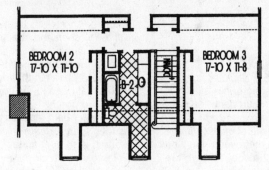

UPPER FLOOR

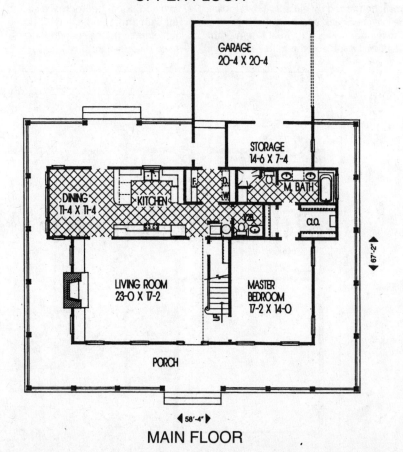

MAIN FLOOR

A Taste of Europe

- This tasteful one-story home is characterized by a European exterior and an ultra-modern interior.
- High 10-ft. ceilings grace the central living areas, from the foyer to the Great Room, and from the nook through the kitchen to the dining room.
- The inviting Great Room showcases a fireplace framed by glass that overlooks the covered back porch.
- A snack bar unites the Great Room with the bayed nook and the galley-style kitchen. A spacious utility room is just off the kitchen and accessible from the two-car garage as well.
- The secluded master suite boasts a luxurious private bath and French doors that open to the covered backyard porch.
- The master bath features a raised garden spa tub set into an intimate corner, with a separate shower nearby. A large walk-in closet and two sinks separated by a built-in makeup table are also included.
- Two additional bedrooms, a second full bath and a front study or home office make up the remainder of this up-to-date design.

Plan VL-2162	
Bedrooms: 3	**Baths:** 2
Living Area:	
Main floor	2,162 sq. ft.
Total Living Area:	**2,162 sq. ft.**
Garage	498 sq. ft.
Exterior Wall Framing:	2x4
Foundation Options:	
Crawlspace	
Slab	

(All plans can be built with your choice of foundation and framing. A generic conversion diagram is available. See order form.)

BLUEPRINT PRICE CODE:	C

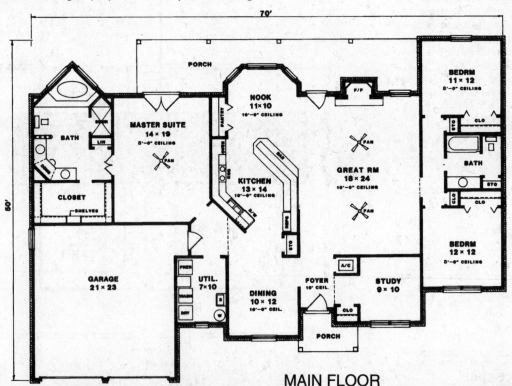

MAIN FLOOR

Plan VL-2162

Welcoming Curb Appeal

- A covered porch, a bay window and decorative trim create a pleasant curb appeal for this country-style home.
- Inside, a formal living room and dining room flank the two-story foyer with its central open-railed stairway.
- A spectacular sunken family room with a masonry fireplace and a three-sided backyard view sits at the rear of the home.
- At the center of the floor plan, the roomy island kitchen and dinette combine for a spacious setting. A closet pantry, a work desk and outdoor access through sliding glass doors are featured.
- A handy main-floor laundry closet is located near the powder room at the garage entrance.
- Three nice-sized secondary bedrooms and a big master bedroom with a personal bath and a walk-in closet are included in the upper level.

Plan GL-2164-P

Bedrooms: 4	Baths: 2½
Living Area:	
Upper floor	1,062 sq. ft.
Main floor	1,102 sq. ft.
Total Living Area:	**2,164 sq. ft.**
Standard basement	1,102 sq. ft.
Garage	525 sq. ft.
Exterior Wall Framing:	2x6

Foundation Options:

Standard basement

(All plans can be built with your choice of foundation and framing. A generic conversion diagram is available. See order form.)

BLUEPRINT PRICE CODE:	C

UPPER FLOOR

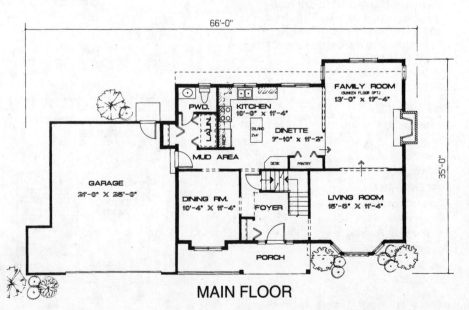

MAIN FLOOR

Updated Classic

- Light-filled and airy, this classic country-style home is filled with modern amenities.
- Brightened by high transom windows, the inviting two-story-high foyer flows into the spacious living room and the formal dining room.
- The efficient kitchen features a breakfast bar and a window over the sink. The adjoining dinette offers sliding glass doors to a backyard terrace. The nearby mudroom/laundry room has garage and backyard access.
- The friendly family room enjoys a view of the backyard through a row of three windows. The handsome fireplace is flanked by glass.
- Upstairs, the spectacular master bedroom boasts a 10-ft. cathedral ceiling and a roomy walk-in closet. The skylighted master bath showcases a whirlpool tub, a separate shower and a dual-sink vanity.
- Another skylighted bath services the three remaining bedrooms.

Plan AHP-9402

Bedrooms: 4	Baths: 2½
Living Area:	
Upper floor	1,041 sq. ft.
Main floor	1,129 sq. ft.
Total Living Area:	**2,170 sq. ft.**
Standard basement	1,129 sq. ft.
Garage and storage	630 sq. ft.
Exterior Wall Framing:	2x4 or 2x6

Foundation Options:

Standard basement

Crawlspace

Slab

(All plans can be built with your choice of foundation and framing. A generic conversion diagram is available. See order form.)

BLUEPRINT PRICE CODE: C

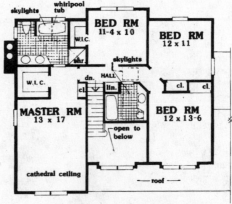

UPPER FLOOR

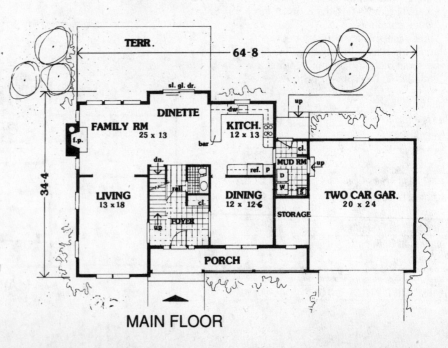

MAIN FLOOR

Plan AHP-9402

PRICES AND DETAILS
ON PAGES 12-15

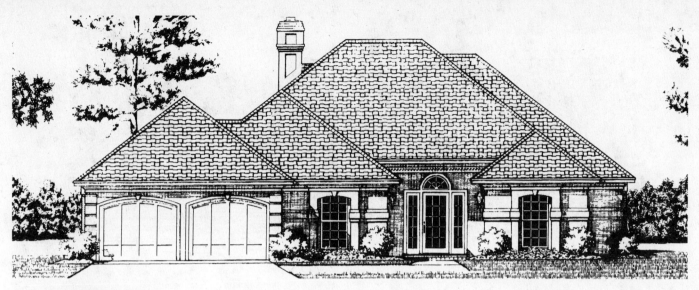

Luxurious Master Suite

- The inviting facade of this gorgeous one-story design boasts a sheltered porch, symmetrical architecture and elegant window treatments.
- Inside, beautiful arched openings frame the living room, which features a 12-ft. ceiling, a dramatic fireplace and a wet bar that is open to the deluxe kitchen.
- The roomy kitchen is highlighted by an island cooktop, a built-in desk and a snack bar that faces the bayed eating area and the covered back porch.
- Isolated to the rear of the home, the master suite is a romantic retreat, offering an intimate sitting area and a luxurious bath. Entered through elegant double doors, the private bath showcases a skylighted corner tub, a separate shower, his-and-hers vanities, and a huge walk-in closet.
- The two remaining bedrooms have walk-in closets and share a hall bath.
- Unless otherwise specified, the home has 9-ft. ceilings throughout.

Plan E-2106

Bedrooms: 3	Baths: 2
Living Area:	
Main floor	2,177 sq. ft.
Total Living Area:	**2,177 sq. ft.**
Standard basement	2,177 sq. ft.
Garage and storage	570 sq. ft.
Exterior Wall Framing:	2x4

Foundation Options:

Standard basement
Crawlspace
Slab

(All plans can be built with your choice of foundation and framing. A generic conversion diagram is available. See order form.)

BLUEPRINT PRICE CODE: C

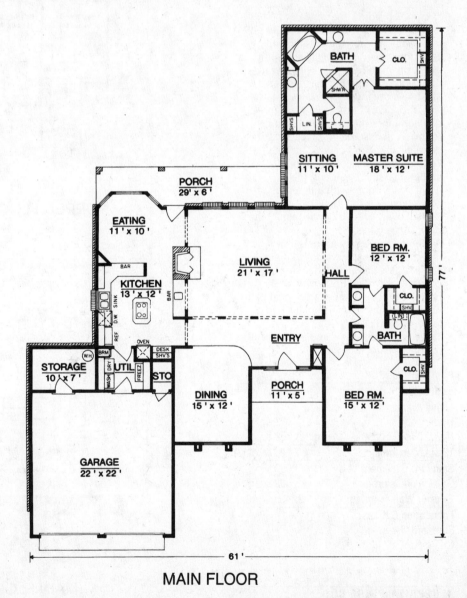

MAIN FLOOR

A Move Up

- Narrow lap siding and repeated half-round windows with divided panes give this traditional home a different look.
- The roomy interior offers space for the upwardly mobile family, with four to five bedrooms and large activity areas.
- The two-story foyer welcomes guests into a spacious formal living expanse that combines the living and dining rooms. A handsome fireplace and a dramatic cathedral ceiling are featured.
- Behind double doors is a cozy study or an optional fifth bedroom.
- A big family room with a fireplace and a media center is the focus of the informal areas. Lovely French doors open to the backyard terrace.
- Adjoining the family room is a well-designed kitchen and a bayed dinette.
- The master suite is secluded in a quiet corner of the main floor. The suite boasts a private terrace, a personal bath with a skylighted whirlpool tub and a large walk-in closet.
- Three more bedrooms and another bath occupy the upper floor.

Plan AHP-9396

Bedrooms: 4+	Baths: 2½
Living Area:	
Upper floor	643 sq. ft.
Main floor	1,553 sq. ft.
Total Living Area:	**2,196 sq. ft.**
Standard basement	1,553 sq. ft.
Garage and storage	502 sq. ft.
Exterior Wall Framing:	2x4 or 2x6

Foundation Options:

Standard basement
Crawlspace
Slab

(All plans can be built with your choice of foundation and framing. A generic conversion diagram is available. See order form.)

BLUEPRINT PRICE CODE: C

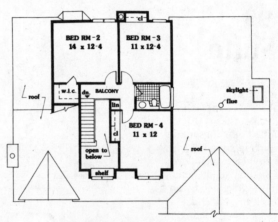

UPPER FLOOR

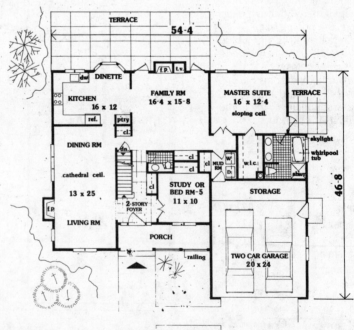

MAIN FLOOR

Plan AHP-9396

PRICES AND DETAILS ON PAGES 12-15

Contemporary Elegance

- This striking contemporary design combines vertical siding with elegant traditional overtones.
- Inside, an expansive activity area is created with the joining of the vaulted living room, the family/dining room and the kitchen. The openness of the rooms creates a spacious, dramatic feeling, which extends to an exciting two-story sun space and a patio beyond.

- A convenient utility/service area near the garage includes a clothes-sorting counter, a deep sink and ironing space.
- Two main-floor bedrooms share a bright bath.
- The master suite includes a sumptuous skylighted bath with two entrances. The tub is uniquely positioned on an angled wall, while the shower and toilet are secluded behind a pocket door. An optional overlook provides views down into the sun space, which is accessed by a spiral staircase.
- A versatile loft area and a bonus room complete this design.

Plan LRD-1971

Bedrooms: 3+	**Baths:** 2

Living Area:	
Upper floor	723 sq. ft.
Main floor	1,248 sq. ft.
Sun space	116 sq. ft.
Bonus room	225 sq. ft.
Total Living Area:	**2,312 sq. ft.**
Standard basement	1,248 sq. ft.
Garage	483 sq. ft.
Exterior Wall Framing:	2x6

Foundation Options:

Standard basement

Crawlspace

(All plans can be built with your choice of foundation and framing. A generic conversion diagram is available. See order form.)

BLUEPRINT PRICE CODE:	C

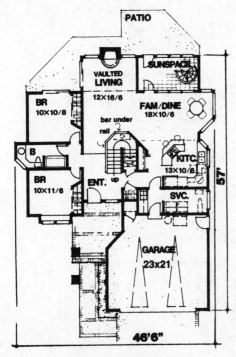

MAIN FLOOR

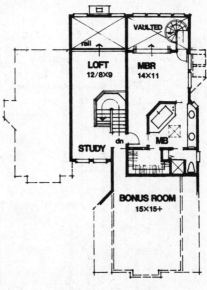

UPPER FLOOR

Classic Styling

- This handsome one-story traditional would look great in town or in the country. The shuttered and paned windows, narrow lap siding and brick accents make it a classic.
- The sprawling design begins with the spacious, central living room, featuring a beamed ceiling that slopes up to 14 feet. A window wall overlooks the covered backyard porch, and an

inviting fireplace includes an extra-wide hearth and built-in bookshelves.
- The galley-style kitchen features a snack bar to the sunny eating area and a raised-panel door to the dining room.
- The isolated master suite is a quiet haven offering a large walk-in closet, a dressing room and a spacious bath.
- Three more bedrooms, two with walk-in closets, and a compartmentalized bath are located at the opposite side of the home.

Plan E-2206

Bedrooms: 4	Baths: 2
Living Area:	
Main floor	2,200 sq. ft.
Total Living Area:	**2,200 sq. ft.**
Standard basement	2,200 sq. ft.
Garage and storage	624 sq. ft.
Exterior Wall Framing:	2x6

Foundation Options:

Standard basement
Crawlspace
Slab
(All plans can be built with your choice of foundation and framing. A generic conversion diagram is available. See order form.)

BLUEPRINT PRICE CODE:	C

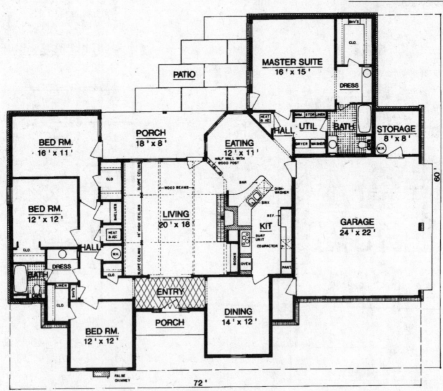

MAIN FLOOR

Plan E-2206

Artful Arches

- This home's wonderful windows and gorgeous gables are accentuated by artful brickwork arches.
- A covered porch with columns leads into the tiled entry, brightened by sidelights and a half-round transom.
- The entry flows into the tray-ceilinged formal dining room, lighted by a stunning arch-top window arangement.
- The sunny island kitchen features a bay window in the breakfast area, a nifty planning desk and corner windows over the sink. Laundry facilities and garage access are also nearby.
- The vaulted Great Room, highlighted by tall casement windows, opens to a rear patio through sliding doors. A unique fireplace warms the entire area.
- The luxurious vaulted master suite, which walks out to its own patio, boasts a large walk-in closet and a generous bath with dual vanities, a whirlpool tub and a separate shower.
- On the upper floor, a balcony with a plant shelf overlooks the Great Room below and three nice bedrooms share two full baths.

Plan AG-2201

Bedrooms: 4	Baths: 3½
Living Area:	
Upper floor	716 sq. ft.
Main floor	1,496 sq. ft.
Total Living Area:	**2,212 sq. ft.**
Standard basement	1,450 sq. ft.
Garage	484 sq. ft.
Exterior Wall Framing:	2x6

Foundation Options:

Standard basement

(All plans can be built with your choice of foundation and framing. A generic conversion diagram is available. See order form.)

BLUEPRINT PRICE CODE:	C

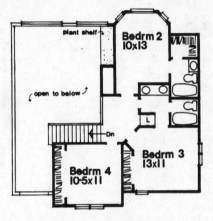

UPPER FLOOR

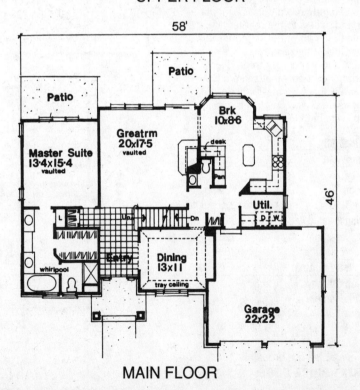

MAIN FLOOR

Tradition Recreated

- Classic traditional styling is recreated in this home with its covered porch, triple dormers and half-round windows.
- A central hall stems from the two-story-high foyer and accesses each of the main living areas.
- A large formal space is created with the merging of the living room and the dining room. The living room boasts a fireplace and a view of the front porch.
- The informal spaces merge at the rear of the home. The kitchen features an oversized cooktop island. The sunny dinette is enclosed with a circular glass wall. The family room boasts a media center and access to the rear terrace.
- A convenient main-floor laundry room sits near the garage entrance.
- The upper floor includes three secondary bedrooms that share a full bath, and a spacious master bedroom that offers dual walk-in closets and a large private bath.

Plan AHP-9393

Bedrooms: 4+	Baths: 3
Living Area:	
Upper floor	989 sq. ft.
Main floor	1,223 sq. ft.
Total Living Area:	**2,212 sq. ft.**
Standard basement	1,223 sq. ft.
Garage and storage	488 sq. ft.
Exterior Wall Framing:	2x4 or 2x6

Foundation Options:
Standard basement
Crawlspace
Slab
(Typical foundation & framing conversion diagram available—see order form.)

BLUEPRINT PRICE CODE: **C**

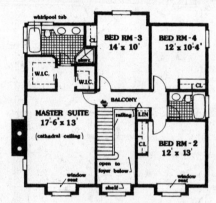

UPPER FLOOR

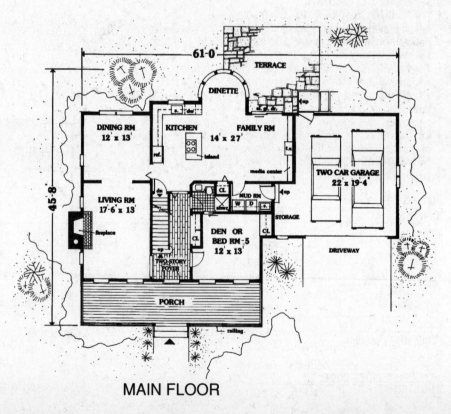

MAIN FLOOR

TO ORDER THIS BLUEPRINT,
CALL TOLL-FREE 1-800-547-5570

Plan AHP-9393

PRICES AND DETAILS
ON PAGES 12-15

A Custom Contemporary

- Clean lines and custom design touches are found throughout this contemporary home.
- A spectacular vaulted Great Room enclosed in windows offers a fireplace and a wraparound deck.
- Open to the Great Room is a cozy dining area and kitchen with island cooktop/eating bar, pantry and view of the adjoining deck.
- The secluded master suite has a coved ceiling, large walk-in closet and private bath with dual vanities, garden tub and separate shower.
- Two additional bedrooms, plus a guest room or den that can be enclosed or informally open, are found on the upper level.

Plan LRD-51391

Bedrooms: 3+	Baths: 3
Living Area:	
Upper floor	550 sq. ft.
Main floor	1,671 sq. ft.
Total Living Area:	**2,221 sq. ft.**
Standard basement	1,671 sq. ft.
Garage	552 sq. ft.
Exterior Wall Framing:	2x6

Foundation Options:
Standard basement
Crawlspace
(Foundation & framing conversion diagram available — see order form.)

BLUEPRINT PRICE CODE:	C

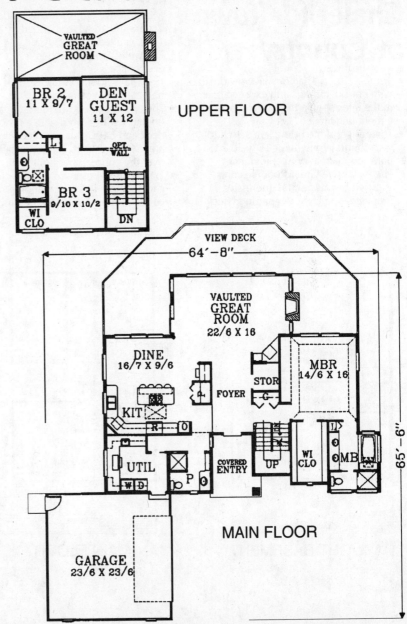

UPPER FLOOR

MAIN FLOOR

Chalet for Town or Country

- Vertical siding, spacious viewing decks with cut-out railings and exposed beams in the interior give this home the look of a mountain chalet.
- The design of the home lends itself to year-round family living as well as to part-time recreational enjoyment.
- The expansive Great Room features exposed beams and an impressive fireplace. The large wraparound deck is accessed through sliding glass doors. The dining area is expanded by an 18-ft. vaulted ceiling.
- The well-planned kitchen is open and easily accessible.
- Two main-floor bedrooms share the hall bath between them.
- The upstairs offers an adult retreat: a fine master bedroom with a private deck and bath, plus a versatile loft area. An airy 13-ft. ceiling presides over the entire upper floor.
- The daylight-basement level includes a garage and a large recreation room with a fireplace and a half-bath.

Plan P-531-2D

Bedrooms: 3+	Baths: 2½
Living Area:	
Upper floor	573 sq. ft.
Main floor	1,120 sq. ft.
Daylight basement	532 sq. ft.
Total Living Area:	**2,225 sq. ft.**
Tuck-under garage	541 sq. ft.
Exterior Wall Framing:	2x6

Foundation Options:

Daylight basement

(All plans can be built with your choice of foundation and framing. A generic conversion diagram is available. See order form.)

BLUEPRINT PRICE CODE: C

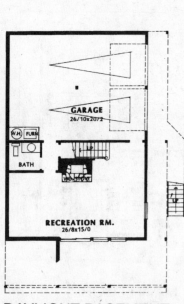

DAYLIGHT BASEMENT

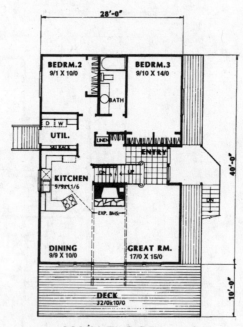

MAIN FLOOR

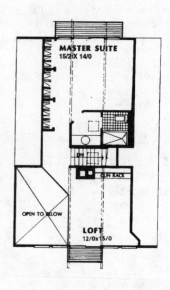

UPPER FLOOR

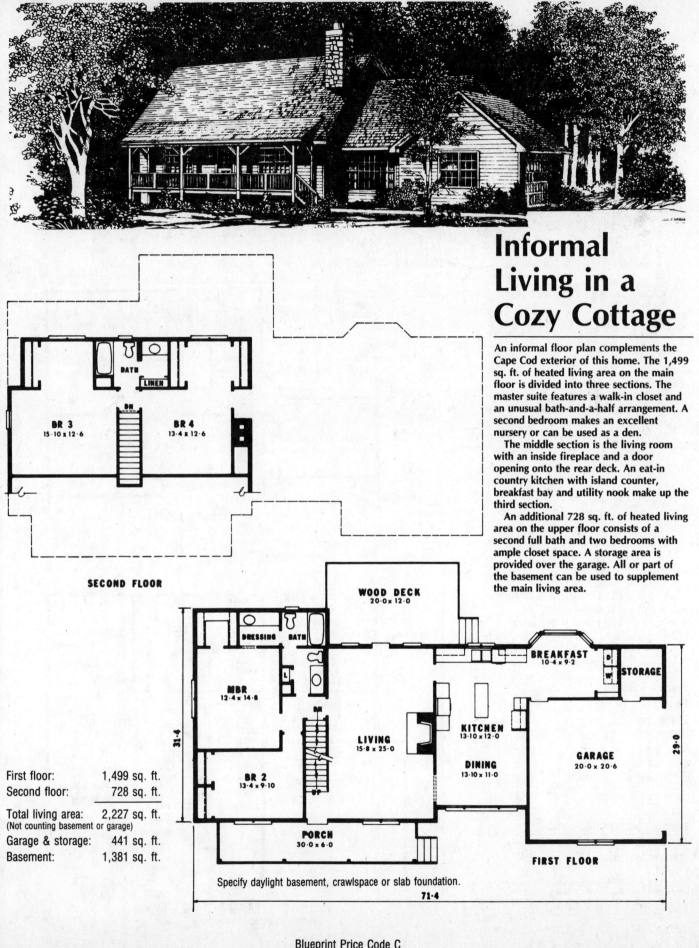

Informal Living in a Cozy Cottage

An informal floor plan complements the Cape Cod exterior of this home. The 1,499 sq. ft. of heated living area on the main floor is divided into three sections. The master suite features a walk-in closet and an unusual bath-and-a-half arrangement. A second bedroom makes an excellent nursery or can be used as a den.

The middle section is the living room with an inside fireplace and a door opening onto the rear deck. An eat-in country kitchen with island counter, breakfast bay and utility nook make up the third section.

An additional 728 sq. ft. of heated living area on the upper floor consists of a second full bath and two bedrooms with ample closet space. A storage area is provided over the garage. All or part of the basement can be used to supplement the main living area.

SECOND FLOOR

BR 3
15·10 x 12·6

BR 4
13·4 x 12·6

BATH

LINEN

DN

FIRST FLOOR

WOOD DECK
20·0 x 12·0

DRESSING   BATH

MBR
12·4 x 14·8

BREAKFAST
10·4 x 9·2

STORAGE

LIVING
15·8 x 25·0

KITCHEN
13·10 x 12·0

GARAGE
20·0 x 20·6

DINING
13·10 x 11·0

BR 2
13·4 x 9·10

DN

UP

PORCH
30·0 x 6·0

31·4

29·0

71·4

First floor: 1,499 sq. ft.
Second floor: 728 sq. ft.

Total living area: 2,227 sq. ft.
(Not counting basement or garage)
Garage & storage: 441 sq. ft.
Basement: 1,381 sq. ft.

Specify daylight basement, crawlspace or slab foundation.

Blueprint Price Code C
Plan C-8030

Appealing and Well-Appointed

- A feature-filled interior and a warm, appealing exterior are the keynotes of this spacious two-story home.
- Beyond the charming front porch, the foyer is brightened by sidelights and an octagonal window. To the right, a cased opening leads into the open living room and dining room. Plenty of windows, including a beautiful boxed-out window, bathe the formal area in light.
- The casual area consists of an extra-large island kitchen, a sizable breakfast area and a spectacular family room with a corner fireplace and a skylighted cathedral ceiling that slopes from 11 ft. to 17 ft. high.
- The upper floor hosts a superb master suite, featuring a skylighted bath with an 11-ft. sloped ceiling, a platform spa tub and a separate shower.
- A balcony hall leads to two more bedrooms, a full bath and an optional bonus room that would make a great loft, study or extra bedroom.

Plan AX-8923-A

Bedrooms: 3+	Baths: 2½
Living Area:	
Upper floor	853 sq. ft.
Main floor	1,199 sq. ft.
Optional loft/bedroom	180 sq. ft.
Total Living Area:	**2,232 sq. ft.**
Standard basement	1,184 sq. ft.
Garage	420 sq. ft.
Exterior Wall Framing:	2x4

Foundation Options:

Standard basement

Slab

(All plans can be built with your choice of foundation and framing. A generic conversion diagram is available. See order form.)

BLUEPRINT PRICE CODE: C

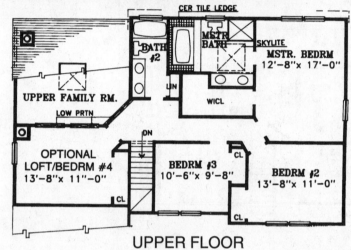

UPPER FLOOR

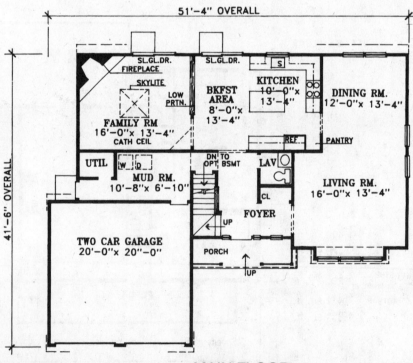

MAIN FLOOR

TO ORDER THIS BLUEPRINT, CALL TOLL-FREE 1-800-547-5570

Plan AX-8923-A

PRICES AND DETAILS ON PAGES 12-15

Luxurious Living on One Level

- The elegant exterior of this spacious one-story presents a classic air of quality and distinction.
- Three French doors brighten the inviting entry, which flows into the spacious living room. Boasting a 13-ft. ceiling, the living room enjoys a fireplace with a wide hearth and adjoining built-in bookshelves. A wall of glass, including a French door, provides views of the sheltered backyard porch.
- A stylish angled counter joins the spacious kitchen to the sunny bay-windowed eating nook.
- Secluded for privacy, the master suite features a nice dressing area, a large walk-in closet and private backyard access. A convenient laundry/utility room is adjacent to the master bath.
- At the opposite end of the home, double doors lead to three more bedrooms, a compartmentalized bath and lots of closet space.

Plan E-2208

Bedrooms: 4	Baths: 2
Living Area:	
Main floor	2,252 sq. ft.
Total Living Area:	**2,252 sq. ft.**
Standard basement	2,252 sq. ft.
Garage and storage	592 sq. ft.
Exterior Wall Framing:	2x6

Foundation Options:

Standard basement

Crawlspace

Slab

(All plans can be built with your choice of foundation and framing. A generic conversion diagram is available. See order form.)

BLUEPRINT PRICE CODE:	C

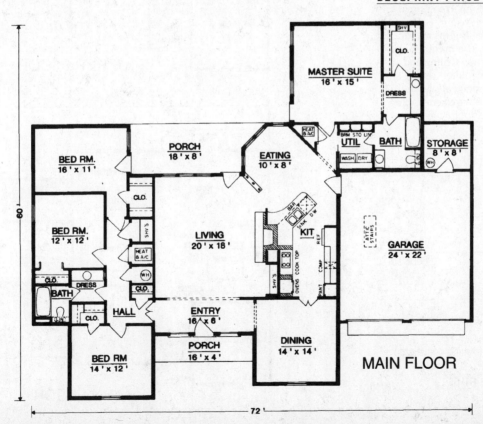

MAIN FLOOR

Family-Oriented Home Design

- From the two-story foyer to the separate guest and family areas, this striking home was designed for formal entertaining and casual family living.
- The heart of the family gathering area is the large family room with a nice fireplace and outdoor access.
- Kneewalls and an angled eating bar visually separate the kitchen, breakfast room and family room without sacrificing the light, open feeling of the entire area.
- The home's three bedrooms are located on the upper floor. The master suite is highlighted with a tray ceiling and a private bath with a vaulted ceiling and an oval tub. Knee space allows the vanity to be used as a makeup table.
- The optional bonus room can be used as a study or playroom.

Plan FB-5055-MANS

Bedrooms: 3+	Baths: 2½
Living Area:	
Upper floor	874 sq. ft.
Main floor	1,008 sq. ft.
Optional bonus room	378 sq. ft.
Total Living Area:	**2,260 sq. ft.**
Daylight basement	1,008 sq. ft.
Garage	415 sq. ft.
Exterior Wall Framing:	2x4

Foundation Options:
Daylight basement
Slab
(Typical foundation & framing conversion diagram available—see order form.)

BLUEPRINT PRICE CODE:	**C**

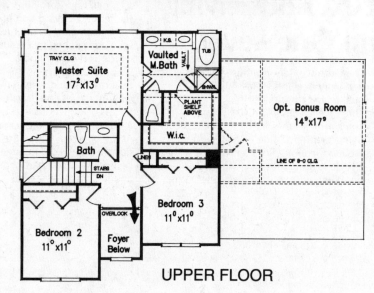

UPPER FLOOR

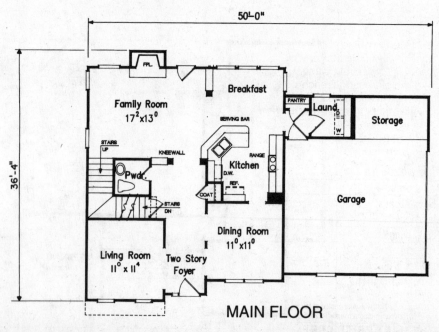

MAIN FLOOR

TO ORDER THIS BLUEPRINT, CALL TOLL-FREE 1-800-547-5570

Plan FB-5055-MANS

PRICES AND DETAILS ON PAGES 12-15

Arranged for Family Living

- This distinguished ranch home has a neatly arranged floor plan with a large activity area at the center and a strategically placed master bedroom.
- The formal living room and dining room flank the entry. The dining room provides views out to the covered front porch and a decorative planter with brick veneer. The living room boasts corner windows and a display niche with shelves.
- The double-doored entry also opens to a large sunken family room with a 13-ft. cathedral ceiling, a handsome fireplace, a patio view and a 10-ft.-high decorative bridge.
- The huge modern kitchen offers a handy snack counter to the adjacent family room. The bayed breakfast room has French-door access to an expansive covered patio.
- Secluded to one end of the home is the deluxe master bedroom, which offers an 11-ft. cathedral ceiling, a spacious walk-in closet and French-door patio access. The master bath has a dual-sink vanity and outdoor access.
- Three additional bedrooms and two more baths are located at the opposite end of the home.

Plan Q-2266-1A

Bedrooms: 4	Baths: 3
Living Area:	
Main floor	2,266 sq. ft.
Total Living Area:	**2,266 sq. ft.**
Garage	592 sq. ft.
Exterior Wall Framing:	2x4

Foundation Options:

Slab
(All plans can be built with your choice of foundation and framing. A generic conversion diagram is available. See order form.)

BLUEPRINT PRICE CODE: C

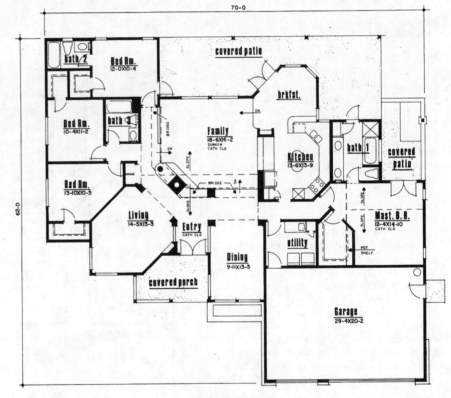

MAIN FLOOR

A Palette of Pleasures

- This stylish traditional brick home has a palette of popular features that serves to enhance family living.
- The formal living spaces are located at the front of the home, flanking the foyer. The dining room is enhanced by a 9-ft. tray ceiling, while the living room boasts a 12-ft. cathedral ceiling.
- A combination kitchen, breakfast nook and family room is oriented to the rear of the home. A pass-through and a snack bar open to the family room, which features a fireplace, a 14-ft.-high vaulted ceiling and deck access.
- The secluded master bedroom offers a 9-ft. tray ceiling and private deck access. The posh master bath boasts a 13-ft. cathedral ceiling and his-and-hers walk-in closets. Dual vanities sit opposite a garden tub and a separate shower.
- Across the home, two secondary bedrooms have walk-in closets and share another full bath. A laundry/utility room and garage access are nearby.

Plan APS-2309

Bedrooms: 3	Baths: 2
Living Area:	
Main floor	2,275 sq. ft.
Total Living Area:	**2,275 sq. ft.**
Standard basement	2,275 sq. ft.
Garage	418 sq. ft.
Exterior Wall Framing:	2x4

Foundation Options:

Standard basement

(All plans can be built with your choice of foundation and framing. A generic conversion diagram is available. See order form.)

BLUEPRINT PRICE CODE:	C

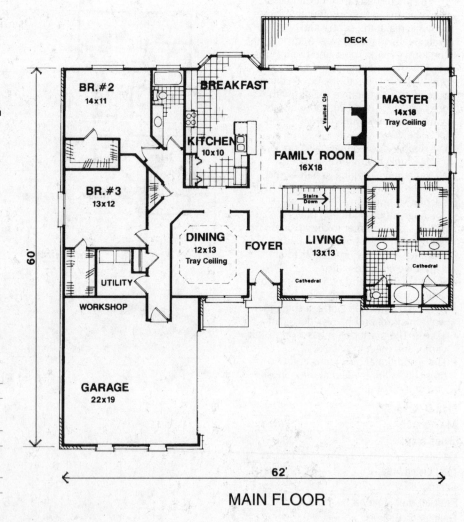

MAIN FLOOR

Plan APS-2309

PRICES AND DETAILS ON PAGES 12-15

Classy Contemporary

- Steep rooflines accented by diagonal wood siding and tall windows give this home dramatic curb appeal.
- Inside, visitors are greeted by a view of the living room, with its 14½-ft. vaulted ceiling and inviting fireplace.
- The dining room is enhanced by a 12-ft. vaulted ceiling.
- The gourmet kitchen area flaunts an eating bar, a writing desk, a large recessed lighting panel, and a large utility room with a pantry.
- The adjacent breakfast nook offers access to the outdoors through lovely French doors.
- Brightened by three beautiful windows, the family room features a woodstove centered on a brick wall. The quiet den could double as an extra bedroom.
- Upstairs, the master suite is graced with a large window, a walk-in closet, a dressing area and a skylighted bath with a sunken tub.
- A hall bath serves the remaining two bedrooms.

Plans P-7627-4A & -4D

Bedrooms: 3+	Baths: 3
Living Area:	
Upper floor	900 sq. ft.
Main floor	1,389 sq. ft.
Total Living Area:	**2,289 sq. ft.**
Daylight basement	1,389 sq. ft.
Garage	462 sq. ft.
Exterior Wall Framing:	2x4
Foundation Options:	**Plan #**
Daylight basement	P-7627-4D
Crawlspace	P-7627-4A

(All plans can be built with your choice of foundation and framing. A generic conversion diagram is available. See order form.)

BLUEPRINT PRICE CODE: C

UPPER FLOOR

BASEMENT STAIRWAY LOCATION

MAIN FLOOR

Homey Hacienda

- This stylish home combines visual impact with an easy-living floor plan.
- Appealing arched windows attract the eye, while the low-sloping tiled roof and deep overhangs protect the home from the sun's rays.
- The tiled front entry is flanked by the dining room and a quiet study.

- Straight ahead, the spacious sunken living room features a fireplace bordered by bright windows.
- The adjoining breakfast area has sliding glass doors to a covered rear patio. The kitchen features a snack bar and a pass-through to the living room.
- The secluded master suite offers a large walk-in closet and a private bath with a luxurious spa tub. French doors lead to the patio.
- The two remaining bedrooms enjoy private access to another full bath.

Plan Q-2298-1A

Bedrooms: 3+	Baths: 2½
Living Area:	
Main floor	2,298 sq. ft.
Total Living Area:	**2,298 sq. ft.**
Garage	433 sq. ft.
Exterior Wall Framing:	2x4

Foundation Options:

Slab
(All plans can be built with your choice of foundation and framing. A generic conversion diagram is available. See order form.)

BLUEPRINT PRICE CODE: **C**

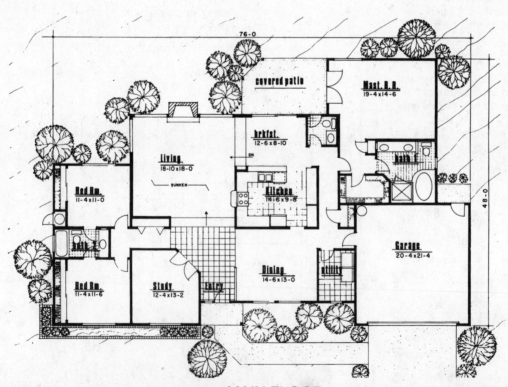

MAIN FLOOR

Plan Q-2298-1A

Luxurious Country Home

- This country cottage hosts many luxuries, such as an expansive Great Room, good-sized sleeping areas and a large screened back porch.
- The rustic front porch opens into the Great Room, which offers a handsome fireplace and access to the large screened back porch.
- The bright kitchen features a huge work island, and unfolds to both the formal dining room and the breakfast bay. A handy laundry closet and access to the garage are also offered.
- The removed master suite has views of the front porch and offers a private bath with two walk-in closets, a dual-sink vanity, a spa tub and a separate shower.
- Upstairs are two oversized bedrooms, each with a dressing room that accesses a common bath.

Plan C-8535

Bedrooms: 3	Baths: 2½
Living Area:	
Upper floor	765 sq. ft.
Main floor	1,535 sq. ft.
Total Living Area:	**2,300 sq. ft.**
Daylight basement	1,535 sq. ft.
Garage	424 sq. ft.
Exterior Wall Framing:	2x4

Foundation Options:

Daylight basement
(All plans can be built with your choice of foundation and framing. A generic conversion diagram is available. See order form.)

BLUEPRINT PRICE CODE: C

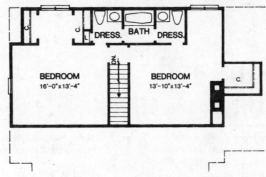

UPPER FLOOR

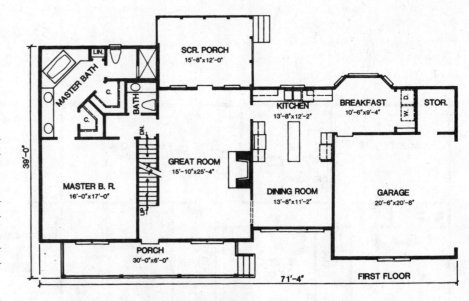

MAIN FLOOR

Spacious and Inviting

The four-column front porch, picture window, siding, brick, stone and cupola combine for a pleasing exterior for this three-bedroom home.

Extra features include a fireplace, screen porch, deluxe master bath and a large separate breakfast room.

Total living area: 2,306 sq. ft.
(Not counting basement or garage)

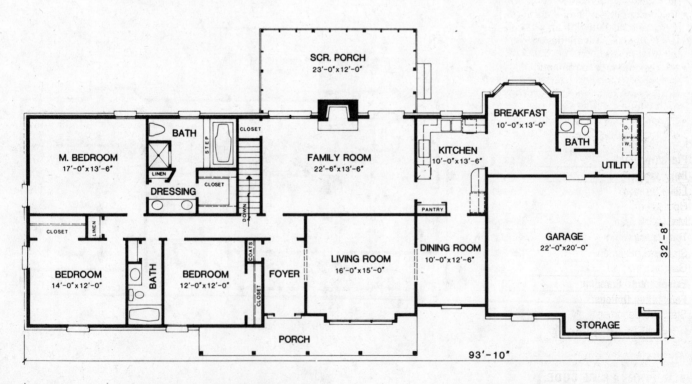

Specify daylight basement, crawlspace or slab foundation.

Blueprint Price Code C
Plan C-8625

PRICES AND DETAILS ON PAGES 12-15

Grand Colonial Home

- This grand Colonial home boasts a porch entry framed by bay windows and gable towers.
- The two-story foyer flows to the dining room on the left and adjoins the bayed living room on the right, with its warm fireplace and flanking windows.
- At the rear, the family room features a 17-ft. ceiling, a media wall, a bar and terrace access through French doors.
- Connected to the family room is a high-tech kitchen with an island work area, a pantry, a work desk and a circular dinette.
- A private terrace, a romantic fireplace, a huge walk-in closet and a lavish bath with a whirlpool tub are featured in the main-floor master suite.
- Three bedrooms and two full baths share the upper floor.

Plan AHP-9120

Bedrooms: 4	Baths: 3
Living Area:	
Upper floor	776 sq. ft.
Main floor	1,551 sq. ft.
Total Living Area:	**2,327 sq. ft.**
Standard basement	1,580 sq. ft.
Garage	440 sq. ft.
Exterior Wall Framing:	2x4 or 2x6

Foundation Options:

Standard basement

Crawlspace

Slab

(All plans can be built with your choice of foundation and framing. A generic conversion diagram is available. See order form.)

BLUEPRINT PRICE CODE: C

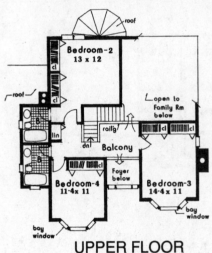

UPPER FLOOR

MAIN FLOOR

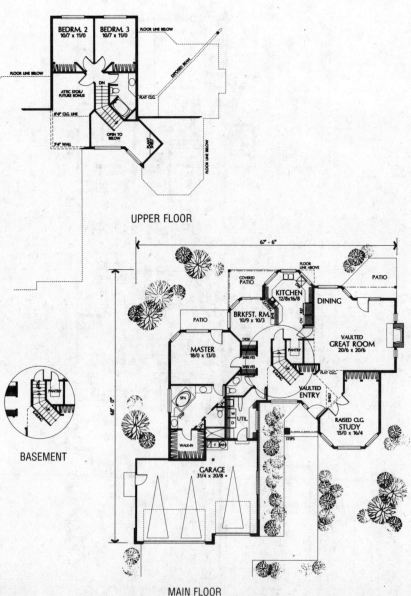

UPPER FLOOR

BASEMENT

MAIN FLOOR

Unique Octagonal Styling

- Volume ceilings and multiple angled windows add style and luxury to this two-level, brick-accented home.
- The vaulted entry reveals double doors that access the study with raised ceiling and a large bay window.
- A vaulted Great Room and dining area share a fireplace and a patio view.
- A second patio joins the bayed kitchen and breakfast room, which share an eating bar. A large pantry is secluded near the stairway.
- The spacious main-level master bedroom offers a private patio and generous bath with walk-in closet, spa tub and separate vanities.

Plans P-6613-3A & -3D	
Bedrooms: 3	**Baths: 2 ½**
Space:	
Upper floor	410 sq. ft.
Main floor	1,925 sq. ft.
Total Living Area	**2,335 sq. ft.**
Basement	1,925 sq. ft.
Garage	648 sq. ft.
Exterior Wall Framing	**2x6**
Foundation options:	**Plan #**
Daylight Basement	P-6613-3D
Crawlspace	P-6613-3A
(Foundation & framing conversion diagram available—see order form.)	
Blueprint Price Code	**C**

Flamboyant Floor Plan

- A host of architectural styles went into the making of this interesting design, from country and Victorian to contemporary. A mixture of gable and hip roofs, a bayed front porch and several differently shaped windows give the exterior plenty of impact.
- A dramatic open floor plan combines to make the home stylishly up to date. High ceilings throughout much of the main level add to the flamboyant floor plan.
- The fantastic family room features a soaring ceiling, a fireplace and an abundance of windows. The adjoining breakfast room has a cathedral ceiling and is open to the kitchen. The attached sun porch is enclosed in glass, with skylights in the sloped ceiling. Formal dining is reserved for the unusual dining room at the front of the home.
- The first-floor master suite boasts a cathedral ceiling, lots of closet space and an irresistible garden tub.
- Three bedrooms and a full bath make up the second level. Each of the bedrooms has a walk-in closet.

Plan AX-1318

Bedrooms: 4	Baths: 2 ½
Space:	
Upper floor	697 sq. ft.
Main floor	1,642 sq. ft.
Total Living Area	**2,339 sq. ft.**
Basement	1,384 sq. ft.
Garage	431 sq. ft.
Exterior Wall Framing	2x4

Foundation options:
Standard Basement
Crawlspace
Slab
(Foundation & framing conversion diagram available—see order form.)

Blueprint Price Code	C

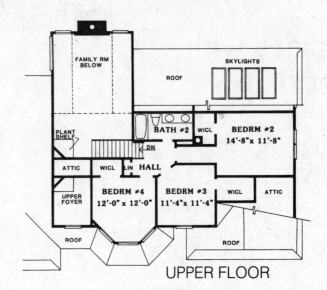

UPPER FLOOR

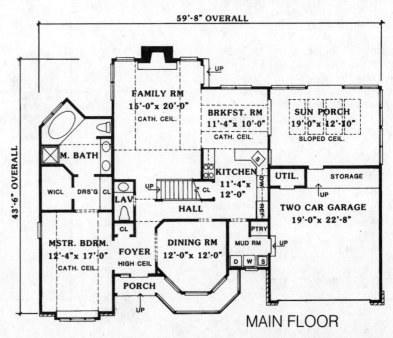

MAIN FLOOR

Loaded with Livability

- The attractive exterior of this home packages a marvelous floor plan that provides the utmost in livability.
- The gorgeous entry sports a 17-ft.-high vaulted ceiling. A 12-ft. vaulted ceiling presides over the spacious living room, which is enhanced by a dramatic boxed-out window. The adjoining dining room opens to a delightful covered patio.
- The kitchen features an island cooktop, a bright angled sink and a sunny nook that accesses another patio. A woodstove in the family room radiates warmth to the entire area.
- A half-bath, laundry facilities and garage access are nearby.
- Upstairs, the sumptuous master suite includes a deluxe bath and a large wardrobe closet.
- Two secondary bedrooms share a compartmentalized bath. A large bonus room above the garage offers a myriad of possible uses.

Plan R-2111

Bedrooms: 3+	Baths: 2½
Living Area:	
Upper floor	945 sq. ft.
Main floor	1,115 sq. ft.
Bonus room	285 sq. ft.
Total Living Area:	**2,345 sq. ft.**
Garage	851 sq. ft.
Exterior Wall Framing:	2x6

Foundation Options:

Crawlspace
(All plans can be built with your choice of foundation and framing. A generic conversion diagram is available. See order form.)

BLUEPRINT PRICE CODE: C

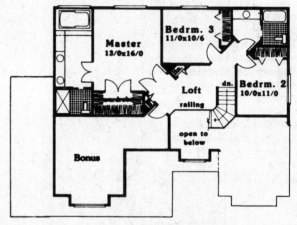

UPPER FLOOR

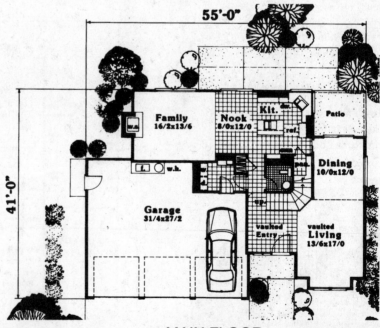

MAIN FLOOR

Ultra-Modern Mediterranean

- Soaring ceilings, a luxurious master suite and a clean stucco exterior with stylish arched windows give this nouveau-Mediterranean home its unique appeal.
- The magnificent living room and the elegant dining room combine to form one large, open area. The dining room has a tall, arched window and a 12-ft. coffered ceiling. The living room boasts a flat ceiling that is over 12 ft. high, a convenient wet bar and sliding glass doors to the covered patio.
- The informal family room is warmed by a fireplace and shares a soaring 12-ft. flat ceiling with the sunny breakfast area and the large, modern kitchen.
- The kitchen is easily accessible from the family area and the formal dining room, and features an eating bar and a spacious pantry.
- The luxurious master suite offers patio access and is enhanced by an elegant 11-ft., 6-in. tray ceiling and his-and-hers walk-in closets. The huge master bath features a dual-sink vanity, a large tiled shower and a whirlpool tub.

Plan HDS-99-158

Bedrooms: 4	Baths: 3

Living Area:.	
Main floor	2,352 sq. ft.
Total Living Area:	**2,352 sq. ft.**
Garage	440 sq. ft.

Exterior Wall Framing:
8-in. concrete block and 2x4

Foundation Options:
Slab
(All plans can be built with your choice of foundation and framing. A generic conversion diagram is available. See order form.)

BLUEPRINT PRICE CODE:	C

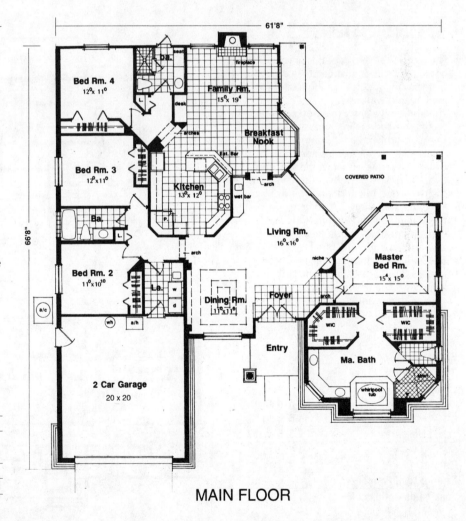

MAIN FLOOR

Great Spaces

- The dynamic exterior of this unique home includes an eye-catching arched window and a cutout in the roof above the covered walkway.
- The impressive entry features a dramatic 15½-ft. vaulted ceiling and opens to the stunning sunken Great Room. A 9-ft. ceiling with wood beams and floor-to-ceiling windows enhance the sunken Great Room. A warm woodstove with a built-in wood bin and a nearby wet bar are other attractions found here.
- The skylighted kitchen offers a convenient snack bar, a greenhouse sink and an adjoining breakfast area.
- The main-floor master suite boasts a large walk-in closet, a private bath with a garden tub and private access to a covered patio or deck.
- A balcony hall upstairs leads to two more bedrooms and another bath.

Plan LRD-22884

Bedrooms: 3	Baths: 2½
Living Area:	
Upper floor	674 sq. ft.
Main floor	1,686 sq. ft.
Total Living Area:	**2,360 sq. ft.**
Standard basement	1,686 sq. ft.
Garage	450 sq. ft.
Exterior Wall Framing:	2x6

Foundation Options:

Standard basement

Crawlspace

(All plans can be built with your choice of foundation and framing. A generic conversion diagram is available. See order form.)

BLUEPRINT PRICE CODE: C

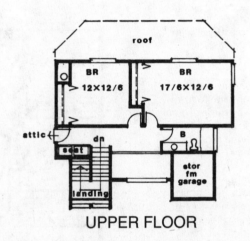

UPPER FLOOR

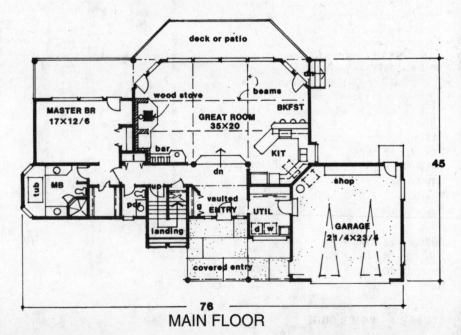

MAIN FLOOR

Plan LRD-22884

Striking Countrypolitan

- This home's eye-catching exterior encloses a modern interior to provide a great family plan for any setting.
- A pleasant covered porch leads into the entry, which adjoins a half-bath.
- Around the corner, the spacious living room boasts a 14-ft.-high vaulted ceiling with an exposed beam, plus a handsome stone fireplace and a wet bar. A French door opens to a covered back porch.
- A large eating area and country kitchen are the focal point of the home. The roomy kitchen offers an oversized island work counter and a handy pantry. The formal dining room and a neatly organized laundry/utility room are conveniently nearby.
- The secluded master bedroom includes three wardrobe closets. Double doors access the private master bath, which shows off a spa tub, a separate shower and a stylish dual-sink vanity.
- Upstairs, three additional bedrooms are serviced by a second full bath.

Plan E-2303

Bedrooms: 4	Baths: 2½
Living Area:	
Upper floor	814 sq. ft.
Main floor	1,553 sq. ft.
Total Living Area:	**2,367 sq. ft.**
Standard basement	1,553 sq. ft.
Garage and storage	626 sq. ft.
Exterior Wall Framing:	2x6

Foundation Options:

Standard basement
Crawlspace
Slab

(All plans can be built with your choice of foundation and framing. A generic conversion diagram is available. See order form.)

BLUEPRINT PRICE CODE: C

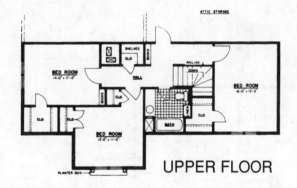

UPPER FLOOR

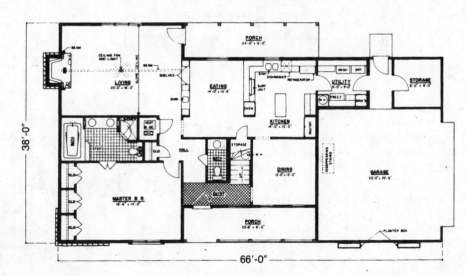

MAIN FLOOR

Spacious Kitchen/Family Room Area

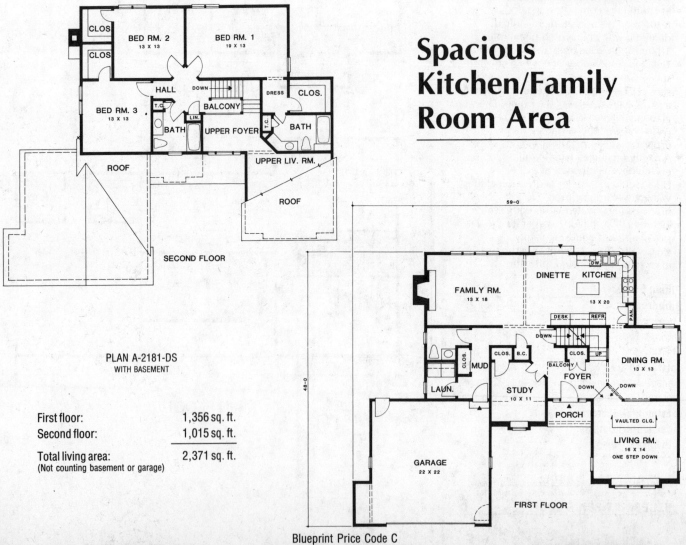

PLAN A-2181-DS
WITH BASEMENT

First floor:	1,356 sq. ft.
Second floor:	1,015 sq. ft.
Total living area:	2,371 sq. ft.

(Not counting basement or garage)

SECOND FLOOR

FIRST FLOOR

Blueprint Price Code C

Plan A-2181-DS

Classic Lines, Elegant Flair

- The rich brick arches and classic lines of this home lend an elegant look that will never become outdated.

- Inside, graceful archways lead from the two-story-high entry to the living and dining rooms, both of which feature 10-ft., 9-in. ceilings.

- The kitchen offers abundant counter space, an expansive window over the sink, a large island cooktop, a desk and a pantry. The adjoining nook has sliding glass doors to a backyard deck or patio, while the entire area is warmed by the fireplace in the family room.

- A nice study with a bay window is entered through double doors.

- Upstairs, the master suite is a real treat, with a luxurious whirlpool tub and his-and-hers walk-in closets.

- Two more bedrooms, a full bath and a storage room are also included. The storage room could be used as an exercise or hobby room.

Plan R-2083

Bedrooms: 3+	Baths: 2½
Living Area:	
Upper floor	926 sq. ft.
Main floor	1,447 sq. ft.
Total Living Area:	**2,373 sq. ft.**
Garage	609 sq. ft.
Storage	138 sq. ft.
Exterior Wall Framing:	2x6

Foundation Options:

Crawlspace

(All plans can be built with your choice of foundation and framing. A generic conversion diagram is available. See order form.)

BLUEPRINT PRICE CODE: C

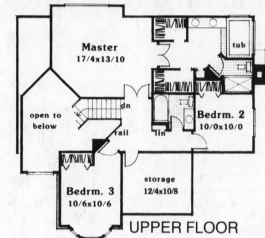

UPPER FLOOR

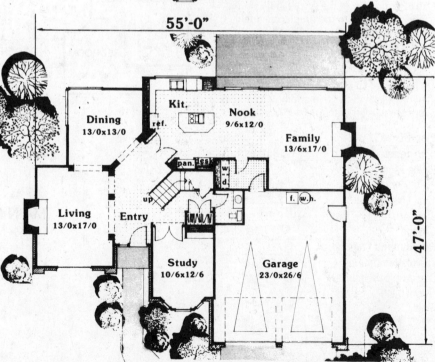

MAIN FLOOR

Light and Bright

- This outstanding home has a light, inviting facade with arched windows, unique transoms and twin dormers.
- The sheltered front porch opens to an airy entry with a dramatic view to the backyard. High 10-ft. ceilings adorn the study and the dining and living rooms.
- A well-designed kitchen is strategically placed near the entrance from the garage and adjoins a sunny morning room. The kitchen is equipped with a pantry, a central island and a nice corner window. The morning room features a lovely window seat, a built-in hutch, a snack bar and a 10-ft. ceiling.
- An inviting fireplace with a tile hearth is the focal point of the cozy family room. The niche next to the fireplace is ideal for an entertainment center. Sliding glass doors open to a large deck.
- The sleeping wing houses three bedrooms, each with a walk-in closet. The master suite has a 10-ft. ceiling and two walk-in closets, in addition to a private garden bath and deck access.

Plan DD-2372

Bedrooms: 3	Baths: 2½
Living Area:	
Main floor	2,376 sq. ft.
Total Living Area:	**2,376 sq. ft.**
Standard basement	2,376 sq. ft.
Garage	473 sq. ft.
Exterior Wall Framing:	2x4

Foundation Options:

Standard basement

Crawlspace

Slab

(All plans can be built with your choice of foundation and framing. A generic conversion diagram is available. See order form.)

BLUEPRINT PRICE CODE:	C

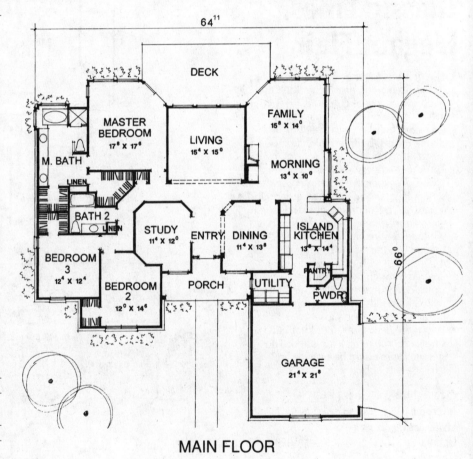

MAIN FLOOR

TO ORDER THIS BLUEPRINT, CALL TOLL-FREE 1-800-547-5570

Plan DD-2372

PRICES AND DETAILS ON PAGES 12-15

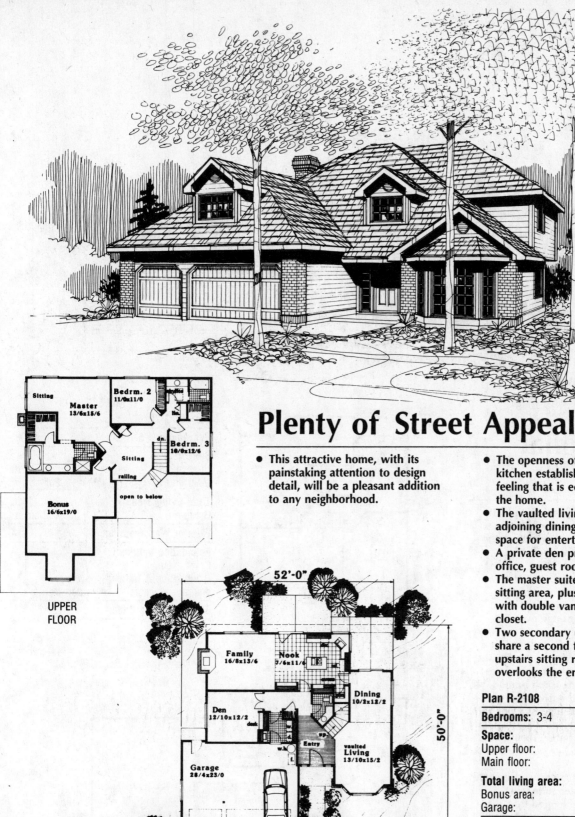

UPPER FLOOR

MAIN FLOOR

52'-0"

50'-0"

Family 16/8x13/6
Nook 7/6x11/6
Dining 10/2x12/2
Den 12/10x12/2
vaulted Living 13/10x15/2
Entry
up
w.h.
Garage 28/4x23/0

Sitting
Master 13/6x15/6
Bedrm. 2 11/0x11/0
Bedrm. 3 10/0x12/6
Sitting
dn.
railing
open to below
Bonus 16/6x19/0

Plenty of Street Appeal

- This attractive home, with its painstaking attention to design detail, will be a pleasant addition to any neighborhood.

- The openness of the country kitchen establishes an expansive feeling that is echoed throughout the home.
- The vaulted living room and adjoining dining area make a great space for entertaining guests.
- A private den provides space for an office, guest room or library.
- The master suite includes a cozy sitting area, plus a private bath with double vanities, and a large closet.
- Two secondary upstairs bedrooms share a second full bath, and an upstairs sitting room/balcony overlooks the entry hall below.

Plan R-2108

Bedrooms: 3-4	Baths: 2½
Space:	
Upper floor:	1,048 sq. ft.
Main floor:	1,335 sq. ft.
Total living area:	2,383 sq. ft.
Bonus area:	445 sq. ft.
Garage:	652 sq. ft.
Exterior Wall Framing:	2x4

Foundation options:
Crawlspace only.
(Foundation & framing conversion diagram available — see order form.)

Blueprint Price Code:	C

Traditional Treat

- A covered front porch with ornamental columns and brackets provides a traditional treat on the exterior of this four-bedroom two-story home.
- Entering the front door, a dramatic view awaits guests of a vaulted foyer with double-back stairs leading up to a bridge overlook above.
- To the left of the foyer, through an arched, columned opening, lies the formal living room with fireplace and formal dining room beyond.
- To the right of the foyer is a double-doored den/guest room with built-in desk.
- The rear-facing family room opens to the island kitchen and breakfast nook.
- The four upstairs bedrooms include an exciting master suite with private bath highlighted by a spa tub.

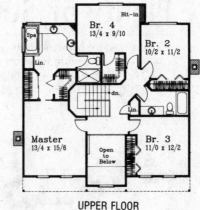

UPPER FLOOR

Plan CDG-2026

Bedrooms: 4-5	Baths: 2½

Space:

Upper floor:	1,089 sq. ft.
Main floor:	1,295 sq. ft.
Total living area:	2,384 sq. ft.
Garage:	452 sq. ft.

Exterior Wall Framing:	2x4

Foundation options:
Crawlspace.
(Foundation & framing conversion diagram available — see order form.)

Blueprint Price Code:	C

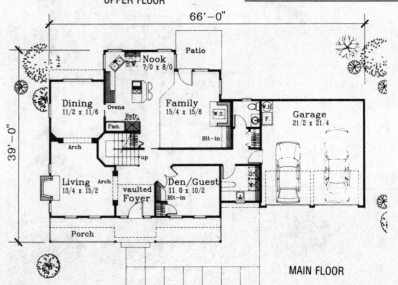

MAIN FLOOR

Simple and Comfortable

- It's hard to beat a design like this for simple comfort.
- The wide, welcoming front porch dresses up the home's basic rectangular shape, adding grace and eye appeal.
- Inside, the formal dining room opens off the foyer, which leads to a spacious living room with a handsome fireplace.
- The open country kitchen includes a cooktop island and a spacious, sunny breakfast area. A utility room and access to the carport are nearby.
- The deluxe master-bedroom suite includes a luxurious master bath with two walk-in closets and double sinks.
- Upstairs, two dormered bedrooms share a double bath and are connected by a balcony loft overlooking the living room below.

Plan J-86113

Bedrooms: 3	Baths: 2½
Living Area:	
Upper floor	658 sq. ft.
Main floor	1,740 sq. ft.
Total Living Area:	**2,398 sq. ft.**
Standard basement	1,740 sq. ft.
Carport	440 sq. ft.
Exterior Wall Framing:	2x4

Foundation Options:

Standard basement

Crawlspace

Slab

(All plans can be built with your choice of foundation and framing. A generic conversion diagram is available. See order form.)

BLUEPRINT PRICE CODE: C

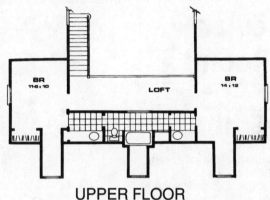

UPPER FLOOR

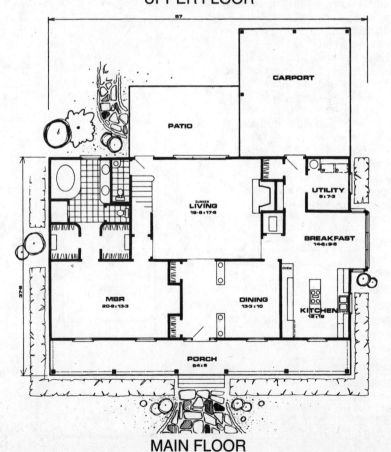

MAIN FLOOR

Spectacular Great Room!

- Open, light-filled spaces centered around a spectacular Great Room mark this updated traditional design.
- The tiled foyer opens to the dining room, which is defined by columns and an overhead plant shelf and enhanced by a 9½-ft.-high flat ceiling.
- The huge central Great Room features a wall of windows, a 17-ft.-high vaulted ceiling and a see-through fireplace with an adjacent wet bar. Sliding glass doors access a delightful deck.
- The kitchen offers a built-in desk, a large pantry, an angled snack bar and a gazebo-like breakfast nook.
- The master suite boasts a 9½-ft. ceiling and a spa bath that includes a separate shower and a huge walk-in closet.
- Double doors open to a quiet den or extra bedroom. The vaulted ceiling soars to a height of 12 ft. above a gorgeous arched window.
- An open, skylighted stairway leads to the upper floor, where two more bedrooms share another full bath.

Plan AG-2401

Bedrooms: 3+	Baths: 2½
Living Area:	
Upper floor	550 sq. ft.
Main floor	1,855 sq. ft.
Total Living Area:	**2,405 sq. ft.**
Standard basement	1,815 sq. ft.
Garage	441 sq. ft.
Exterior Wall Framing:	2x6

Foundation Options:

Standard basement

(All plans can be built with your choice of foundation and framing. A generic conversion diagram is available. See order form.)

BLUEPRINT PRICE CODE:	C

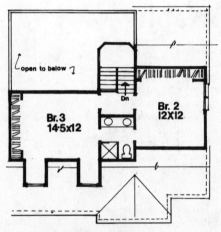

UPPER FLOOR

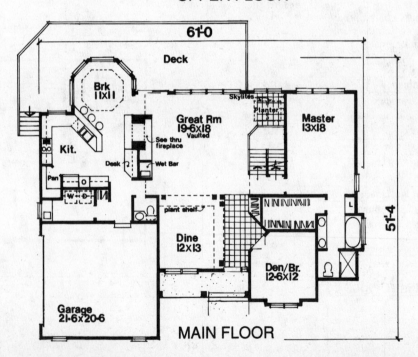

MAIN FLOOR

Open Spaces, Elegant Places

- Past its inviting columned entry, the stunning 19-ft.-high foyer of this beautiful modern home is brightened by high transom windows.
- Off the foyer, the vaulted dining room opens to a backyard patio through sliding glass doors. A decorative rail provides views into the sunken and vaulted living room.
- The spacious island kitchen offers a sunny bay-windowed breakfast nook, a roomy walk-in pantry and a corner sink.
- The adjacent family room features a handsome fireplace and patio access. A French door leads into a quiet den.
- Up the skylighted staircase, double doors lead into the luxurious master bedroom. The elegant master bath is highlighted by skylights and boasts a step-up spa tub, a separate shower and a sit-down, dual-sink vanity.
- Two additional bedrooms have private access to a shared skylighted bath. Both rooms also include separate dressing areas with walk-in closets and individual vanities.

Plan CDG-2047

Bedrooms: 3+	Baths: 3
Living Area:	
Upper floor	1,112 sq. ft.
Main floor	1,295 sq. ft.
Total Living Area:	**2,407 sq. ft.**
Garage	620 sq. ft.
Exterior Wall Framing:	2x6

Foundation Options:

Crawlspace

(All plans can be built with your choice of foundation and framing. A generic conversion diagram is available. See order form.)

BLUEPRINT PRICE CODE:	**C**

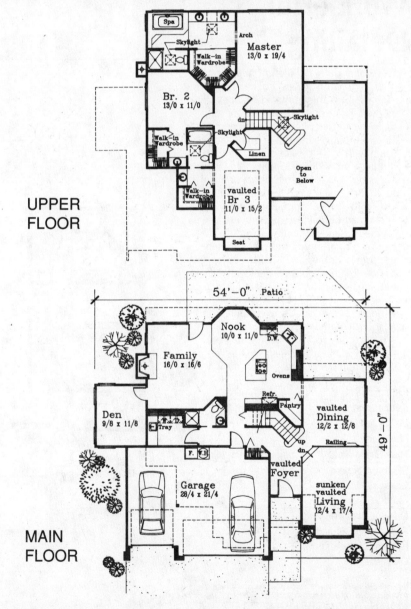

UPPER FLOOR

MAIN FLOOR

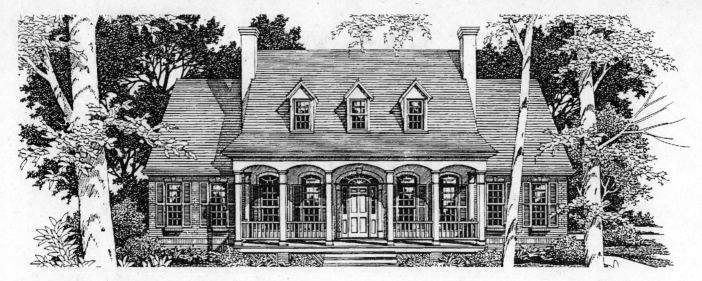

Wonderful Detailing

- The wonderfully detailed front porch, with its graceful arches, columns and railings, gives this home a character all its own. Dormer windows and arched transoms further accentuate the porch.
- The floor plan features a central living room with a 10-ft.-high ceiling and a fireplace framed by French doors. These doors open to a covered porch or a sun room, and a sheltered deck beyond.
- Just off the living room, the island kitchen and breakfast area provide a spacious place for family or guests. The nearby formal dining room has arched transom windows and a 10-ft. ceiling, as does the bedroom off the foyer. All of the remaining rooms have 9-ft. ceilings.
- The unusual master suite includes a window alcove, access to the porch and a fantastic bath with a garden tub.
- A huge utility room, a storage area off the garage and a 1,000-sq.-ft. attic space are other bonuses of this design.

Plan J-90019

Bedrooms: 3	Baths: 2½
Living Area:	
Main floor	2,410 sq. ft.
Total Living Area:	**2,410 sq. ft.**
Standard basement	2,410 sq. ft.
Garage	512 sq. ft.
Storage	86 sq. ft.
Exterior Wall Framing:	2x6

Foundation Options:

Standard basement
Crawlspace
Slab

(All plans can be built with your choice of foundation and framing. A generic conversion diagram is available. See order form.)

BLUEPRINT PRICE CODE:	C

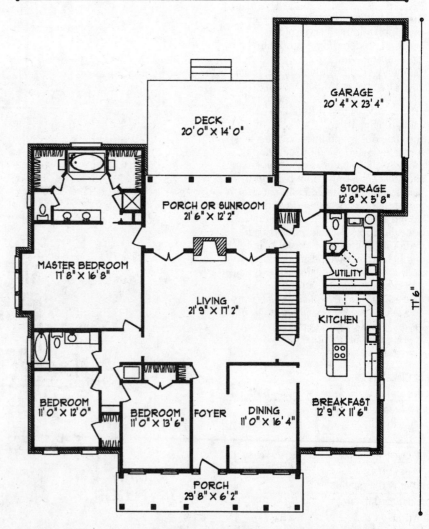

MAIN FLOOR

Plan J-90019

PRICES AND DETAILS ON PAGES 12-15

ALT. STUDIO PLAN

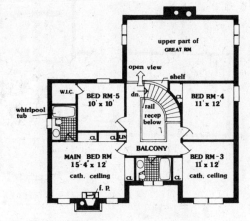

UPPER FLOOR

Floor Plan Offers Options

- This exquisite design offers elegant exterior detailing and a versatile interior floor plan.
- The open, two-story reception area reveals a classic curved staircase.
- A formal living room with a brick fireplace and an open dining room flanks the foyer.
- The roomy gourmet kitchen opens to a dinette/Great Room combination enhanced by a fireplace, a sloped ceiling and wooden French doors that open to the rear terrace.
- The main level may also include the master bedroom with private bath. The alternate floor plan uses this space as a home office or studio.
- The upper level houses three secondary bedrooms and the alternate master bedroom with fireplace and cathedral ceiling.

Plan AHP-9350

Bedrooms: 4-5	**Baths:** 3½
Space:	
Upper floor	870 sq. ft.
Main floor	1,541 sq. ft.
Total Living Area	**2,411 sq. ft.**
Basement	1,090 sq. ft.
Garage	442 sq. ft.
Exterior Wall Framing	**2x4 or 2x6**

Foundation options:
Partial Basement
Crawlspace
Slab
(Foundation & framing conversion diagram available—see order form.)

BLUEPRINT PRICE CODE	C

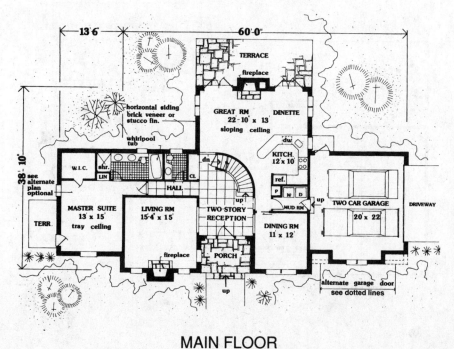

MAIN FLOOR

Five-Bedroom Traditional

- This sophisticated traditional home makes a striking statement both inside and out.
- The dramatic two-story foyer is flanked by the formal living spaces. The private dining room overlooks the front porch, while the spacious living room has outdoor views on two sides.
- A U-shaped kitchen with a snack bar, a sunny dinette area and a large family room flow together at the back of the home. The family room's fireplace warms the open, informal expanse, while sliding glass doors in the dinette access the backyard terrace.
- The second floor has five roomy bedrooms and two skylighted bathrooms. The luxurious master suite has a high ceiling with a beautiful arched window, a dressing area and a huge walk-in closet. The private bath offers dual sinks, a whirlpool tub and a separate shower.
- Attic space is located above the garage.

Plan AHP-9392

Bedrooms: 5	Baths: 2½
Living Area:	
Upper floor	1,223 sq. ft.
Main floor	1,193 sq. ft.
Total Living Area:	**2,416 sq. ft.**
Standard basement	1,130 sq. ft.
Garage	509 sq. ft.
Storage	65 sq. ft.
Exterior Wall Framing:	2x4 or 2x6

Foundation Options:
Standard basement
Crawlspace
Slab
(Typical foundation & framing conversion diagram available—see order form.)

BLUEPRINT PRICE CODE:	C

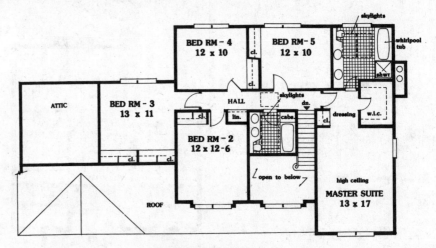

UPPER FLOOR

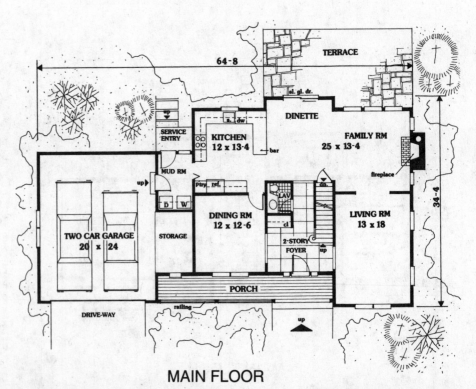

MAIN FLOOR

Plan AHP-9392

PRICES AND DETAILS ON PAGES 12-15

Classy Country

- A classy portico and a dramatic five-sided bay pique interest for this grand country-style home.
- The interior commands attention with its own delights. The two-story gallery soars to a height of 18 ft. and hosts an elegant curved stairway.
- The spectacular five-sided living room is enclosed in glass and warmed by an alluring fireplace angled into a niche off the stairway. The living room flows into the formal dining room, which is also accented by a bay window.
- A corner pantry and a circular snack bar are offered in the spacious U-shaped kitchen. The adjoining dinette opens to a backyard terrace.
- For casual comfort, the family will enjoy the open family room, complete with another fireplace.
- Four big bedrooms and two baths occupy the upper floor. The master bedroom is highlighted by a 13-ft. cathedral ceiling and a unique boxed-out window arrangement. The private master bath boasts a skylighted whirlpool tub, a dual-sink vanity and a skylighted dressing area.

Plan K-697-T

Bedrooms: 4	Baths: 2½
Living Area:	
Upper floor	1,105 sq. ft.
Main floor	1,319 sq. ft.
Total Living Area:	**2,424 sq. ft.**
Daylight basement	1,250 sq. ft.
Garage	430 sq. ft.
Exterior Wall Framing:	2x4 or 2x6

Foundation Options:
Daylight basement
Slab
(All plans can be built with your choice of foundation and framing. A generic conversion diagram is available. See order form.)

BLUEPRINT PRICE CODE:	C

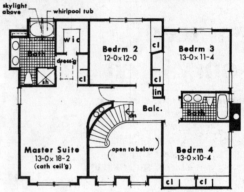

UPPER FLOOR

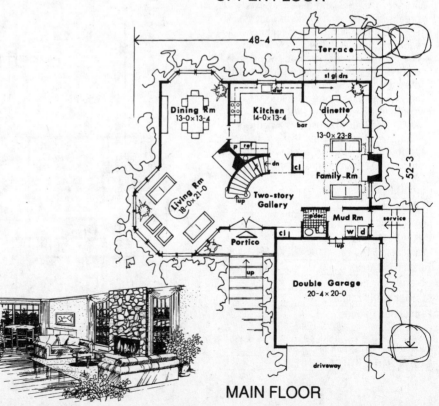

MAIN FLOOR

VIEW INTO FAMILY ROOM AND DINETTE

Magnificent Masonry Arch

- This beautiful brick home attracts the eye with its magnificent masonry arch over the recessed entry.
- The two-story-high foyer is highlighted by a huge half-round transom as it spreads between a bayed study and the formal dining room.
- The fabulous kitchen boasts a walk-in pantry closet, a snack bar, handy laundry facilities and a sunny bayed breakfast nook with backyard access.
- The adjoining family room features a soothing fireplace flanked by windows.
- The main-floor master suite includes a cathedral-ceilinged bath with a walk-in closet, a garden tub, a separate shower and two vanities, one with knee space.
- Another full bath serves the study, which may also be used as a bedroom.
- An upper-floor balcony leads to two additional bedrooms, each with private access to a common full bath.

Plan KLF-9309

Bedrooms: 3+	Baths: 3
Living Area:	
Upper floor	574 sq. ft.
Main floor	1,863 sq. ft.
Total Living Area:	**2,437 sq. ft.**
Garage	519 sq. ft.
Exterior Wall Framing:	2x4

Foundation Options:

Slab

(All plans can be built with your choice of foundation and framing. A generic conversion diagram is available. See order form.)

BLUEPRINT PRICE CODE: C

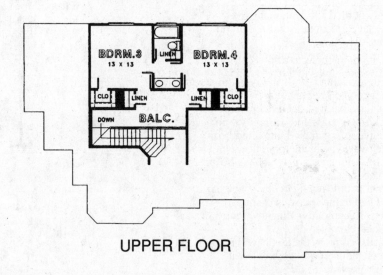

UPPER FLOOR

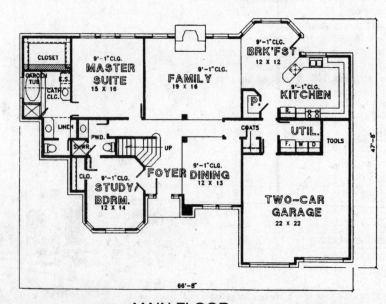

MAIN FLOOR

Spacious Home for Scenic Lots

- Vertical wood siding, stone accents, large windows and a spectacular deck make this home ideal for a mountain, lake, golf course or other scenic site.
- The front porch opens to a spacious foyer, which unfolds to the formal dining room.
- The sunken family room is set off from the hall with an open rail and boasts a 20-ft. cathedral ceiling, a stone fireplace and access to a large deck.

- The U-shaped kitchen opens to a bright breakfast room with deck access.
- A laundry/utility room is conveniently located between the breakfast room and the two-car garage.
- The master suite is removed from the secondary bedrooms and offers a roomy walk-in closet. The compartmentalized master bath includes a separate dressing area with a dual-sink vanity.
- Two additional bedrooms share a unique bath with separate vanities and dressing areas.
- A fabulous upstairs studio is brightened by tall, angled windows and could provide extra space for guests.

Plan C-7710

Bedrooms: 3+	**Baths:** 2

Living Area:	
Upper floor	248 sq. ft.
Main floor	2,192 sq. ft.
Total Living Area:	**2,440 sq. ft.**
Daylight basement	2,192 sq. ft.
Garage	431 sq. ft.
Storage and utility	132 sq. ft.
Exterior Wall Framing:	2x4

Foundation Options:

Daylight basement
Crawlspace
Slab
(All plans can be built with your choice of foundation and framing. A generic conversion diagram is available. See order form.)

BLUEPRINT PRICE CODE:	C

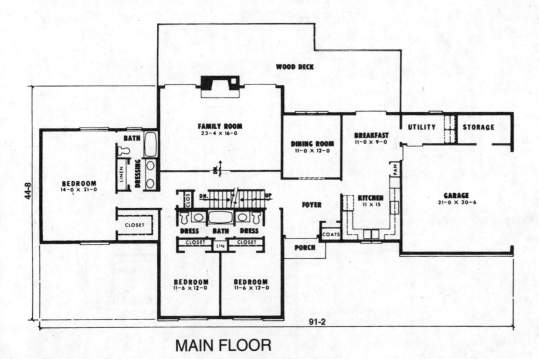

MAIN FLOOR

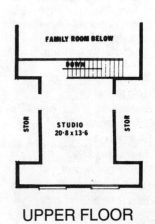

UPPER FLOOR

Timeless Styling

- This home's timeless gables and classic front porch conceal an expansive interior with modern styling.
- Sidelighted double doors open from the porch to the elegant two-story gallery and its curved, open-railed staircase.
- The living room boasts stylish windows, a fireplace with built-in wood storage and a 14-ft., 6-in. cathedral ceiling.
- The semi-circular dining room basks in light from a radiant arrangement of windows, offering a panoramic view.
- The kitchen features a bright sink, a nifty snack bar and a sunny half-circle dinette with views to the backyard.
- Another fireplace warms the family room, which also features sliding glass doors to a backyard terrace.
- The mudroom has laundry facilities, plus access to a half-bath and to the two-car garage.
- The upper-floor master suite offers a balcony and a private bath with a whirlpool tub and a separate shower. A skylighted bath serves the three secondary bedrooms.

Plan K-692-T

Bedrooms: 4	Baths: 2½
Living Area:	
Upper floor	950 sq. ft.
Main floor	1,498 sq. ft.
Total Living Area:	**2,448 sq. ft.**
Daylight basement	1,430 sq. ft.
Garage	440 sq. ft.
Exterior Wall Framing:	2x4 or 2x6

Foundation Options:

Daylight basement
Slab

(All plans can be built with your choice of foundation and framing. A generic conversion diagram is available. See order form.)

BLUEPRINT PRICE CODE:	**C**

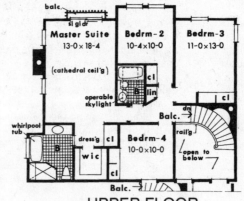

UPPER FLOOR

VIEW INTO FAMILY ROOM

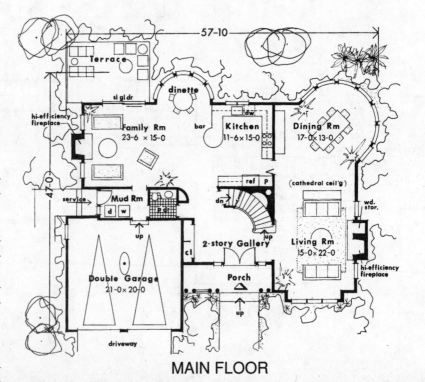

MAIN FLOOR

Plan K-692-T

PRICES AND DETAILS ON PAGES 12-15

Tasteful Style

- Traditional lines and a contemporary floor plan combine to make this home a perfect choice for the '90s.
- The two-story-high entry introduces the formal living room, which is warmed by a fireplace and brightened by a round-top window arrangement. The living room's ceiling rises to 13 ft., 9 inches.
- A handy pocket door separates the formal dining room from the kitchen for special occasions. The U-shaped kitchen features an eating bar, a work desk and a bayed nook with access to an outdoor patio.
- The spacious family room includes a second fireplace and outdoor views.
- Ceilings in all main-floor rooms are at least 9 ft. high for added spaciousness.
- Upstairs, the master suite features a 12-ft. vaulted ceiling, two walk-in closets and a compartmentalized bath with a luxurious tub in a window bay.
- Two additional bedrooms share a split bath. A versatile bonus room could serve as an extra bedroom or as a sunny area for hobbies or paperwork.

Plan S-8389

Bedrooms: 3+	Baths: 2½
Living Area:	
Upper floor	932 sq. ft.
Main floor	1,290 sq. ft.
Bonus room	228 sq. ft.
Total Living Area:	**2,450 sq. ft.**
Standard basement	1,290 sq. ft.
Garage	429 sq. ft.
Exterior Wall Framing:	2x6

Foundation Options:

Standard basement
Crawlspace
Slab

(All plans can be built with your choice of foundation and framing.
A generic conversion diagram is available. See order form.)

BLUEPRINT PRICE CODE: C

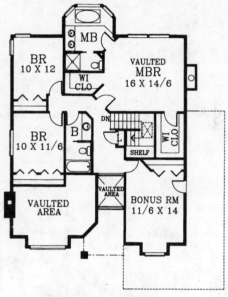

UPPER FLOOR

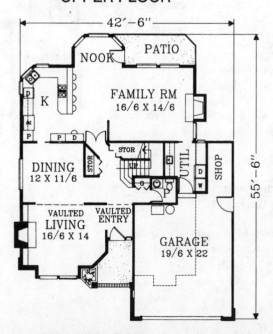

MAIN FLOOR

Captivating Interior Space

- Attractive stucco, ornate windows and tropical design accents add to the appeal of this captivating home.
- The tiled foyer has arched entries to the living room, dining room and family room. The living and dining rooms have dramatic window treatments. The spacious family room boasts a dramatic corner fireplace, a vaulted ceiling and sliding glass doors to the covered patio.
- The exciting skylighted kitchen offers a vaulted ceiling, ample counter space, a serving bar and a bayed breakfast nook with a pantry closet.
- The removed master suite boasts a romantic two-way fireplace shared with the private bath. The elegant bath shows off an oval tub, a separate corner shower and a vaulted ceiling.
- Raised 10-ft. ceilings are featured in the three secondary bedrooms at the opposite end of the home. Two large baths serve these bedrooms.

Plan HDS-99-135

Bedrooms: 4	Baths: 3
Living Area:	
Main floor	2,454 sq. ft.
Total Living Area:	**2,454 sq. ft.**
Garage	448 sq. ft.

Exterior Wall Framing: 8-in. concrete block

Foundation Options:

Slab

(Typical foundation & framing conversion diagram available—see order form.)

BLUEPRINT PRICE CODE: C

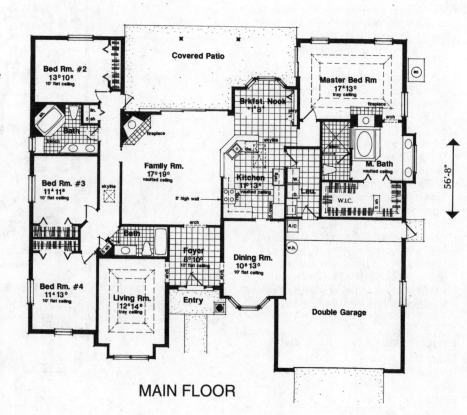

MAIN FLOOR

TO ORDER THIS BLUEPRINT, CALL TOLL-FREE 1-800-547-5570   Plan HDS-99-135   *PRICES AND DETAILS ON PAGES 12-15*

Contemporary Colonial

- A Palladian window and a half-round window above the entry door give this Colonial a new look. Inside, the design maximizes space while creating an open, airy atmosphere.
- The two-story-high foyer flows between the formal areas at the front of the home. Straight ahead, the exciting family room features a built-in wet bar and a fireplace framed by French doors.
- A bay window brightens the adjoining breakfast nook and kitchen. An angled counter looks to the nook and the family room, keeping the cook in touch with the family activities.
- The four bedrooms on the upper floor include a luxurious master suite with an 11-ft. vaulted ceiling and a skylighted bathroom. The upper-floor laundry also makes this a great family home.
- The basement plan (not shown) has room for an optional den or bedroom, a recreation room with a fireplace, a storage room and a utility area.

Plan CH-320-A

Bedrooms: 4+	Baths: 3
Living Area:	
Upper floor	1,164 sq. ft.
Main floor	1,293 sq. ft.
Total Living Area:	**2,457 sq. ft.**
Basement	1,293 sq. ft.
Garage	462 sq. ft.
Exterior Wall Framing:	2x4

Foundation Options:

Daylight basement

Standard basement

Crawlspace

(All plans can be built with your choice of foundation and framing. A generic conversion diagram is available. See order form.)

BLUEPRINT PRICE CODE: C

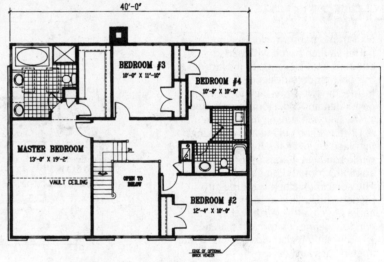

UPPER FLOOR

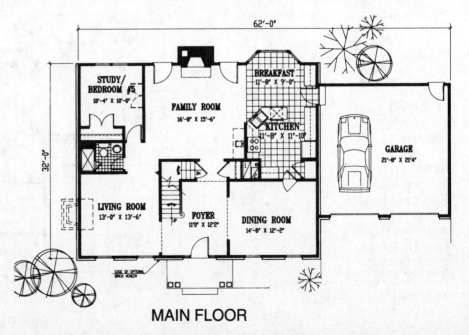

MAIN FLOOR

Modern Elegance

- Half-round transom windows and a barrel-vaulted porch with paired columns lend elegance to the facade of this post-modern design.
- Inside, the two-story-high foyer leads past a den and a diagonal, open-railed stairway to the sunken living room.
- A 17-ft. vaulted ceiling and a striking fireplace enhance the living room, while square columns introduce the adjoining formal dining room.
- The adjacent kitchen is thoroughly modern, including an island cooktop and a large pantry. A sunny bay window defines the breakfast area, where a sliding glass door opens to the angled backyard deck.
- Columns preface the sunken family room, which also sports a 17-ft.-high vaulted ceiling and easy access to the deck. A half-bath, a laundry room and access to the garage are nearby.
- Upstairs, the master suite features a 10-ft. vaulted ceiling, a private bath and a large walk-in closet.

Plan B-89005

Bedrooms: 4	Baths: 2½
Living Area:	
Upper floor	1,083 sq. ft.
Main floor	1,380 sq. ft.
Total Living Area:	**2,463 sq. ft.**
Standard basement	1,380 sq. ft.
Garage	483 sq. ft.
Exterior Wall Framing:	2x4

Foundation Options:

Standard basement

(All plans can be built with your choice of foundation and framing. A generic conversion diagram is available. See order form.)

BLUEPRINT PRICE CODE:	C

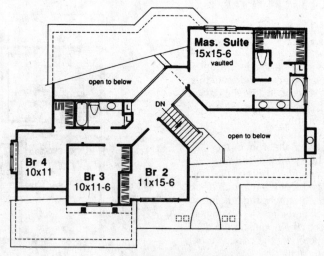

UPPER FLOOR

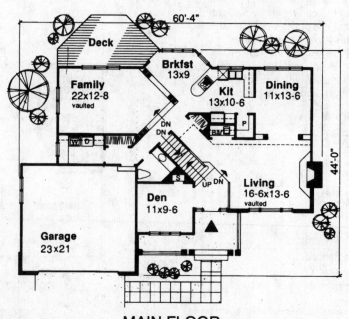

MAIN FLOOR

 Plan B-89005 *PRICES AND DETAILS ON PAGES 12-15*

Rustic Four-Bedroom Home

This 2,467 sq. ft. rustic design includes a deluxe master suite with walk-in and walk-thru closets, linen closet, large double vanity and both a tub and separate shower stall.

The U-shaped kitchen features a counter bar open to the Great Room, which has a raised-hearth fireplace. A large utility room and a second bedroom and full bath with linen closet are located on the 1,694 sq. ft. main floor.

Two additional bedrooms and a third full bath with linen closet are located upstairs. A built-in bookcase, window seats and access to attic storage areas are also included on the 773 sq. ft. upper floor.

Front porch, dormers, shutters, multi-paned windows and a combination of wood and stone materials combine for a rustic exterior. The screened-in porch doubles as a covered breezeway connecting house and garage.

Specify crawlspace or daylight basement foundation when ordering.

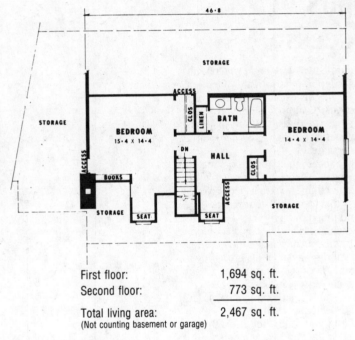

First floor: 1,694 sq. ft.
Second floor: 773 sq. ft.

Total living area: 2,467 sq. ft.
(Not counting basement or garage)

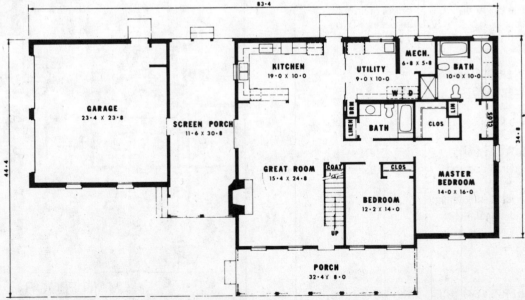

Blueprint Price Code C

Plan C-7746

Pillars of Success

- A stunning two-story entry porch with heavy support pillars creates a look of success for this exciting new design.
- The covered entrance gives way to an open entry foyer with closets for coats and general storage. A powder room is just steps away.
- Straight ahead, the Great Room features a fireplace, a TV niche and a 16-ft. vaulted ceiling. A French door gives access to a view deck that wraps around much of the home.
- The kitchen's island boasts a cooktop and a convenient snack counter. The adjacent dining bay offers great views.
- The main-floor master suite has a 10-ft. coved ceiling, private deck access, built-in shelves, a dressing area and a private skylighted bath.
- A den or guest room includes a 9-ft. vaulted ceiling and deck access.
- The upper floor has a central hobby area with a 13-ft. vaulted ceiling. Two bedrooms feature views to the Great Room below.

Plan LRD-32190

Bedrooms: 3+	Baths: 3
Living Area:	
Upper floor	606 sq. ft.
Main floor	1,865 sq. ft.
Total Living Area:	**2,471 sq. ft.**
Standard basement	1,865 sq. ft.
Garage	529 sq. ft.
Exterior Wall Framing:	2x6

Foundation Options:

Standard basement
Crawlspace
Slab

(All plans can be built with your choice of foundation and framing. A generic conversion diagram is available. See order form.)

BLUEPRINT PRICE CODE: **C**

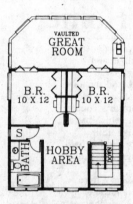

UPPER FLOOR

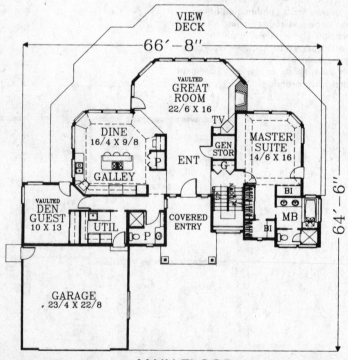

MAIN FLOOR

Fantastic Facade, Stunning Spaces

- Matching dormers and a generous covered front porch give this home its fantastic facade. Inside, the open living spaces are just as stunning.
- A two-story foyer bisects the formal living areas. The living room offers three bright windows, an inviting fireplace and sliding French doors to the Great Room. The formal dining room overlooks the front porch and has easy access to the kitchen.
- The Great Room is truly grand, featuring a fireplace and a TV center flanked by French doors that lead to a large deck.
- A circular dinette connects the Great Room to the kitchen, which is handy to a mudroom and a powder room.
- The main-floor master suite boasts a 14-ft. cathedral ceiling, a walk-in closet and a private bath with a whirlpool tub.
- Upstairs, four large bedrooms share another whirlpool bath. One bedroom offers a 12-ft. sloped ceiling.

Plan AHP-9397

Bedrooms: 5	Baths: 2½
Living Area:	
Upper floor	928 sq. ft.
Main floor	1,545 sq. ft.
Total Living Area:	**2,473 sq. ft.**
Standard basement	1,165 sq. ft.
Garage and storage	432 sq. ft.
Exterior Wall Framing:	2x4 or 2x6

Foundation Options:
Standard basement
Crawlspace
Slab
(All plans can be built with your choice of foundation and framing. A generic conversion diagram is available. See order form.)

BLUEPRINT PRICE CODE:	C

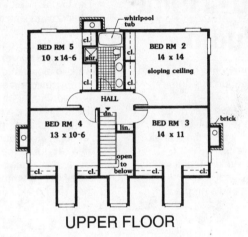

UPPER FLOOR

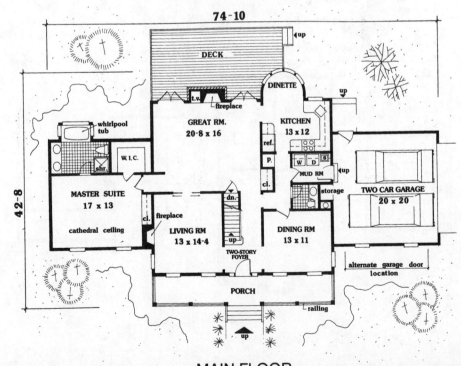

MAIN FLOOR

Spacious Home with Studio

- Rustic exterior overtones of stone and wood siding surround this home's spacious interior.
- A decorative planter serves as an attractive conversation piece that separates the entry from the formal dining room beyond.
- The tremendous sunken living room is highlighted by a breathtaking 20-ft. cathedral ceiling and a fireplace.

- The impressive U-shaped kitchen offers a windowed sink and ample counter space. The adjacent breakfast room boasts a large front window.
- The private master suite includes a walk-in closet and private access to a compartmentalized bath.
- Two additional bedrooms at the rear of the home share a unique bath with twin toilets and sinks.
- An upper-floor studio, study or play area overlooks the living room.
- The two-car garage offers two storage areas, one of which can be accessed from the breakfast room.

Plan C-7113

Bedrooms: 3+	Baths: 2
Living Area:	
Upper floor	260 sq. ft.
Main floor	2,213 sq. ft.
Total Living Area:	**2,473 sq. ft.**
Daylight basement	2,213 sq. ft.
Garage	410 sq. ft.
Storage and utility	120 sq. ft.
Exterior Wall Framing:	2x4

Foundation Options:

Daylight basement
Crawlspace
Slab

(All plans can be built with your choice of foundation and framing. A generic conversion diagram is available. See order form.)

BLUEPRINT PRICE CODE: C

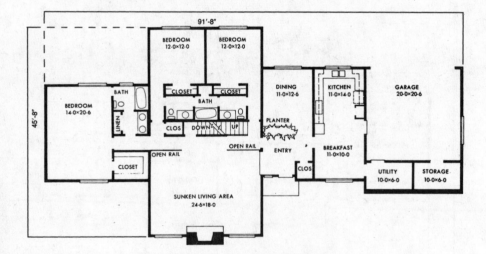

MAIN FLOOR

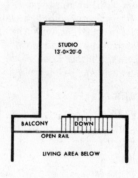

UPPER FLOOR

TO ORDER THIS BLUEPRINT, CALL TOLL-FREE 1-800-547-5570   Plan C-7113   *PRICES AND DETAILS ON PAGES 12-15*

Farmhouse with Character

- The charm of yesterday's farmhouse and the exquisite design of a modern floor plan characterize this four-bedroom ranch.
- At the center of the floor plan is a stunning living room with an 11-ft. stepped-up ceiling, a massive corner fireplace and a door to the rear porch.
- An angled snack bar separates the living room from the adjoining kitchen and bayed breakfast nook. The formal dining room is positioned on the opposite side of the kitchen.
- The isolated master suite offers two walk-in closets and a royal bath with a sunny garden tub, twin vanities and a separate shower. It also offers private access to the porch.
- Three additional bedrooms are located at the opposite end of the home, serviced by two full baths.

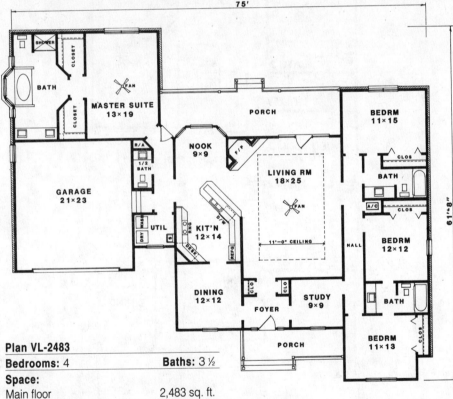

Plan VL-2483

Bedrooms: 4	Baths: 3 ½
Space:	
Main floor	2,483 sq. ft.
Total Living Area	**2,483 sq. ft.**
Garage	504 sq. ft.
Exterior Wall Framing	2x4

Foundation options:

Crawlspace

Slab

(Foundation & framing conversion diagram available—see order form.)

Blueprint Price Code	C

Fabulous Facade

- Beautiful windows, accented with columns and keystones, blanket the facade of this distinguished home.
- The interior spaces are deceptively spacious, beginning with a two-story-high entry and an open staircase.
- The right side of the home is taken up by a bayed living room that stretches to the formal dining room.
- The casual living area includes an island kitchen with a walk-in pantry and an adjoining morning room with access to a rear patio. The family room has a fireplace and plenty of windows.
- Upstairs, the master bedroom has a ceiling that slopes to 10 feet. The master bath offers two walk-in closets separated by a whirlpool bath, plus a shower and a toilet compartment.
- Walk-in closets are also found in the two remaining bedrooms. The front-facing bedroom boasts a 9-ft. ceiling and an arched window. The game room also has a 9-ft. ceiling.

Plan DD-2460

Bedrooms: 3+	Baths: 2½
Living Area:	
Upper floor	1,407 sq. ft.
Main floor	1,085 sq. ft.
Total Living Area:	**2,492 sq. ft.**
Standard basement	1,085 sq. ft.
Garage	410 sq. ft.
Exterior Wall Framing:	2x4

Foundation Options:

Standard basement
Crawlspace
Slab

(All plans can be built with your choice of foundation and framing. A generic conversion diagram is available. See order form.)

BLUEPRINT PRICE CODE:	**C**

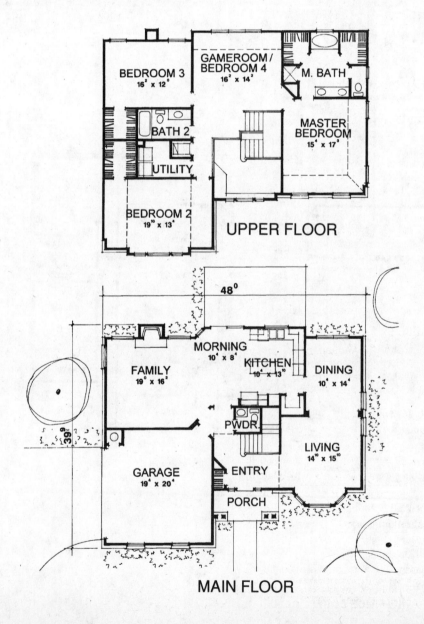

UPPER FLOOR

MAIN FLOOR

Stunning and Sophisticated

- A well-balanced blend of brick, stucco, and glass gives this stunning one-story home a sophisticated look.
- Past the recessed entry, the 16-ft.-high foyer is highlighted by a round-topped transom window. An arched opening introduces the formal dining room.
- The spectacular living room boasts an elegant 16-ft. coffered ceiling and is brightened by a trio of tall windows topped by a radius transom.
- The spacious island kitchen includes a roomy corner pantry and a built-in desk. A serving bar is convenient to the family room and the sunny breakfast area.
- A window-flanked fireplace is the focal point of the family room, which features a 16-ft. vaulted ceiling.
- A tray ceiling adorns the luxurious master suite. The vaulted master bath has a 16-ft. ceiling and includes a garden tub, a separate shower and his-and-hers vanities and walk-in closets.

Plan FB-5074-ARLI

Bedrooms: 3+	Baths: 2½
Living Area:	
Main floor	2,492 sq. ft.
Total Living Area:	**2,492 sq. ft.**
Daylight basement	2,492 sq. ft.
Garage	400 sq. ft.
Exterior Wall Framing:	2x4

Foundation Options:

Daylight basement

Crawlspace

(All plans can be built with your choice of foundation and framing. A generic conversion diagram is available. See order form.)

BLUEPRINT PRICE CODE:	C

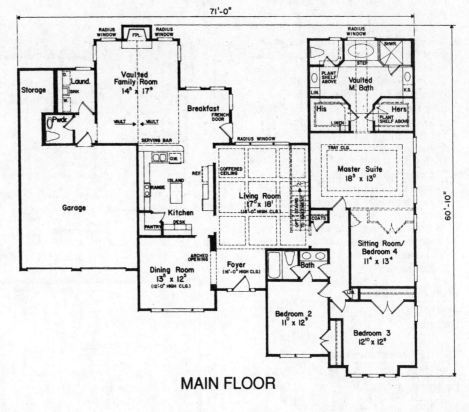

MAIN FLOOR

Full of Surprises

- While dignified and reserved on the outside, this plan presents intriguing angles, vaulted ceilings and surprising spaces throughout the interior.
- The elegant, vaulted living room flows from the expansive foyer and includes a striking fireplace and a beautiful bay.
- The spacious island kitchen offers wide corner windows above the sink and easy service to both the vaulted dining room and the skylighted nook.
- The adjoining vaulted family room features a warm corner woodstove and sliding doors to the backyard patio.
- The superb master suite includes a vaulted sleeping area and an exquisite private bath with a skylighted dressing area, a large walk-in closet, a step-up spa tub and a separate shower.
- Three secondary bedrooms are located near another full bath and a large laundry room with garage access.

Plans P-7711-3A & -3D

Bedrooms: 4	Baths: 2
Living Area:	
Main floor (crawlspace version)	2,510 sq. ft.
Main floor (basement version)	2,580 sq. ft.
Total Living Area:	**2,510/2,580 sq. ft.**
Daylight basement	2,635 sq. ft.
Garage	806 sq. ft.
Exterior Wall Framing:	2x6
Foundation Options:	**Plan #**
Daylight basement	P-7711-3D
Crawlspace	P-7711-3A

(All plans can be built with your choice of foundation and framing. A generic conversion diagram is available. See order form.)

BLUEPRINT PRICE CODE:	D

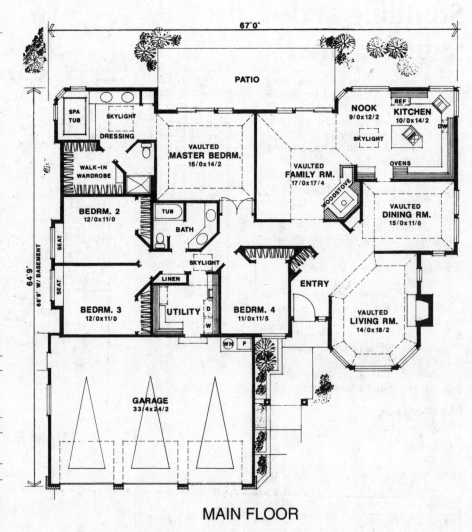

MAIN FLOOR

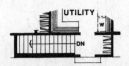

BASEMENT STAIRWAY LOCATION

Zesty Southwestern!

- Elegant arches and a bright stucco exterior add a zesty southwestern flavor to this beautiful one-story home.
- Past the columned front porch, the angled entry is flanked by the living room and the dining room, both of which feature 9½-ft. tray ceilings and lovely bay windows.
- The skylighted island kitchen offers a windowed sink, a built-in planning desk and a sunny breakfast nook.
- The adjacent family room boasts a tray ceiling and a corner fireplace. A French door opens to a covered patio.
- Double doors introduce the luxurious master bedroom, which enjoys patio access and a 9-ft.-high tray ceiling. The skylighted master bath includes a garden spa tub, a separate shower, a walk-in closet and a dual-sink vanity.
- Two additional bedrooms have built-in window seats and share a second skylighted bath. A den off the entry could easily be used as an extra bedroom or as a home office.

Plans P-7752-3A & -3D

Bedrooms: 3+	Baths: 2
Living Area:	
Main floor (crawlspace version)	2,503 sq. ft.
Main floor (basement version)	2,575 sq. ft.
Total Living Area:	**2,503/2,575 sq. ft.**
Daylight basement	2,578 sq. ft.
Garage	962 sq. ft.
Exterior Wall Framing:	2x6
Foundation Options:	**Plan #**
Daylight basement	P-7752-3D
Crawlspace	P-7752-3A

(All plans can be built with your choice of foundation and framing.
A generic conversion diagram is available. See order form.)

BLUEPRINT PRICE CODE:	**D**

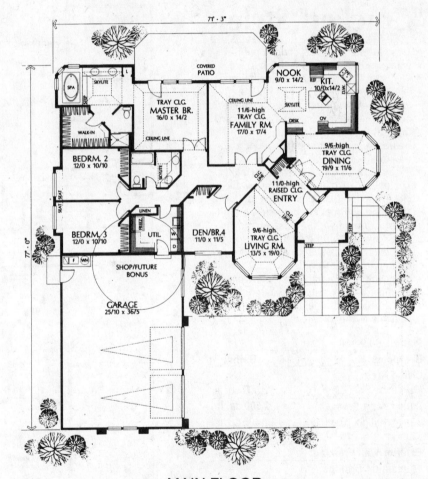

MAIN FLOOR

BASEMENT
STAIRWAY
LOCATION

TO ORDER THIS BLUEPRINT,
CALL TOLL-FREE 1-800-547-5570

Plans P-7752-3A & -3D

PRICES AND DETAILS
ON PAGES 12-15

121

Southern "Cracker" Style

- This Florida "Cracker" style home is warm and inviting. Its walkout lower level can accommodate a sloping lot.
- Expansive front and rear porches are ideal for entertaining. Access to the rear porch is possible from the Great Room, the dining room and the master bedroom. A second bedroom opens to the front porch.
- All three bedrooms have private baths! The master bath also offers dual walk-in closets and a luxurious garden tub.
- The huge gourmet kitchen offers a built-in desk, a pantry closet and a handy work island. Volume ceilings are found in the kitchen as well as in the dining room and Great Room.
- Adjacent to the garage on the lower level is room for a future playroom or home office. Other expansion is possible in the loft area.

Plan HDS-99-160

Bedrooms: 3	Baths: 3
Living Area:	
Main floor	2,500 sq. ft.
Total Living Area:	**2,500 sq. ft.**
Partial daylight basement	492 sq. ft.
Garage	764 sq. ft.
Exterior Wall Framing:	2x4

Foundation Options:

Partial daylight basement

(Typical foundation & framing conversion diagram available—see order form.)

BLUEPRINT PRICE CODE:	D

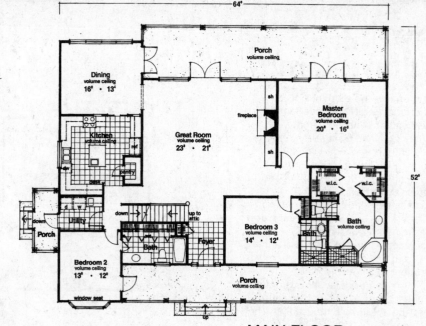

MAIN FLOOR

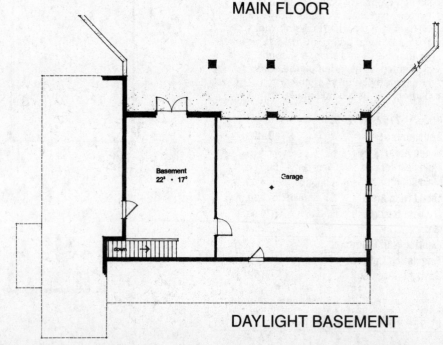

DAYLIGHT BASEMENT

 Plan HDS-99-160

Enjoyable Four-Season Porch

- Outdoor lovers will enjoy the exciting four-season porch and expansive deck this stylish home has to offer.
- Round-top and transom windows adorn the exterior and bring light into the spacious interior. The 14-ft.-high foyer is especially light and airy, offering a view into nearly all of the living areas.
- The huge sunken Great Room has a dramatic see-through fireplace, a stunning back window wall and a 13-ft.-high vaulted ceiling.
- The spacious corner kitchen is highlighted by a functional cooktop island and is open to both the casual and the formal dining areas. Double doors access the porch and deck.
- Two bedrooms and two baths occupy the sleeping wing. The master bedroom is enhanced by a tray ceiling as well as the see-through fireplace. The stunning master bath features a dual-sink vanity and a whirlpool tub under glass.
- The den off the foyer can be used for reading or sleeping overnight guests.

Plan PI-92-535	
Bedrooms: 2	**Baths:** 2½
Living Area:	
Main floor	2,302 sq. ft.
Four-season porch	208 sq. ft.
Total Living Area:	**2,510 sq. ft.**
Daylight basement	2,302 sq. ft.
Garage	912 sq. ft.
Exterior Wall Framing:	2x6
Foundation Options:	

Daylight basement
(All plans can be built with your choice of foundation and framing. A generic conversion diagram is available. See order form.)

BLUEPRINT PRICE CODE:	D

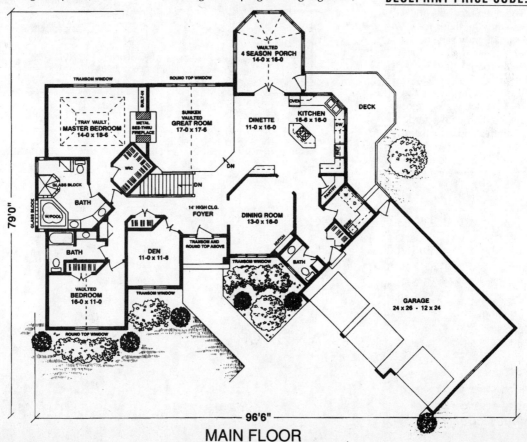

MAIN FLOOR

Facade is Best on the Block

- This stylish facade will dress up any neighborhood with its symmetrical bay windows and dramatic rooflines.
- At the center of the interior is a spacious living room with a 10-ft. ceiling, a corner fireplace and a window wall that adjoins a pair of sliders leading to the rear deck.
- The powder room off the hall could also open to the deck, serving as a pool bath.
- Across the hall are the kitchen and morning room, which feature a cooktop island, a step-in pantry and a bayed eating area. The opening above the sink provides a view into the living room as well as access to a handy serving/snack counter.
- The formal dining room is located opposite the foyer.
- The bayed master suite overlooks the rear deck and offers two walk-in closets and a large private bath with a garden tub, separate vanities and an isolated toilet.
- The home also offers two additional bedrooms and a large three-car garage.

Plan DD-2513

Bedrooms: 3	Baths: 2½
Living Area:	
Main floor	2,513 sq. ft.
Total Living Area:	**2,513 sq. ft.**
Standard basement	2,513 sq. ft.
Garage	529 sq. ft.
Exterior Wall Framing:	2x4

Foundation Options:
Standard basement
Crawlspace
Slab
(Typical foundation & framing conversion diagram available—see order form.)

BLUEPRINT PRICE CODE: D

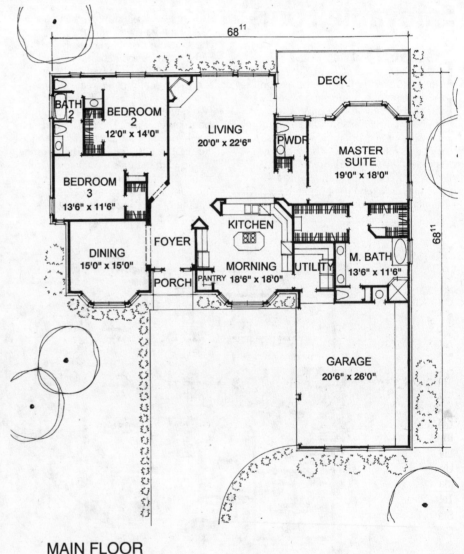

MAIN FLOOR

Formal Meets Informal

- The charming, columned front porch of this appealing home leads visitors into a two-story-high foyer with a beautiful turned staircase.
- The gracious formal living room shares a 15-ft. cathedral ceiling and a dramatic see-through fireplace with the adjoining family room.
- A railing separates the family room from the spacious breakfast area and the island kitchen. A unique butler's pantry joins the kitchen to the dining room, which is enhanced by a tray ceiling.
- A convenient laundry room is located between the kitchen and the entrance to the garage .
- All four bedrooms are located on the upper level. The master suite boasts an 11-ft. cathedral ceiling, a walk-in closet and a large, luxurious bath.

Plan OH-132

Bedrooms: 4	Baths: 2½
Living Area:	
Upper floor	1,118 sq. ft.
Main floor	1,396 sq. ft.
Total Living Area:	**2,514 sq. ft.**
Standard basement	1,396 sq. ft.
Garage	413 sq. ft.
Storage/workshop	107 sq. ft.
Exterior Wall Framing:	2x4

Foundation Options:

Standard basement

(All plans can be built with your choice of foundation and framing. A generic conversion diagram is available. See order form.)

BLUEPRINT PRICE CODE: D

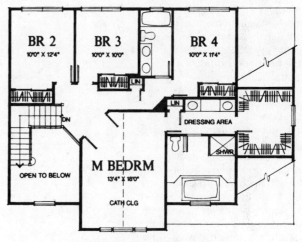

UPPER FLOOR

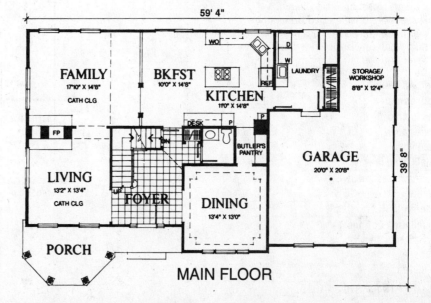

MAIN FLOOR

Nostalgic Exterior Appeal

- A covered front porch, large half-round windows and Victorian gable details give this nostalgic home classic appeal.
- A stunning two-story foyer awaits guests at the entry, which is flooded with light from the half-round window above.
- The central island kitchen is brightened by the bay-windowed breakfast room, which looks into the family room over a low partition.
- Highlighted by a skylight and a corner fireplace, the cathedral-ceilinged family room is sure to be a high-traffic area. Sliding glass doors allow activities to be extended to the backyard patio.
- Upstairs, the master bedroom boasts a unique sloped ceiling and a lovely boxed-out window. The master bath has a spa tub, a corner shower and a dual-sink vanity. A dressing area and a walk-in closet are also offered.
- Three more upstairs bedrooms share two linen closets and a hallway bath. A railed balcony bridge overlooks the foyer and the family room.

Plan AX-90305

Bedrooms: 4	Baths: 2½
Living Area:	
Upper floor	1,278 sq. ft.
Main floor	1,237 sq. ft.
Total Living Area:	**2,515 sq. ft.**
Standard basement	1,237 sq. ft.
Garage	400 sq. ft.
Exterior Wall Framing:	2x4

Foundation Options:

Standard basement
Slab
(All plans can be built with your choice of foundation and framing. A generic conversion diagram is available. See order form.)

BLUEPRINT PRICE CODE: D

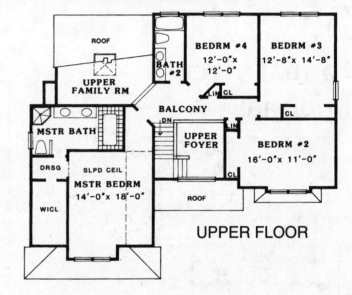

UPPER FLOOR

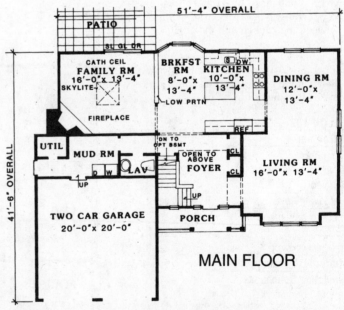

MAIN FLOOR

All the Best

- This unique home offers the best of both worlds, with its charming, old-time exterior and modern, luxurious interior.
- The covered front porch leads to a two-story foyer with a beautiful open staircase. To the right, the large formal dining room showcases a boxed-out window. To the left, the living room overlooks the front porch and has the option of a cased opening or a solid wall facing the family room.
- The expansive family room is brightened by a dramatic window wall and has a French door to the backyard. The fireplace is positioned so it can be enjoyed from the adjoining kitchen.
- The deluxe kitchen boasts a double oven, a huge walk-in pantry and a long serving bar. The 11½-ft.-high vaulted breakfast room is illuminated by a gorgeous arched window.
- The upper floor includes a dynamite master suite, which features a 9½-ft. tray ceiling in the sleeping area and a 16-ft. vaulted ceiling in the luxurious bath.
- The big bonus room could serve as a playroom or an extra bedroom.

Plan FB-2516

Bedrooms: 3+	Baths: 2½
Living Area:	
Upper floor	1,057 sq. ft.
Main floor	1,212 sq. ft.
Bonus room	247 sq. ft.
Total Living Area:	**2,516 sq. ft.**
Daylight basement	1,212 sq. ft.
Garage and storage	504 sq. ft.
Exterior Wall Framing:	2x4

Foundation Options:

Daylight basement

Crawlspace

(All plans can be built with your choice of foundation and framing. A generic conversion diagram is available. See order form.)

BLUEPRINT PRICE CODE: D

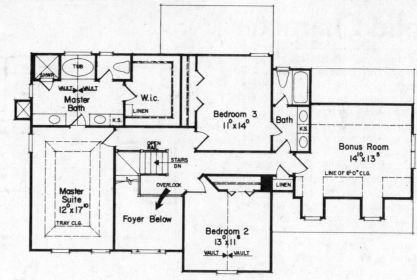

UPPER FLOOR

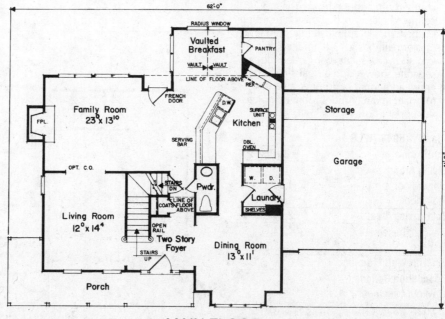

MAIN FLOOR

TO ORDER THIS BLUEPRINT, CALL TOLL-FREE 1-800-547-5570

Plan FB-2516

PRICES AND DETAILS ON PAGES 12-15 127

Solid Character

- A dramatic, stately roofline and a distinguished brick facade give a solid look to this distinctive family home.
- The impressive two-story-high foyer boasts an elegant tray ceiling.
- A columned arch introduces the formal dining room, where French doors bring the outside in.
- The central kitchen includes a pantry and features an arched opening over the sink. The nearby breakfast bay offers a built-in serving shelf with an arched pass-through to the family room.
- Flanked by tall windows, a handsome fireplace is the focal point of the two-story-high family room.
- Ceilings in all main-floor rooms are 9 ft. high unless otherwise specified.
- Upstairs, a railed balcony overlooks the family room and the foyer. The tray-ceilinged master suite boasts a morning kitchen and a vaulted sitting room. The master bath has a 13-ft. vaulted ceiling and showcases a corner garden tub, a separate shower and a dual-sink vanity.
- Three additional bedrooms, a second full bath and a laundry room complete the upper floor.

Plan FB-5048-NELS

Bedrooms: 4	**Baths:** 2½
Living Area:	
Upper floor	1,309 sq. ft.
Main floor	1,240 sq. ft.
Total Living Area:	**2,549 sq. ft.**
Daylight basement	1,240 sq. ft.
Garage	400 sq. ft.
Exterior Wall Framing:	2x4
Foundation Options:	

Daylight basement

(All plans can be built with your choice of foundation and framing. A generic conversion diagram is available. See order form.)

BLUEPRINT PRICE CODE: **D**

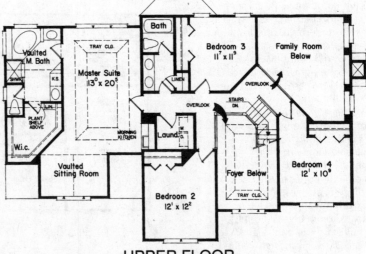

UPPER FLOOR

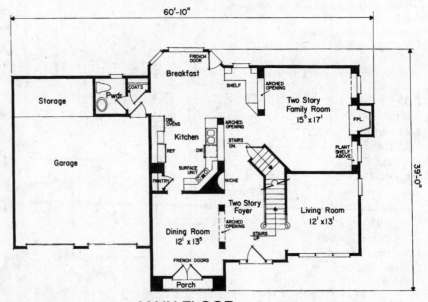

MAIN FLOOR

 TO ORDER THIS BLUEPRINT, CALL TOLL-FREE 1-800-547-5570 Plan FB-5048-NELS *PRICES AND DETAILS ON PAGES 12-15*

Dynamic Design

- Angled walls, vaulted ceilings and lots of glass set the tempo for this dynamic home.
- The covered front entry opens to a raised foyer and a beautiful staircase with a bayed landing.
- One step down, a spectacular see-through fireplace with a raised hearth and built-in wood storage is visible from both the bayed dining room and the stunning Great Room.
- The Great Room also showcases an 18-ft.-high vaulted ceiling, wraparound windows and access to a deck or patio.
- The adjoining nook has a door to the deck and is served by the kitchen's snack bar. The kitchen is enhanced by a 9-ft. ceiling, corner windows and a pass-through to the dining room.
- Upstairs, the master suite offers a 10-ft.-high coved ceiling, a splendid bath, a large walk-in closet and a private deck.

Plan S-41587

Bedrooms: 3+	Baths: 3
Living Area:	
Upper floor	1,001 sq. ft.
Main floor	1,550 sq. ft.
Total Living Area:	**2,551 sq. ft.**
Basement	1,550 sq. ft.
Garage (three-car)	773 sq. ft.
Exterior Wall Framing:	2x6

Foundation Options:
Daylight basement
Standard basement
Crawlspace
Slab
(All plans can be built with your choice of foundation and framing. A generic conversion diagram is available. See order form.)

BLUEPRINT PRICE CODE: D

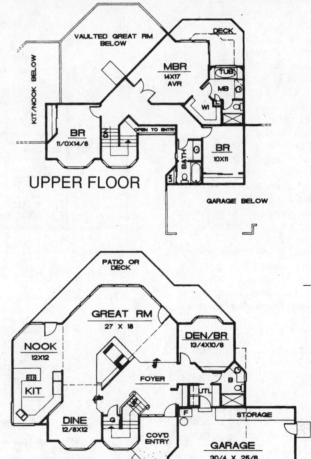

UPPER FLOOR

MAIN FLOOR

Hot Tub, Deck Highlighted

- Designed for indoor/outdoor living, this home features a skylighted spa room with a hot tub and a backyard deck that spans the width of the home.
- A central hall leads to the sunny kitchen and nook, which offer corner windows, a snack bar and a pantry.
- Straight ahead, the open dining and living rooms form one huge space, further pronounced by expansive windows. The 16-ft. vaulted living room also features a fireplace and sliding glass doors to the deck.
- The master suite includes a cozy window seat, a large walk-in closet, a private bath and access to the tiled spa room. The spa may also be entered from the deck and an inner hall.
- Upstairs, two more bedrooms share a full bath and a balcony that overlooks the living room below.
- The optional daylight basement offers a deluxe sauna, a fourth bedroom, a laundry room and a wide recreation room with a fireplace. A large game room and storage are also included.

REAR VIEW

Plans H-2114-1A & -1B

Bedrooms: 3+	Baths: 2½-3½
Living Area:	
Upper floor	732 sq. ft.
Main floor	1,682 sq. ft.
Spa room	147 sq. ft.
Daylight basement	1,386 sq. ft.
Total Living Area:	**2,561/3,947 sq. ft.**
Garage	547 sq. ft.
Exterior Wall Framing:	2x6
Foundation Options:	**Plan #**
Daylight basement	H-2114-1B
Crawlspace	H-2114-1A

(All plans can be built with your choice of foundation and framing. A generic conversion diagram is available. See order form.)

BLUEPRINT PRICE CODE: D/F

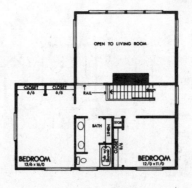

UPPER FLOOR

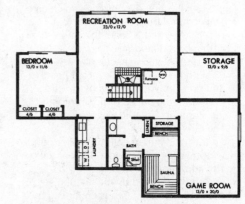

DAYLIGHT BASEMENT

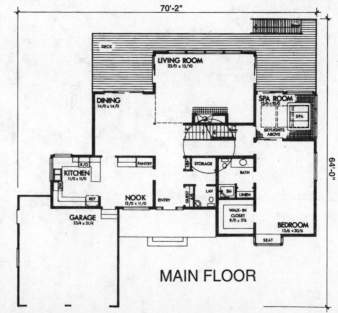

MAIN FLOOR

STAIRWAY AREA IN CRAWLSPACE VERSION

Photo by Felice Photographers

Classic Country-Style

- Almost completely surrounded by an expansive porch, this classic plan exudes warmth and grace.
- The foyer is liberal in size and leads guests to a formal dining room to the left or the large living room to the right.
- The open country kitchen includes a sunny, bay-windowed breakfast nook. A utility area, a full bath and garage access are nearby.
- Upstairs, the master suite is impressive, with its large sleeping area, walk-in closet and magnificent garden bath.
- Three secondary bedrooms share a full bath with a dual-sink vanity.
- Also note the stairs leading up to an attic, which is useful for storage space.

**NOTE:
The above photographed home may have been modified by the homeowner. Please refer to floor plan and/or drawn elevation shown for actual blueprint details.

Plan J-86134

Bedrooms: 4	Baths: 3
Living Area:	
Upper floor	1,195 sq. ft.
Main floor	1,370 sq. ft.
Total Living Area:	**2,565 sq. ft.**
Standard basement	1,370 sq. ft.
Garage	576 sq. ft.
Exterior Wall Framing:	2x4

Foundation Options:

Standard basement
Crawlspace
Slab

(All plans can be built with your choice of foundation and framing. A generic conversion diagram is available. See order form.)

BLUEPRINT PRICE CODE: D

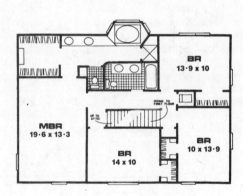

UPPER FLOOR

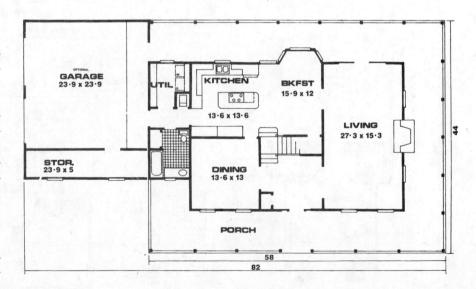

MAIN FLOOR

Photo by Mark Englund/HomeStyles

Extraordinary Estate Living

- Extraordinary estate living is at its best in this palatial beauty.
- The double-doored entry opens to a large central living room that overlooks a covered patio with a vaulted ceiling. Volume 14-ft. ceilings are found in the living room, in the formal dining room and in the den or study, which may serve as a fourth bedroom.
- The gourmet chef will enjoy the spacious kitchen, which flaunts a

cooktop island, a walk-in pantry and a peninsula snack counter shared with the breakfast room and family room.
- This trio of informal living spaces also shares a panorama of glass and a corner fireplace centered between TV and media niches.
- Isolated at the opposite end of the home is the spacious master suite, which offers private patio access. Dual walk-in closets define the entrance to the adjoining master bath, complete with a garden Jacuzzi and separate dressing areas.
- The hall bath also opens to the outdoors for use as a pool bath.

Plan HDS-99-177	
Bedrooms: 3+	**Baths:** 3
Living Area:	
Main floor	2,597 sq. ft.
Total Living Area:	**2,597 sq. ft.**
Garage	761 sq. ft.
Exterior Wall Framing:	2x4
Foundation Options:	
Slab	

(All plans can be built with your choice of foundation and framing. A generic conversion diagram is available. See order form.)

BLUEPRINT PRICE CODE: **D**

NOTE:
The above photographed home may have been modified by the homeowner. Please refer to floor plan and/or drawn elevation shown for actual blueprint details.

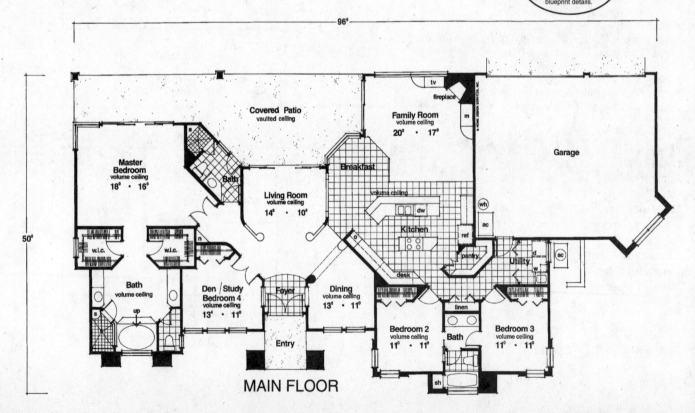

MAIN FLOOR

Plan HDS-99-177

PRICES AND DETAILS
ON PAGES 12-15

Photo by Kevin Haslip

Privacy and Luxury

- This home's large roof planes and privacy fences enclose a thoroughly modern, open floor plan.
- A beautiful courtyard greets guests on their way to the secluded entrance. Inside, a two-story-high entry area leads directly into the living and dining rooms, which boast an 11-ft. vaulted ceiling, plus floor-to-ceiling windows and a fireplace with a stone hearth.
- The angular kitchen features a snack bar to the adjoining family room and a passive-solar sun room that offers natural brightness.
- A 14½-ft. vaulted ceiling presides over the family room. Sliding glass doors access a backyard patio with a sun deck and a hot tub.
- The luxurious master suite opens to both the front courtyard and the backyard hot tub area. The 11-ft.-high vaulted bath includes a dual-sink vanity, a raised garden tub, a separate shower and a corner walk-in closet.
- Two secondary bedrooms and another bath share the upper floor, which boasts commanding views of main-floor areas.

Plans P-7663-3A & -3D

Bedrooms: 3+	Baths: 3
Living Area:	
Upper floor	569 sq. ft.
Main floor	2,039 sq. ft.
Total Living Area:	**2,608 sq. ft.**
Daylight basement	2,039 sq. ft.
Garage	799 sq. ft.
Exterior Wall Framing:	2x4
Foundation Options:	**Plan #**
Daylight basement	P-7663-3D
Crawlspace	P-7663-3A

(All plans can be built with your choice of foundation and framing. A generic conversion diagram is available. See order form.)

BLUEPRINT PRICE CODE:	D

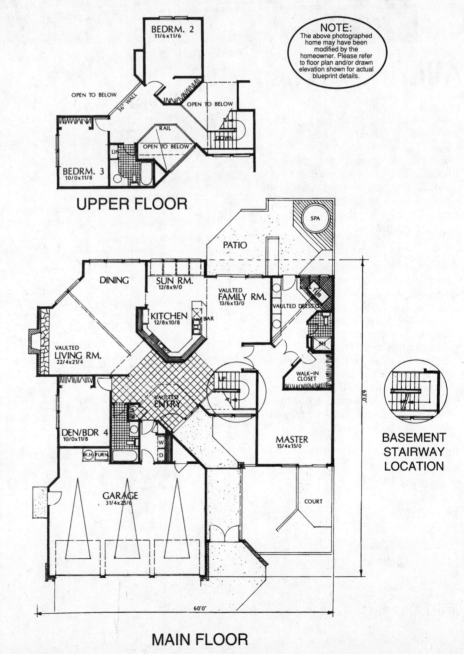

UPPER FLOOR

BEDRM. 2
11/6 x 11/6

OPEN TO BELOW

3/6 WALL

OPEN TO BELOW

RAIL

OPEN TO BELOW

DOWN

BEDRM. 3
10/0 x 11/8

NOTE:
The above photographed home may have been modified by the homeowner. Please refer to floor plan and/or drawn elevation shown for actual blueprint details.

SPA

PATIO

DINING

SUN RM.
12/8 x 9/0

VAULTED FAMILY RM.
13/6 x 13/0

VAULTED DRESS

KITCHEN
12/8 x 10/8

BAR

TUB

VAULTED LIVING RM.
22/4 x 21/4

WALK-IN CLOSET

VAULTED ENTRY

MASTER
15/4 x 15/0

DEN/BDR 4
10/0 x 11/8

W.H. FURN.

GARAGE
31/4 x 25/6

COURT

60'0"

63'0"

MAIN FLOOR

BASEMENT STAIRWAY LOCATION

Photo by Mark Englund/HomeStyles

Alluring Arches

- Massive columns, high, dramatic arches and expansive glass attract passersby to this alluring one-story home.
- Inside, 12-ft. coffered ceilings are found in the foyer, dining room and living room. A bank of windows in the living room provides a sweeping view of the covered backyard patio, creating a bright, open effect that is carried throughout the home.
- The informal, family activity areas are oriented to the back of the home as well. Spectacular window walls in the breakfast room and family room offer tremendous views. The family room's inviting corner fireplace is positioned to be enjoyed from the breakfast area and the spacious island kitchen.
- Separated from the secondary bedrooms, the superb master suite is entered through double doors and features a sitting room and a garden bath. Another full bath is across the hall from the den, which would also make a great guest room or nursery.

Plan HDS-99-179

Bedrooms: 3+	Baths: 3
Living Area:	
Main floor	2,660 sq. ft.
Total Living Area:	**2,660 sq. ft.**
Garage	527 sq. ft.
Exterior Wall Framing:	2x4

Foundation Options:

Slab

(All plans can be built with your choice of foundation and framing. A generic conversion diagram is available. See order form.)

BLUEPRINT PRICE CODE: D

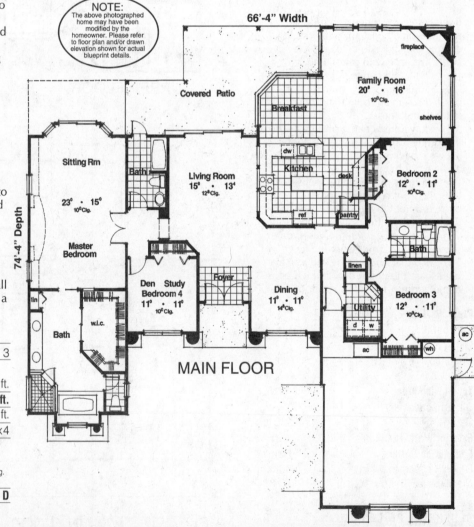

NOTE:
The above photographed home may have been modified by the homeowner. Please refer to floor plan and/or drawn elevation shown for actual blueprint details.

66'-4" Width

74'-4" Depth

Covered Patio

fireplace

Family Room
20⁸ · 16⁸
10⁰Clg.

shelves

Breakfast

dw

Kitchen

desk

Bedroom 2
12⁰ · 11⁰
10⁰Clg.

ref

pantry

Sitting Rm

Bath

Living Room
15⁰ · 13⁰
12⁸Clg.

23⁰ · 15⁰
10⁰Clg.

Bath

linen

Master Bedroom

w.i.c.

Bath

Den Study
Bedroom 4
11⁰ · 11⁰
10⁰Clg.

Foyer

Dining
11⁰ · 11⁰
14⁸Clg.

Utility

d w

Bedroom 3
12⁰ · 11⁰
10⁰Clg.

ac

ac

wh

MAIN FLOOR

Plan HDS-99-179

PRICES AND DETAILS
ON PAGES 12-15

Luxurious Interior

- This luxurious home is introduced by an exciting tiled entry with a 17½-ft. vaulted ceiling and a skylight.
- The highlight of the home is the expansive Great Room and dining area, with its fireplace, planter, 17½-ft. vaulted ceiling and bay windows. The fabulous wraparound deck with a step-up hot tub is the perfect complement to this large entertainment space.
- The kitchen features lots of counter space, a large pantry and an adjoining bay-windowed breakfast nook.
- The exquisite master suite flaunts a sunken garden tub, a separate shower, a dual-sink vanity, a walk-in closet and private access to the deck area.
- The game room downstairs is perfect for casual entertaining, with its warm woodstove, oversized wet bar and patio access. Two bedrooms, a full bath and a large utility area are also included.

Plan P-6595-3D

Bedrooms: 3	Baths: 2½
Living Area:	
Main floor	1,530 sq. ft.
Daylight basement	1,145 sq. ft.
Total Living Area:	**2,675 sq. ft.**
Garage	462 sq. ft.
Exterior Wall Framing:	2x6

Foundation Options:

Daylight basement

(All plans can be built with your choice of foundation and framing. A generic conversion diagram is available. See order form.)

BLUEPRINT PRICE CODE: D

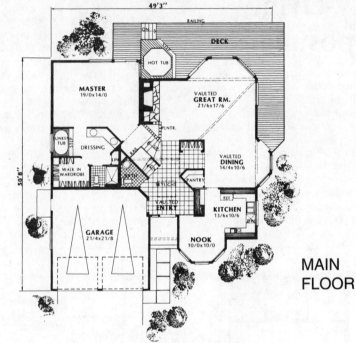

MAIN FLOOR

DAYLIGHT BASEMENT

Easy-Living Atmosphere

- Clean lines and a functional, well-designed floor plan create a relaxed, easy-living atmosphere for this sprawling ranch-style home.
- An inviting front porch with attractive columns and planter boxes opens to an airy entry, which flows into the living room and the family room.
- The huge central family room features a 14-ft. vaulted, exposed-beam ceiling and a handsome fireplace with a built-in wood box. A nice desk and plenty of bookshelves give the room a distinguished feel. A French door opens to a versatile covered rear porch.
- The large gourmet kitchen is highlighted by an arched brick pass-through to the family room. Double doors open to the intimate formal dining room, which hosts a built-in china hutch. The sunny informal eating area features lovely porch views on either side.
- The isolated sleeping wing includes four bedrooms. The enormous master bedroom has a giant walk-in closet and a private bath. A compartmentalized bath with two vanities serves the remaining bedrooms.

Plan E-2700	
Bedrooms: 4	**Baths:** 2½
Living Area:	
Main floor	2,719 sq. ft.
Total Living Area:	**2,719 sq. ft.**
Garage	533 sq. ft.
Storage	50 sq. ft.
Exterior Wall Framing:	2x6

Foundation Options:

Crawlspace
Slab
(All plans can be built with your choice of foundation and framing. A generic conversion diagram is available. See order form.)

BLUEPRINT PRICE CODE:	D

MAIN FLOOR

TO ORDER THIS BLUEPRINT,
CALL TOLL-FREE 1-800-547-5570

Plan E-2700

PRICES AND DETAILS
ON PAGES 12-15

Photo by Kevin Robinson

Striking Hillside Home Design

- This striking home is designed for a sloping site. The two-car garage and sideyard deck are nestled into the hillside, while cedar siding and a shake roof blend in nicely with the terrain.
- Clerestory windows brighten the entry and the living room, which unfold from the covered front porch. The huge living/dining area instantly catches the eye, with its corner fireplace, 17-ft. sloped ceiling and exciting window treatments. The living room also offers an inviting window seat, while the dining room has sliding glass doors to the large deck.
- The adjoining nook and kitchen also have access to the deck, along with lots of storage and work space.
- The isolated bedroom wing includes a master suite with his-and-hers closets and a private bath. The two smaller bedrooms share a hall bath.
- The daylight basement hosts a laundry room, a recreation room with a fireplace and a bedroom with two closets, plus a large general-use area.

Plan H-2045-5

Bedrooms: 4	**Baths:** 3
Living Area:	
Main floor	1,602 sq. ft.
Daylight basement	1,133 sq. ft.
Total Living Area:	**2,735 sq. ft.**
Tuck-under garage	508 sq. ft.
Exterior Wall Framing:	2x4

Foundation Options:

Daylight basement

(All plans can be built with your choice of foundation and framing. A generic conversion diagram is available. See order form.)

BLUEPRINT PRICE CODE:	D

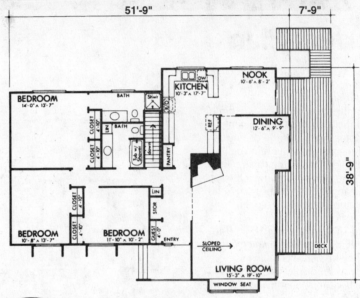

MAIN FLOOR

NOTE: The above photographed home may have been modified by the homeowner. Please refer to floor plan and/or drawn elevation shown for actual blueprint details.

DAYLIGHT BASEMENT

TO ORDER THIS BLUEPRINT,
CALL TOLL-FREE 1-800-547-5570

Plan H-2045-5

PRICES AND DETAILS
ON PAGES 12-15

137

A Perfect Plan

- This home's dramatic architecture and thoughtful room arrangement are a perfect combination.
- Seen from the stunning foyer, the dining room is enhanced by a 17-ft. ceiling. Double doors introduce the den or study, which also has a volume ceiling.
- Straight ahead is the living room, with its 16-ft., 9-in. vaulted ceiling. One set of doors leads to an expansive covered patio and another set leads to the informal region of the home.
- The island kitchen boasts a 16-ft., 9-in. vaulted ceiling, as well as a nice pantry and a sunny breakfast area.
- The family room displays a gorgeous fireplace, built-in shelving and a ceiling that vaults to 15 feet.
- The three secondary bedrooms have easy access to a full bath and a large laundry room.
- On the opposite side of the home, the stunning master suite opens to the patio and features his-and-hers walk-in closets and a private bath with a step-up tub, a separate shower and a bright solarium. Each of the four bedrooms has a 10-ft. ceiling.

Plan HDS-99-171

Bedrooms: 4+	Baths: 3
Living Area:	
Main floor	2,799 sq. ft.
Total Living Area:	**2,799 sq. ft.**
Garage	575 sq. ft.

Exterior Wall Framing:
8-in. concrete block

Foundation Options:
Slab
(All plans can be built with your choice of foundation and framing. A generic conversion diagram is available. See order form.)

BLUEPRINT PRICE CODE: D

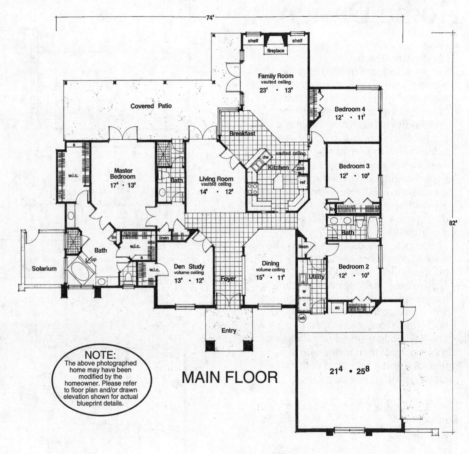

NOTE:
The above photographed home may have been modified by the homeowner. Please refer to floor plan and/or drawn elevation shown for actual blueprint details.

MAIN FLOOR

Home with Sparkle

- This dynamite design simply sparkles, with the main living areas geared toward a gorgeous greenhouse at the back of the home.
- At the front of the home, a sunken foyer introduces the formal dining room, which is framed by a curved half-wall. The sunken living room boasts a 17-ft. vaulted ceiling and a nice fireplace.
- The spacious kitchen features a bright, two-story skywell above the island. The family room's ceiling rises to 17 feet. These rooms culminate at a solar greenhouse with an indulgent hot tub and a 12-ft. vaulted ceiling. The neighboring bath has a raised spa tub.
- Upstairs, the impressive master suite includes its own deck and a stairway to the greenhouse. A vaulted library with a woodstove augments the suite. Ceilings soar to 16 ft. in both areas.

Plan S-8217

Bedrooms: 3+	Baths: 2
Living Area:	
Upper floor	789 sq. ft.
Main floor	1,709 sq. ft.
Bonus room	336 sq. ft.
Total Living Area:	**2,834 sq. ft.**
Partial basement	1,242 sq. ft.
Garage	441 sq. ft.
Exterior Wall Framing:	2x6

Foundation Options:

Partial basement
Crawlspace
Slab
(All plans can be built with your choice of foundation and framing. A generic conversion diagram is available. See order form.)

BLUEPRINT PRICE CODE: D

UPPER FLOOR

50'-6"
MAIN FLOOR

62'

Photo by Mark Englund/HomeStyles

Take the Plunge!

- From the elegant porte cochere to the striking rooflines, this home's facade is magnificent. But the rear area is equally fine, with its spa, waterfall and pool.
- Double doors lead from the entry into a columned foyer. Beyond the living room is a sunken wet bar that extends into the pool area, allowing guests to swim up to the bar for refreshments.
- The stunning master suite offers views of the pool through a curved window wall, access to the patio and an opulent bath.
- A secluded den, study or guest room is conveniently close to the hall bath.
- The dining room boasts window walls and a tiered pedestal ceiling. The island kitchen easily services both the formal and the informal areas of the home.
- A large breakfast room flows into a warm family room with a fireplace and sliders to the patio and pool.
- A railed staircase leads to the upper floor, where there are two bedrooms, a continental bath and a shared balcony deck overlooking the pool area.
- The observatory features high windows to accommodate an amateur stargazer's telescope. This room could also be used as an activity area for hobbies or games.

Plan HDS-99-154

Bedrooms: 3-4	Baths: 3
Living Area:	
Upper floor	675 sq. ft.
Main floor	2,212 sq. ft.
Total Living Area:	**2,887 sq. ft.**
Garage	479 sq. ft.
Exterior Wall Framing:	2x4

Foundation Options:

Slab

(Typical foundation & framing conversion diagram available—see order form.)

BLUEPRINT PRICE CODE: D

NOTE:
The above photographed home may have been modified by the homeowner. Please refer to floor plan and/or drawn elevation shown for actual blueprint details.

UPPER FLOOR

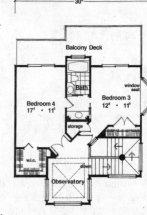

MAIN FLOOR

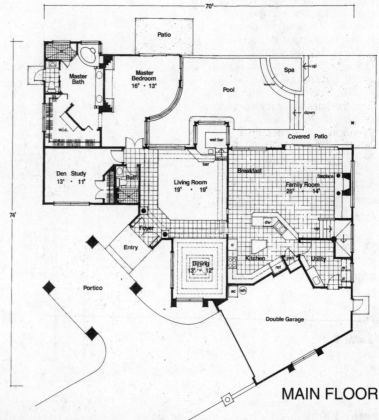

Photo by Mark Englund/HomeStyles

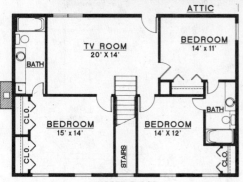

UPPER FLOOR

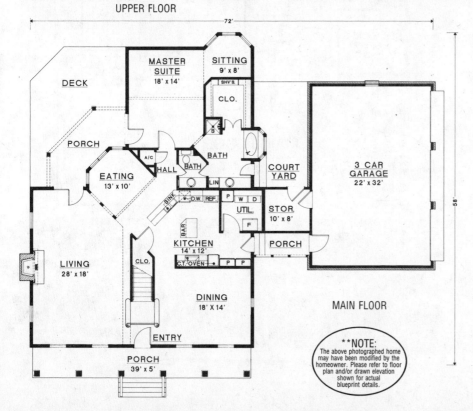

MAIN FLOOR

**NOTE:
The above photographed home
may have been modified by the
homeowner. Please refer to floor
plan and/or drawn elevation
shown for actual
blueprint details.

Plantation Perfected

- The stately plantation style with two-story columns, triple dormers, full-width porch and shuttered windows, is perfected with a modern, exciting floor plan.
- A vast living room lies to the left of the entry and stairs, complete with a fireplace and access to the rear porch and deck.
- The formal dining room is located to the right of the entry.
- The island kitchen overlooks the eating bay, and has glimpses of the living room through columns.
- The stunning main floor master suite features sloped ceilings, a garden bath overlooking a private courtyard, and a bay windowed sitting room.
- The three bedrooms upstairs share a large TV/playroom.

Plan E-2800

Bedrooms: 4	Baths: 3

Space:

Upper floor:	1,120 sq. ft.
Main floor:	1,768 sq. ft.

Total living area:	2,888 sq. ft.
Basement:	1,768 sq. ft.
Garage:	726 sq. ft.

Exterior Wall Framing:	2x6

Ceiling Heights:

Upper floor:	8'
Main floor:	9'

Foundation options:
Crawlspace.
Standard basement.
Slab.
(Foundation & framing conversion diagram available — see order form.)

Blueprint Price Code:	D

Photo by Mark Englund/HomeStyles

Angled Interior

- This plan gives new dimension to one-story living. The exterior has graceful arched windows and a sweeping roofline. The interior is marked by unusual angles and stately columns.
- The living areas are clustered around a large lanai, or covered porch. French doors provide lanai access from the family room, the living room and the master bedroom.
- The central living room also offers arched windows and shares a two-sided fireplace with the family room.
- The island kitchen and the bayed morning room are open to the family room, which features a wet bar next to the striking fireplace.
- The master bedroom features an irresistible bath with a spa tub, a separate shower, dual vanities and two walk-in closets. Two more good-sized bedrooms share another full bath.
- A 12-ft. cathedral ceiling enhances the third bedroom. Standard 8-ft. ceilings are found in the second bedroom and the hall bath. All other rooms boast terrific 10-ft. ceilings.

Plan DD-2802

Bedrooms: 3+	Baths: 2½
Living Area:	
Main floor	2,899 sq. ft.
Total Living Area:	**2,899 sq. ft.**
Standard basement	2,899 sq. ft.
Garage	568 sq. ft.
Exterior Wall Framing:	2x4

Foundation Options:

Standard basement
Crawlspace
Slab
(All plans can be built with your choice of foundation and framing. A generic conversion diagram is available. See order form.)

BLUEPRINT PRICE CODE:	D

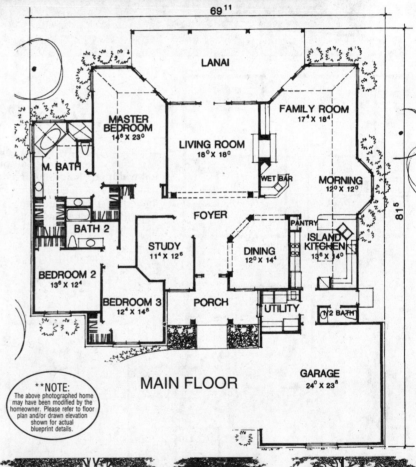

MAIN FLOOR

NOTE: The above photographed home may have been modified by the homeowner. Please refer to floor plan and/or drawn elevation shown for actual blueprint details.

REAR VIEW

Plan DD-2802

Dramatic Backyard Views

- Columned front and rear porches offer country styling to this elegant two-story.
- A dramatic array of windows stretches along the informal, rear-oriented living areas, including the central family room, the adjoining kitchen and morning room and the secluded master suite.
- The modern kitchen features an angled snack counter, a walk-in pantry, and a work island, in addition to the bayed morning room.
- The formal dining room and living room flank the two-story-high foyer.
- The exciting master suite has a sunny bayed sitting area with its own fireplace, large walk-in closets and a luxurious private bath with dual vanities, spa tub and separate shower.
- The centrally located stairway leads to three extra bedrooms and two full baths on the upper level.

Plan DD-2912

Bedrooms: 4	Baths: 3½
Space:	
Upper floor	916 sq. ft.
Main floor	2,046 sq. ft.
Total Living Area	**2,962 sq. ft.**
Basement	1,811 sq. ft.
Garage	513 sq. ft.
Exterior Wall Framing	2x4

Foundation options:

Standard Basement
Crawlspace
Slab
(All plans can be built with your choice of foundation and framing. A generic conversion diagram is available. See order form.))

BLUEPRINT PRICE CODE	D

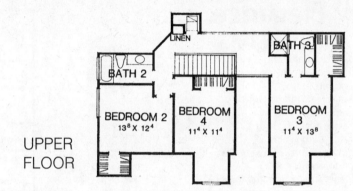

UPPER FLOOR

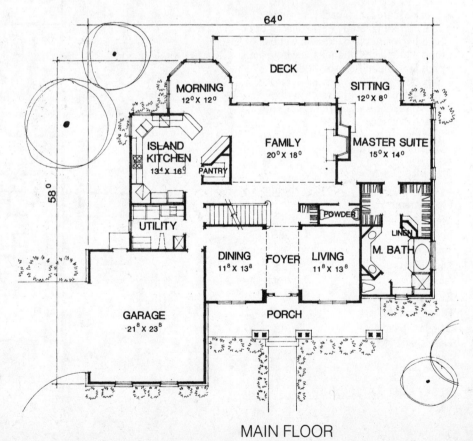

MAIN FLOOR

Stately Elegance

- The elegant interior of this home is introduced by a dramatic barrel-vaulted entry with stately columns.
- Double doors open to the 19-ft.-high foyer, where a half-round transom window brightens an attractive open-railed stairway.
- Off the foyer, the living room is separated from the sunny dining room by impressive columns.
- The island kitchen offers a bright corner sink, a walk-in pantry and a bayed breakfast area with backyard views.
- The adjoining family room offers a door to a backyard patio, while a wet bar and a fireplace enhance the whole area.
- Upstairs, the master suite boasts a private bath with two walk-in closets, a garden spa tub and a separate shower.
- Three secondary bedrooms have private bathroom access.
- Ceilings in all rooms are 9 ft. high for added spaciousness.

Plan DD-2968-A

Bedrooms: 4+	Baths: 3½
Living Area:	
Upper floor	1,382 sq. ft.
Main floor	1,586 sq. ft.
Total Living Area:	**2,968 sq. ft.**
Standard basement	1,586 sq. ft.
Garage	521 sq. ft.
Exterior Wall Framing:	2x4

Foundation Options:

Standard basement

Crawlspace

Slab

(All plans can be built with your choice of foundation and framing. A generic conversion diagram is available. See order form.)

BLUEPRINT PRICE CODE: **D**

**NOTE:
The above photographed home may have been modified by the homeowner. Please refer to floor plan and/or drawn elevation shown for actual blueprint details.

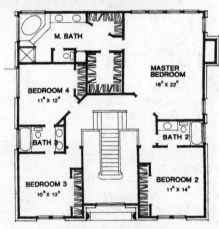

UPPER FLOOR

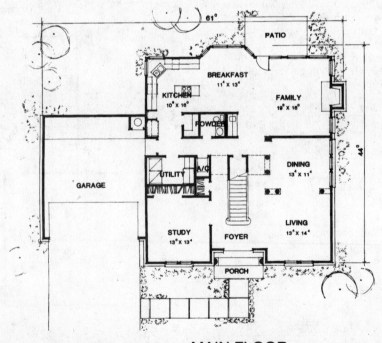

MAIN FLOOR

Stately Colonial

- This stately Colonial features a covered front entry and a secondary entry near the garage and the utility room.
- The main foyer opens to a comfortable den with elegant double doors.
- The formal living areas adjoin to the left of the foyer and culminate in a lovely bay window overlooking the backyard.
- The open island kitchen has a great central location, easily accessed from each of the living areas. Informal dining can be extended to the outdoors through sliding doors in the dinette.
- A half-wall introduces the big family room, which boasts a high 16-ft., 9-in. vaulted ceiling, an inviting fireplace and optional built-in cabinets.
- The upper floor is shared by four bedrooms, including a spacious master bedroom with a large walk-in closet, a dressing area for two and a private bath. An alternate bath layout is included in the blueprints.
- A bonus room may be added above the garage for additional space.

Plan A-2283-DS

Bedrooms: 4+	Baths: 2½
Living Area:	
Upper floor	1,137 sq. ft.
Main floor	1,413 sq. ft.
Total Living Area:	**2,550 sq. ft.**
Optional bonus room	280 sq. ft.
Standard basement	1,413 sq. ft.
Garage	484 sq. ft.
Exterior Wall Framing:	2x6

Foundation Options:

Standard basement

(All plans can be built with your choice of foundation and framing. A generic conversion diagram is available. See order form.)

BLUEPRINT PRICE CODE: D

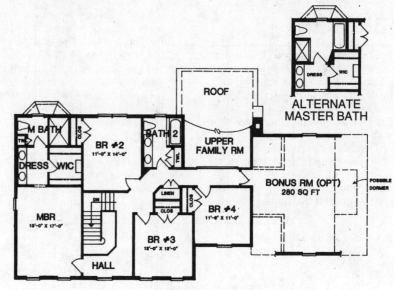

UPPER FLOOR

ALTERNATE MASTER BATH

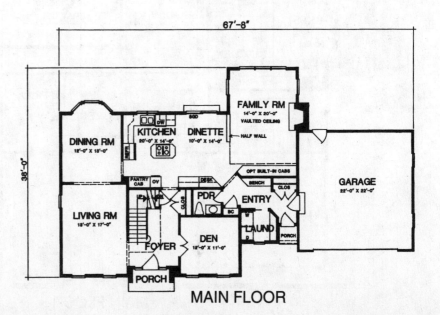

MAIN FLOOR

Beautifully Balanced

- The beautifully balanced facade of this warm one-story wraps around a central courtyard. Inside, exciting window treatments and high ceilings brighten and expand the spaces.
- The elegant front entrance leads to an impressive foyer with a 17-ft.-high ceiling and a clerestory window above. The adjoining dining room boasts a 10-ft.-high tray ceiling.
- A step down from the foyer, the living room is defined by a railing, a 10-ft.

tray ceiling and a fireplace flanked by windows. Another fireplace, this one with an extended hearth for extra seating, can be found in the neighboring family room. The family room also has French doors to the backyard.
- The efficient U-shaped kitchen is paired with a spectacular breakfast room that features a 10½-ft.-high domed ceiling and a built-in brick barbecue.
- The huge master suite boasts a 10-ft. tray ceiling, a walk-in closet and a clever compartmentalized bathroom with a dressing area and a spa tub.
- Three additional bedrooms, one of which would make an ideal office, share a hall bath.

Plan AX-93302

Bedrooms: 3+	**Baths:** 2½
Living Area:	
Main floor	2,553 sq. ft.
Total Living Area:	**2,553 sq. ft.**
Standard basement	2,424 sq. ft.
Garage	438 sq. ft.
Exterior Wall Framing:	2x6

Foundation Options:

Standard basement
Slab
(All plans can be built with your choice of foundation and framing. A generic conversion diagram is available. See order form.)

BLUEPRINT PRICE CODE: D

MAIN FLOOR

77'-8" OVERALL
53'-0" OVERALL

FRENCH DRS.
FIREPLACE
LIVING RM 19'-4"x15'-0" TRAY CEIL
FIREPLACE
FAMILY RM 14'-0"x19'-0"
BKFST 9'-2"x11'-2" DOMED CEIL
BATH #2
CL
BEDRM #4 13'-0"x11'-0"
KITCHEN 10'-6"x13'-2"
DN
HALL
REF
VAULTED CEIL
LIN
LAUN/MUD RM
DINING RM 14'-0"x12'-0" TRAY CEIL
FOYER
OFFICE/ BEDRM #2 10'-0"x 12'-0"
CL
WICL
BEDRM #3 13'-0"x11'-0"
LAV
D W CL DN
DN
PANT
CL
PORCH
CL CL
UTIL W/O BSMT
DRSG
LIN CU
MASTER BEDRM 13'-0"x19'-2" TRAY CEIL
TWO CAR GARAGE 21'-4"x20'-0"
COURTYARD
MSTR BATH
ALT GAR DR LOCAT

Gabled Manor

- Distinctive gables and a distinguished stone facade give a classic look to this richly detailed family home.
- The inviting entry vaults to 16 ft. and unfolds to the cozy living room and its warm fireplace.
- The intimate formal dining room is easily serviced by the island kitchen, which features a pantry and corner windows above the sink. French doors in the adjoining breakfast area open to a backyard patio.
- Under a spectacular vaulted ceiling that slopes to 18 ft., the fantastic family room boasts patio access and a handsome fireplace flanked by glass.
- The luxurious master suite is expanded by an 11-ft., 8-in.-high flat ceiling and includes a roomy walk-in closet and a relaxing sitting area with a clever juice bar. The master bath showcases a corner garden tub, a separate shower and an L-shaped dual-sink vanity.
- Three more bedrooms and a second full bath are located upstairs.

Plan B-91035

Bedrooms: 4	Baths: 2½
Living Area:	
Upper floor	583 sq. ft.
Main floor	1,982 sq. ft.
Total Living Area:	**2,565 sq. ft.**
Standard basement	1,982 sq. ft.
Garage	508 sq. ft.
Exterior Wall Framing:	2x6

Foundation Options:

Standard basement

(All plans can be built with your choice of foundation and framing. A generic conversion diagram is available. See order form.)

BLUEPRINT PRICE CODE:	D

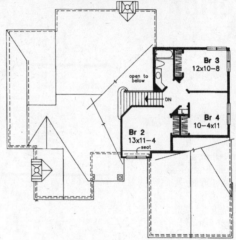

UPPER FLOOR

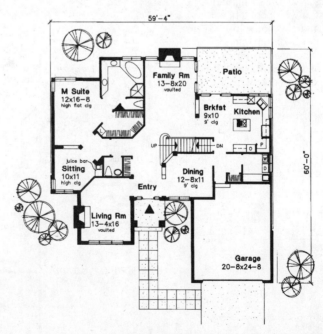

MAIN FLOOR

Elegant Interior

- An inviting covered porch welcomes guests into the elegant interior of this spectacular country home.
- Just past the entrance, the formal dining room boasts a stepped ceiling and a nearby server with a sink.
- The adjoining island kitchen has an eating bar that serves the breakfast room, which is enhanced by a 12-ft. cathedral ceiling and a bayed area of 8- and 9-ft.-high windows. Sliding glass doors lead to a covered side porch.
- Brightened by a row of 8-ft.-high windows and a glass door to the backyard, the spacious Great Room features a stepped ceiling, a built-in media center and a corner fireplace.
- The master bedroom has a tray ceiling and a cozy sitting area. The skylighted master bath boasts a whirlpool tub, a separate shower and a walk-in closet.
- A second main-floor bedroom offers private access to a compartmentalized bath. Two more bedrooms share a third bathroom on the upper floor.

Plan AX-3305-B

Bedrooms: 3+	Baths: 3
Living Area:	
Upper floor	550 sq. ft.
Main floor	2,017 sq. ft.
Total Living Area:	**2,567 sq. ft.**
Upper-floor storage	377 sq. ft.
Standard basement	2,017 sq. ft.
Garage	415 sq. ft.
Exterior Wall Framing:	2x4

Foundation Options:
Standard basement
Crawlspace
Slab
(All plans can be built with your choice of foundation and framing. A generic conversion diagram is available. See order form.)

BLUEPRINT PRICE CODE: D

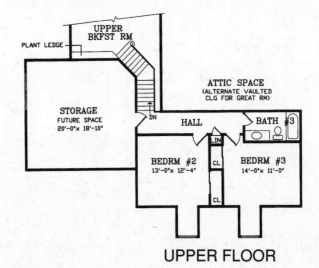

UPPER FLOOR

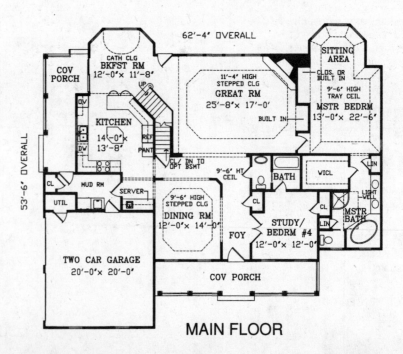

MAIN FLOOR

Tradition Reacquainted

- This home's paneled shutters, rustic columns and oval-glassed front door reacquaint passersby with traditional homes from days gone by.
- The floor plan's airy kitchen, spacious family room and distinct formal spaces are also designed for traditional ease and comfort.
- The two-story foyer features two coat closets with plant shelves above. French doors in the adjoining living room open to the front porch.

- The formal dining room unfolds from the living room, creating a large expanse for entertaining.
- The island kitchen features a handy serving bar, a sunny breakfast area and decorative half-walls leading to the adjacent family room.
- Stunning window walls highlight both the breakfast room and the family room, where a striking fireplace offers comfort and ambience.
- Upstairs, an exciting master suite offers a tray ceiling and built-in shelves. The vaulted master bath boasts a corner spa tub, a make-up table with knee space and his-and-hers walk-in closets. Three more bedrooms share a split bath.

Plan FB-5344-MADR

Bedrooms: 4	Baths: 2½
Living Area:	
Upper floor	1,372 sq. ft.
Main floor	1,210 sq. ft.
Total Living Area:	**2,582 sq. ft.**
Daylight basement	1,210 sq. ft.
Garage and storage	450 sq. ft.
Exterior Wall Framing:	2x4

Foundation Options:

Daylight basement
(All plans can be built with your choice of foundation and framing. A generic conversion diagram is available. See order form.)

BLUEPRINT PRICE CODE:	D

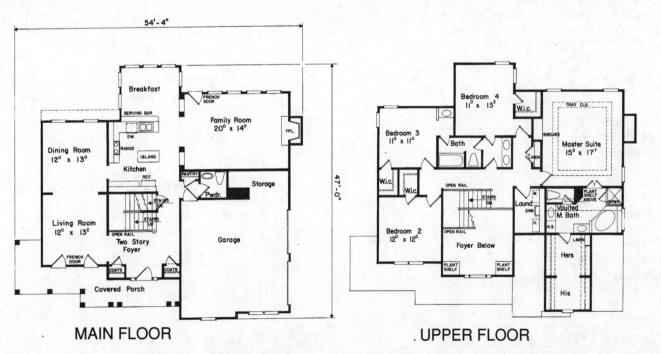

MAIN FLOOR

UPPER FLOOR

Inside Angles

- This cleverly designed home offers a space-efficient floor plan that is well suited for building on a narrow lot.
- Past the columned porch, the vaulted entry orients guests to the home's angled interior.
- Beyond the entry, the spectacular Great Room features a 17-ft.-high vaulted ceiling, a corner fireplace and French doors to an inviting patio.
- The adjoining formal dining room is convenient to the kitchen and offers access to a sizable backyard deck.
- The kitchen serves the Great Room via a handy pass-through above the sink. The sunny morning room accesses the deck through sliding glass doors.
- A turned stairway brightened by tall windows leads to the upper floor. The elegant master bedroom is enhanced by a 10-ft. gambrel ceiling. The master bath showcases a spa tub, a separate shower, a dual-sink vanity and his-and-hers walk-in closets.

Plan DD-2594

Bedrooms: 2+	Baths: 2½
Living Area:	
Upper floor	1,127 sq. ft.
Main floor	1,467 sq. ft.
Total Living Area:	**2,594 sq. ft.**
Standard basement	1,467 sq. ft.
Garage	488 sq. ft.
Exterior Wall Framing:	2x4

Foundation Options:

Standard basement

Crawlspace

Slab

(All plans can be built with your choice of foundation and framing. A generic conversion diagram is available. See order form.)

BLUEPRINT PRICE CODE:	D

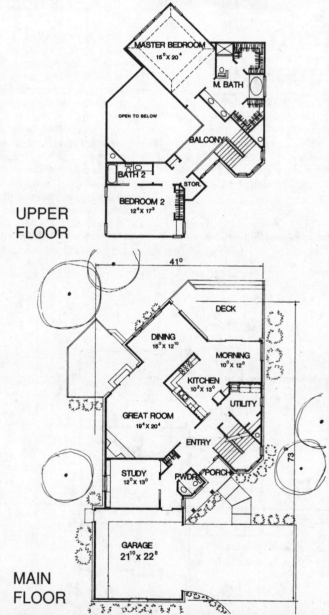

UPPER FLOOR

MAIN FLOOR

Highlighted by Skylights

- The traditional country exterior of this attractive brick home encloses an airy, light-filled interior.
- The inviting covered porch opens into the foyer, which features a 15-ft.-high sloped ceiling. Off the foyer is the sunken living room with a boxed-out bay and a window seat.
- Opposite the living room, the formal dining room boasts a 9-ft. tray ceiling.
- The skylighted island kitchen includes a bayed breakfast area. Defined by columns and half-walls, the skylighted family room enjoys a dramatic corner fireplace and French doors to a backyard deck. A 13-ft. sloped ceiling enhances the entire area.
- The master bedroom boasts a roomy walk-in closet and a spectacular skylighted bath with a 14-ft. cathedral ceiling and a corner platform tub.
- Upstairs, two more bedrooms have private access to a shared full bath.
- Plans for both a two-car and a three-car garage are included in the blueprints.

VIEW INTO FAMILY ROOM, BREAKFAST ROOM AND KITCHEN

Plan AX-1310-B

Bedrooms: 4	Baths: 3½
Living Area:	
Upper floor	625 sq. ft.
Main floor	1,973 sq. ft.
Total Living Area:	**2,598 sq. ft.**
Standard basement	1,973 sq. ft.
Two-car garage	407 sq. ft.
Three-car garage	617 sq. ft.
Exterior Wall Framing:	2x4

Foundation Options:

Standard basement
Crawlspace
Slab

(All plans can be built with your choice of foundation and framing. A generic conversion diagram is available. See order form.)

BLUEPRINT PRICE CODE: D

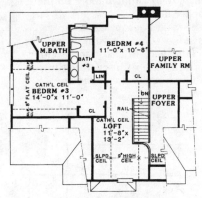

UPPER FLOOR

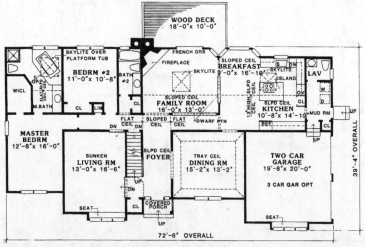

MAIN FLOOR

Established Character

- A charming front porch with support pillars, palladian windows, dormers, and brick all give this home an established character.
- The formal living and dining rooms overlook the rear deck with plenty of glass and feature a tall fireplace rising up to meet the vaulted ceiling.
- The kitchen has a work island overlooking the octagonal morning room and the informal family living space.
- There are two bedrooms on the main floor and two more on the upper floor.
- The main floor master suite overlooks the rear yard. It features a large walk-in closet and exciting private bath with separate shower and tub under the palladian window.

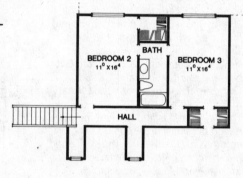

UPPER FLOOR

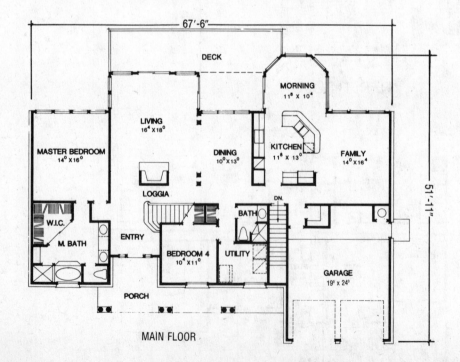

MAIN FLOOR

Plan DD-2509

Bedrooms: 4	Baths: 3
Space:	
Upper floor:	588 sq. ft.
Main floor:	2,011 sq. ft.
Total living area:	2,599 sq. ft.
Standard basement:	2,011 sq. ft.
Garage:	456 sq. ft.
Exterior Wall Framing:	2x4
Ceiling Heights:	
Upper floor:	8'
Main floor:	9'

Foundation options:
Standard basement.
Crawlspace.
Slab.
(Foundation & framing conversion diagram available — see order form.)

Blueprint Price Code:	D

Quaint Detailing

- Quaint windows accented by keystones and shutters exemplify the detailing found in this stately brick home.
- The columned front entry leads to the two-story foyer that flows between the front-oriented formal areas.
- The 18-ft. ceiling extends past an open-railed stairway to the expansive family room, which boasts a fireplace and a French door to the backyard.
- The bayed breakfast nook features an angled serving counter/desk that wraps around to the adjoining island kitchen. A pantry, a laundry room, a half-bath and the garage entrance are all nearby.
- Ceilings in all main-floor rooms are 9 ft. high unless otherwise specified.
- Upstairs, the master suite includes a 10-ft. tray ceiling, a see-through fireplace and his-and-hers walk-in closets. The posh bath flaunts a 12-ft. vaulted ceiling and a garden spa tub.
- A balcony bridge connects three more bedrooms, two with walk-in closets, and another full bath.

Plan FB-5237-NORW

Bedrooms: 4	**Baths:** 2½
Living Area:	
Upper floor	1,353 sq. ft.
Main floor	1,248 sq. ft.
Total Living Area:	**2,601 sq. ft.**
Daylight basement	1,248 sq. ft.
Garage	528 sq. ft.
Exterior Wall Framing:	2x4
Foundation Options:	

Daylight basement

(All plans can be built with your choice of foundation and framing. A generic conversion diagram is available. See order form.)

BLUEPRINT PRICE CODE:	**D**

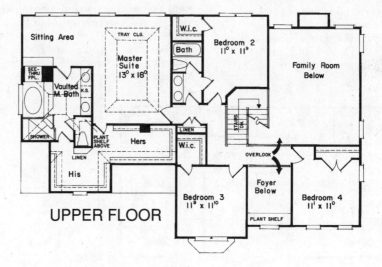

UPPER FLOOR

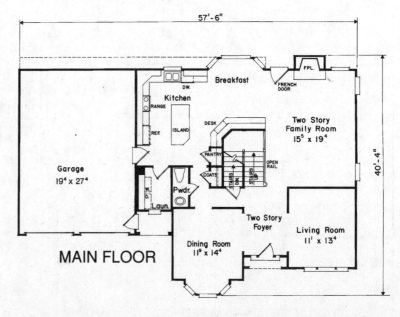

MAIN FLOOR

Large Deck Wraps Home

- A full deck and an abundance of windows surround this exciting two-level contemporary.
- The brilliant living room boasts a huge fireplace and a 14-ft.-high cathedral ceiling, plus a stunning prow-shaped window wall.

- Skywalls brighten the island kitchen and the dining room. A pantry closet and laundry facilities are nearby.
- The master bedroom offers private access to the deck. The master bath includes a dual-sink vanity, a large tub and a separate shower. A roomy hall bath serves a second bedroom.
- A generous-sized family room, another full bath and two additional bedrooms share the lower level with a two-car garage and a shop area.

Plan NW-579	
Bedrooms: 4	**Baths:** 3
Living Area:	
Main floor	1,707 sq. ft.
Daylight basement	901 sq. ft.
Total Living Area:	**2,608 sq. ft.**
Tuck-under garage	588 sq. ft.
Shop	162 sq. ft.
Exterior Wall Framing:	2x6
Foundation Options:	

Daylight basement
(All plans can be built with your choice of foundation and framing. A generic conversion diagram is available. See order form.)

BLUEPRINT PRICE CODE: D

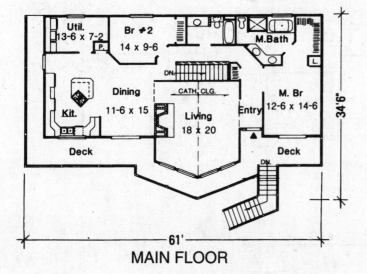

MAIN FLOOR

VIEW INTO LIVING ROOM

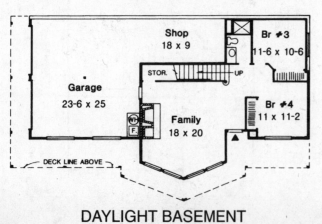

DAYLIGHT BASEMENT

Comfortable Contemporary

- Contemporary lines give this home a bold facade. Its interior is both innovative and comfortable.
- Graced with a beautiful fireplace and three large windows, the living room is open to the dining room. The dining room features a sliding glass door that accesses a partially covered patio.
- The U-shaped kitchen boasts a writing desk, a pantry, a cooktop island and a breakfast nook with patio access.
- Showcasing a beautiful fireplace flanked by windows, the sunken family room is perfect for casual entertaining.
- Double doors introduce a quiet den or extra bedroom. A full bath is nearby.
- The master bedroom is highlighted by a private deck, a walk-in wardrobe, a sunken tub and a dual-sink vanity.
- The three remaining upper-floor bedrooms share another full bath.

Plans P-7644-2A & -2D

Bedrooms: 4+	Baths: 3
Living Area:	
Upper floor	1,101 sq. ft.
Main floor	1,523 sq. ft.
Total Living Area:	**2,624 sq. ft.**
Daylight basement	1,286 sq. ft.
Garage	935 sq. ft.
Exterior Wall Framing:	2x4
Foundation Options:	**Plan #**
Daylight basement	P-7644-2D
Crawlspace	P-7644-2A

(All plans can be built with your choice of foundation and framing. A generic conversion diagram is available. See order form.)

BLUEPRINT PRICE CODE:	**D**

BASEMENT STAIRWAY LOCATION

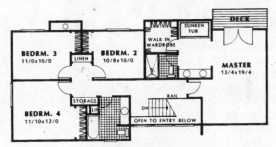

UPPER FLOOR

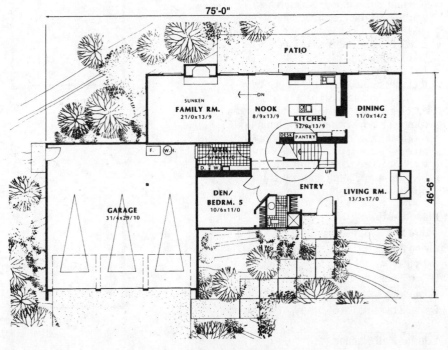

MAIN FLOOR

Well-Planned Walk-Out

- A handsome exterior, combined with an excellent interior design, makes this plan a popular and smart choice.
- The tiled entry opens to the formal dining room and the Great Room, which are separated by stylish columns and heightened by vaulted ceilings.
- A see-through fireplace with an adjacent wet bar highlights the Great Room. A window wall offers wonderful views of the expansive backyard deck.
- The fantastic kitchen, which is also warmed by the fireplace, offers a built-in desk, a walk-in pantry and an angled snack bar that faces an octagonal breakfast bay.
- The spacious main-floor master suite includes a raised ceiling, a huge walk-in closet and a lavish bath.
- An elegant den, a handy half-bath and a roomy laundry complete the main floor.
- A dramatic, open stairway overlooking an eye-catching planter leads to the walk-out basement. Included are two bedrooms and a full bath, plus an optional bonus room or family room.

Plan AG-9105

Bedrooms: 3+	Baths: 2½
Living Area:	
Main floor	1,838 sq. ft.
Daylight basement (finished)	800 sq. ft.
Total Living Area:	**2,638 sq. ft.**
Daylight basement (unfinished)	1,038 sq. ft.
Garage	462 sq. ft.
Exterior Wall Framing:	2x6
Foundation Options:	
Daylight basement	

(All plans can be built with your choice of foundation and framing. A generic conversion diagram is available. See order form.)

BLUEPRINT PRICE CODE:	D

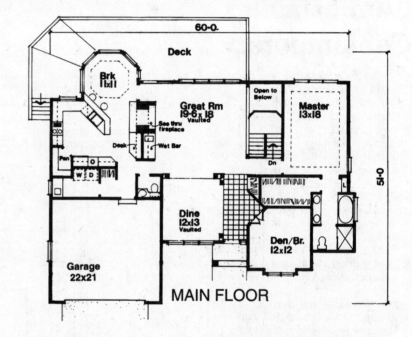

MAIN FLOOR

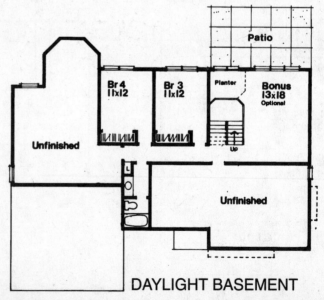

DAYLIGHT BASEMENT

Fantastic
Front Entry

- A fantastic arched window presides over the 18-ft.-high entry of this two-story, giving guests a bright welcome.
- The spacious living room is separated from the dining room by a pair of boxed columns with built-in shelves.
- The kitchen offers a walk-in pantry, a serving bar and a sunny breakfast room with a French door to the backyard.
- A boxed column accents the entry to the 18-ft. vaulted family room, which boasts a dramatic window bank and an inviting fireplace.
- The main-floor den is easily converted into an extra bedroom or guest room.
- The master suite has a 10-ft. tray ceiling, a huge walk-in closet and decorative plant shelves. The 15½-ft. vaulted bath features an oval tub and two vanities, one with knee space.
- Three additional bedrooms share another full bath near the second stairway to the main floor.

Plan FB-2680

Bedrooms: 4+	Baths: 3
Living Area:	
Upper floor	1,256 sq. ft.
Main floor	1,424 sq. ft.
Total Living Area:	**2,680 sq. ft.**
Daylight basement	1,424 sq. ft.
Garage	496 sq. ft.
Exterior Wall Framing:	2x4

Foundation Options:

Daylight basement

(All plans can be built with your choice of foundation and framing. A generic conversion diagram is available. See order form.)

BLUEPRINT PRICE CODE:	D

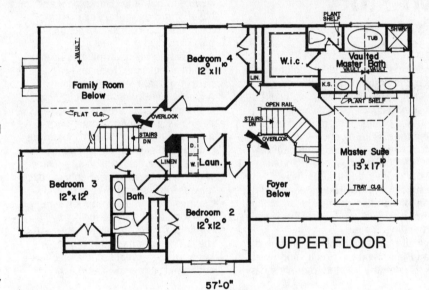

UPPER FLOOR

57'-0"

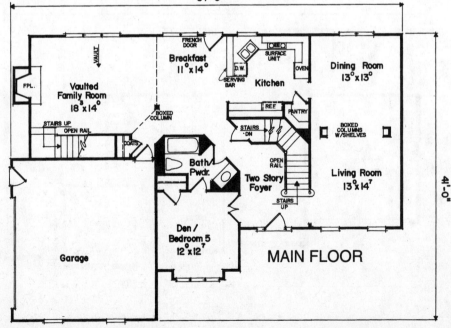

MAIN FLOOR

41'-0"

Two-Story Palace

- Decorative brick borders, a columned porch and dramatic arched windows give a classy look to this magnificent two-story palace.
- The open, sidelighted entry is flanked by the formal dining and living rooms, both of which feature elegant paned-glass windows. A coat closet and a powder room are just steps away.
- The spacious family room is warmed by a fireplace and brightened by a beautiful arched window set into a high-ceilinged area.
- The well-planned kitchen, highlighted by an island worktop and a windowed sink, is centrally located to provide easy service to both the dining room and the bayed morning room. The morning room offers access to a large, inviting backyard deck.
- A bright and heartwarming sun room also overlooks the deck, and is a perfect spot to read or just relax.
- A handy laundry/utility area is located at the entrance to the two-car garage.
- Windows surround the main-floor master suite, which boasts a luxurious bath with a garden tub, a separate shower and a dual-sink vanity. Three walk-in closets provide plenty of space for wardrobe storage.
- Ceilings in all main-floor rooms are 9 ft. high for added spaciousness.
- Upstairs, three good-sized bedrooms share a compartmentalized bath. A large and convenient attic area offers additional storage possibilities.

Plan DD-2689	
Bedrooms: 4	**Baths:** 2½
Living Area:	
Upper floor	755 sq. ft.
Main floor	1,934 sq. ft.
Total Living Area:	**2,689 sq. ft.**
Standard basement	1,934 sq. ft.
Garage	436 sq. ft.
Exterior Wall Framing:	2x4
Foundation Options:	

Standard basement
Crawlspace
Slab
(All plans can be built with your choice of foundation and framing. A generic conversion diagram is available. See order form.)

BLUEPRINT PRICE CODE:	D

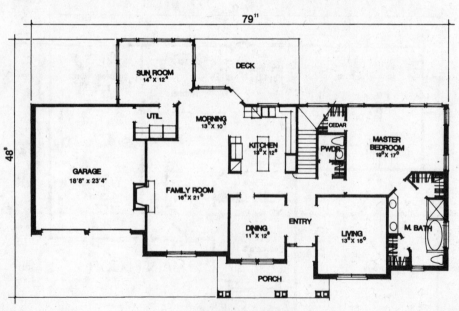

MAIN FLOOR

UPPER FLOOR

Plan DD-2689

PRICES AND DETAILS ON PAGES 12-15

REAR VIEW

Stunning Estate for Scenic Sites

- A tiered roofline, expansive windows and a magnificent wraparound deck adorn this fantastic home, which is perfect for scenic building sites.
- The main floor is a masterpiece of open design, beginning with the sunny dining room that flows into the unique kitchen. The kitchen features an angled island cooktop/snack bar, a corner sink framed by windows and a nice pantry closet.
- The sunken living room is bordered by railings on two sides, keeping it visually open. A window-filled bay overlooks the deck, while a 12-ft. ceiling heightens the room's spaciousness. Other highlights include built-in bookshelves and a fireplace with a raised hearth and a built-in log bin.
- The luxurious master suite boasts a cozy window seat, a plush bath and a private sitting room with access to the deck.
- Downstairs, the recreation room offers another fireplace and double doors to a covered driveway or patio. One of the two bedrooms here offers a private bath and walk-in closet.
- Ceilings in most rooms are at least 9-ft. high for added spaciousness.

Plan NW-779

Bedrooms: 3	Baths: 3½
Living Area:	
Main floor	1,450 sq. ft.
Daylight basement	1,242 sq. ft.
Total Living Area:	**2,692 sq. ft.**
Exterior Wall Framing:	2x6

Foundation Options:

Daylight basement
(All plans can be built with your choice of foundation and framing. A generic conversion diagram is available. See order form.)

BLUEPRINT PRICE CODE:	**D**

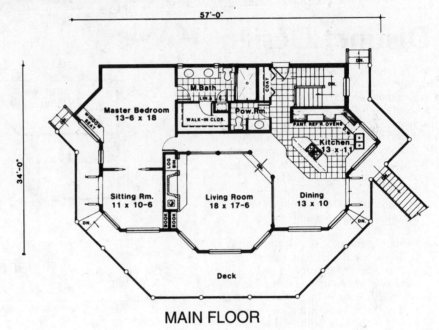

MAIN FLOOR

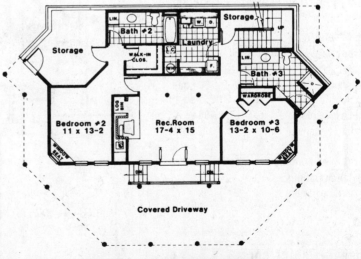

DAYLIGHT BASEMENT

Distinct Design

- This home's distinct design is seen from the curvature of its covered porch to its decorative wrought-iron roof rail.
- The 17-ft.-high foyer is lighted in an oval theme, through the clerestory window, the front door and its flanking sidelights. The broad foyer stretches between the vaulted formal living areas and a casual TV room across from a full bath.
- With its unique corner design, the fireplace in the Great Room also warms the unusual rounded dining room and the breakfast area.
- The dining room boasts a 14-ft-high ceiling, while the kitchen features an angled sink, a nearby pantry and a handy wet bar facing the Great Room.
- The master suite, with its 13-ft.-high tray ceiling, offers a bath with a spa tub and a designer shower, both brightened by glass blocks.
- Upstairs, a balcony hall leads to a turreted recreation room, two bedrooms and a full bath.

Plan AX-92326

Bedrooms: 3+	Baths: 3
Living Area:	
Upper floor	736 sq. ft.
Main floor	1,960 sq. ft.
Total Living Area:	**2,696 sq. ft.**
Standard basement	1,915 sq. ft.
Garage	455 sq. ft.
Exterior Wall Framing:	2x4

Foundation Options:

Standard basement

Crawlspace

Slab

(All plans can be built with your choice of foundation and framing. A generic conversion diagram is available. See order form.)

BLUEPRINT PRICE CODE: D

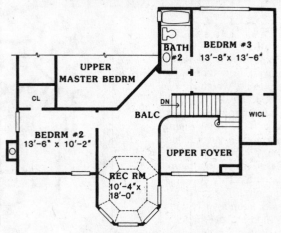

UPPER FLOOR

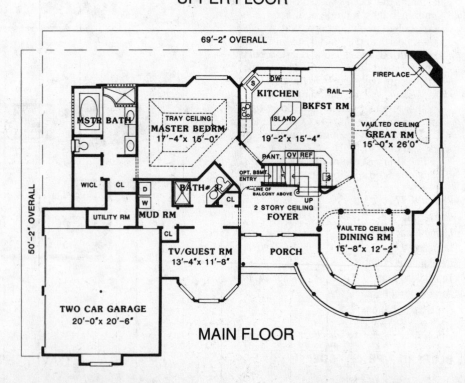

MAIN FLOOR

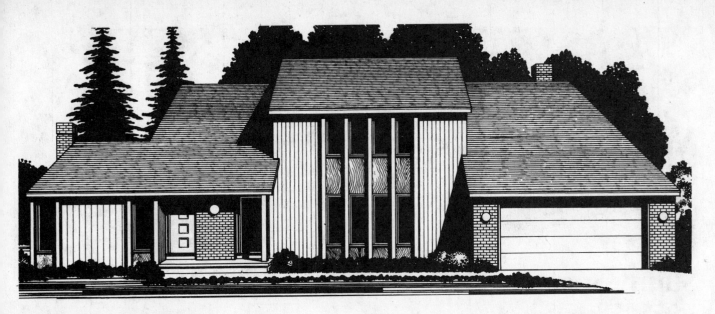

Strong, Bold Contemporary

- Bold vertical lines and eye-catching rooflines give this contemporary home lots of curb appeal.
- The entry foyer warmly receives guests, with its 16½-ft. vaulted ceiling, planter and view to the large living room. The living room boasts a fireplace and a soaring 12-ft. cathedral ceiling.
- The study, with built-in bookshelves, is a perfect place to read or relax.
- The island kitchen features a handy pantry, a work desk and a lazy Susan. The adjoining dinette provides outdoor access through sliding glass doors.
- A second fireplace is the focal point in the sunken family room.
- Upstairs, double doors introduce the master suite, which boasts two closets and a compartmentalized bath.
- A hall bath with a dual-sink vanity is shared by the remaining bedrooms.

Plan A-2108-DS

Bedrooms: 4	**Baths:** 2½

Living Area:	
Upper floor	1,134 sq. ft.
Main floor	1,570 sq. ft.
Total Living Area:	**2,704 sq. ft.**
Standard basement	1,570 sq. ft.
Garage	484 sq. ft.

Exterior Wall Framing: 2x4

Foundation Options:
Standard basement
(All plans can be built with your choice of foundation and framing. A generic conversion diagram is available. See order form.)

BLUEPRINT PRICE CODE: D

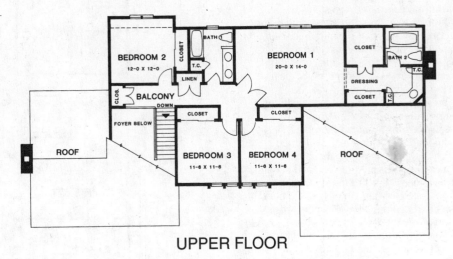

UPPER FLOOR

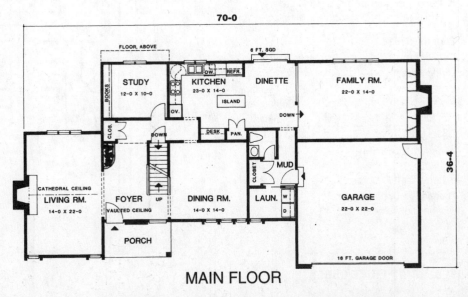

MAIN FLOOR

Sunny Spaces

- Graced by skylights and clerestory windows, this bright and airy home is filled with sunny spaces.
- The skylighted foyer boasts a 12-ft. sloped ceiling and showcases a sunstreaked open-railed stairway.
- Off the foyer, the intimate sunken living room features a 16-ft. cathedral ceiling and tall corner windows. Defined by columns and rails, the adjacent formal dining room is enhanced by an elegant 12-ft. stepped ceiling.
- The skylighted island kitchen includes a sunny breakfast space, which is separated from the family room by a half-wall. Expanded by a skylighted 16-ft. cathedral ceiling, the family room offers a handsome fireplace and access to a sunken rear sun room.
- The deluxe master suite is graced by a stepped ceiling, a bayed sitting room and a private bath. Sliding glass doors open to the sun room, which boasts an 11-ft., 7-in. vaulted ceiling.
- Two more bedrooms, a study alcove and a full bath are found upstairs.

Plan AX-91314

Bedrooms: 3+	Baths: 3
Living Area:	
Upper floor	544 sq. ft.
Main floor	1,959 sq. ft.
Sun room	202 sq. ft.
Total Living Area:	**2,705 sq. ft.**
Standard basement	1,833 sq. ft.
Garage	482 sq. ft.
Exterior Wall Framing:	2x4

Foundation Options:

Standard basement
Crawlspace
Slab

(All plans can be built with your choice of foundation and framing. A generic conversion diagram is available. See order form.)

BLUEPRINT PRICE CODE:	D

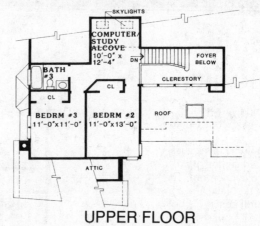

UPPER FLOOR

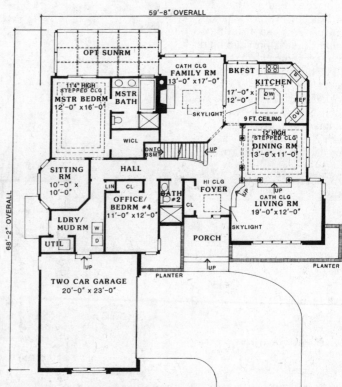

MAIN FLOOR

TO ORDER THIS BLUEPRINT, CALL TOLL-FREE 1-800-547-5570   Plan AX-91314   *PRICES AND DETAILS ON PAGES 12-15*

Unforgettable Floor Plan

- Unusual shapes and exciting features give this home an unforgettable floor plan and a handsome facade.
- The exterior is distinguished by an arched-window entry flanked by columns. Columns are also used on the large L-shaped front porch. Arched windows in the study and in one of the second-story bedrooms echo the graceful lines of the entry.
- To the right of the tiled entry hall lies the vaulted living room, separated by half-walls and columns. To the left is the eye-catching study, with its octagonal tray ceiling. The dining room also has a tray ceiling and is tucked between the living room and the kitchen for easy yet intimate entertaining.
- The showpiece of the main floor is the spectacular kitchen, breakfast room and family room arrangement. A wonderful see-through fireplace warms the entire area. The breakfast room features large bay windows, a tray ceiling and an angled countertop snack bar facing the kitchen. The vaulted family room accesses a large rear patio.
- The crown jewel of the second floor is the stunning master suite, with its romantic fireplace, intimate sitting area and private deck. The plush master bath includes his 'n hers sinks, a garden tub and separate shower.

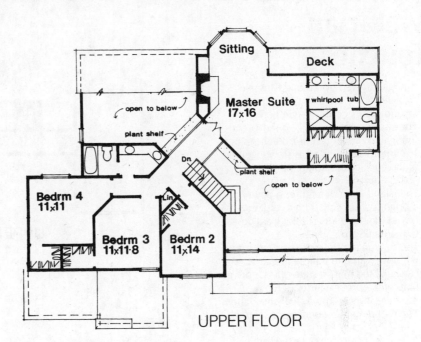

UPPER FLOOR

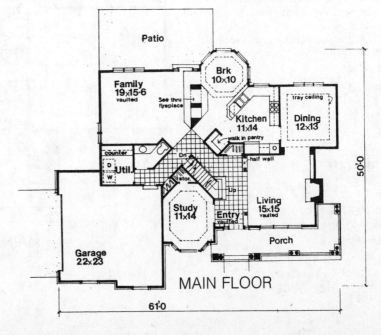

MAIN FLOOR

Plan AG-2701

Bedrooms: 4	**Baths:** 2 ½
Space:	
Upper floor	1,195 sq. ft.
Main floor	1,572 sq. ft.
Total Living Area	**2,767 sq. ft.**
Basement	1,572 sq. ft.
Garage	506 sq. ft.
Exterior Wall Framing	2x6
Foundation options:	
Standard Basement	
(Foundation & framing conversion diagram available—see order form.)	
Blueprint Price Code	D

Victorian Touches

- A huge covered porch and fishscale shingles bring Victorian elements to the facade of this country-style home.
- The spacious foyer leads to the formal living and dining rooms on either side.
- The informal living areas flow together at the back of the home for easy entertaining.
- The island kitchen features a pantry and a bright corner sink. The oversized, bayed dinette offers sliding glass doors to the backyard.
- The sunken family room boasts a rear window wall and a large fireplace.
- Upstairs, the master suite offers a private bath with corner whirlpool tub, a separate shower and a dual-sink vanity. The two remaining bedrooms share a hall bath.
- A large bonus room over the garage could be used as a hobby area, home office or playroom.
- Central to the upper floor is an inviting sitting area with lovely oval window.

Plan PI-91-567

Bedrooms: 3+	Baths: 2½
Living Area:	
Upper floor	1,194 sq. ft.
Main floor	1,258 sq. ft.
Bonus room	369 sq. ft.
Total Living Area:	**2,821 sq. ft.**
Standard basement	1,244 sq. ft.
Garage	672 sq. ft.
Exterior Wall Framing:	2x6

Foundation Options:

Standard basement

(Typical foundation & framing conversion diagram available—see order form.)

BLUEPRINT PRICE CODE:	D

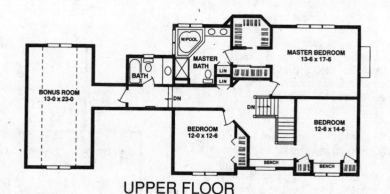

UPPER FLOOR

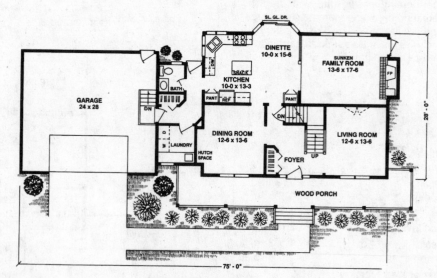

MAIN FLOOR

Spacious Country-Style

- With a minimum of four bedrooms and an open floor plan, this design is perfect for growing families.
- The covered front porch and country-style detailing give the exterior a warm, homey look.
- Inside, an arched opening in the two-story foyer provides a view into the formal dining room. Straight ahead, the vaulted family room offers a fireplace and an arched opening to the breakfast nook and kitchen.
- The spacious nook and kitchen area features a French door to the backyard, a work island and lots of counter space.
- The formal living room, reminiscent of the old-fashioned parlor, overlooks the delightful front porch.
- The upper floor is highlighted by a luxurious master suite, plus includes a balcony hall overlook, a multipurpose loft, three large bedrooms and two additional baths.

Plan FB-5016-MARY

Bedrooms: 4+	Baths: 4
Living Area:	
Upper floor	1,408 sq. ft.
Main floor	1,426 sq. ft.
Total Living Area:	**2,834 sq. ft.**
Daylight basement	1,426 sq. ft.
Garage	240 sq. ft.
Storage	40 sq. ft.
Exterior Wall Framing:	2x4

Foundation Options:
Daylight basement
(Typical foundation & framing conversion diagram available—see order form.)

BLUEPRINT PRICE CODE:	D

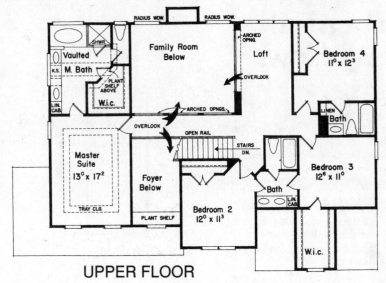

UPPER FLOOR

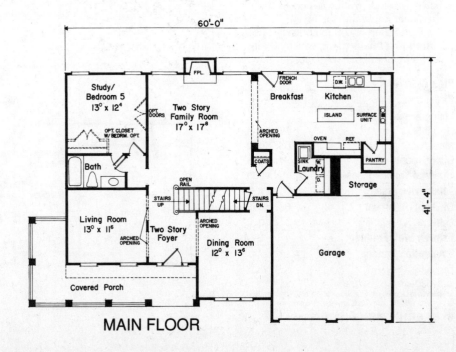

MAIN FLOOR

Symmetrical Bay Windows

- This home's ornate facade proudly displays a pair of symmetrical copper-topped bay windows.
- A bright, two-story-high foyer stretches to the vaulted Great Room, with its fireplace and backyard deck access.
- The island kitchen offers a snack bar and a breakfast nook that opens to the deck and the garage.
- The main-floor master suite features private deck access, dual walk-in closets and a personal bath with a corner garden tub. A laundry room and a bayed study are nearby.
- Upstairs, three secondary bedrooms and another full bath are located off the balcony bridge, which overlooks both the Great Room and the foyer.
- A second stairway off the breakfast nook climbs to a bonus room, which adjoins an optional full bath and closet.

Plan C-9010

Bedrooms: 4+	Baths: 2½-3½
Living Area:	
Upper floor	761 sq. ft.
Main floor	1,637 sq. ft.
Bonus room	347 sq. ft.
Optional bath and closet	106 sq. ft.
Total Living Area:	**2,851 sq. ft.**
Daylight basement	1,637 sq. ft.
Garage	572 sq. ft.
Exterior Wall Framing:	**2x4**

Foundation Options:

Daylight basement

Crawlspace

(All plans can be built with your choice of foundation and framing. A generic conversion diagram is available. See order form.)

BLUEPRINT PRICE CODE: **D**

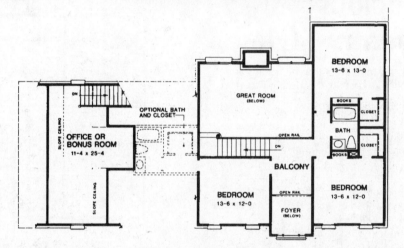

UPPER FLOOR

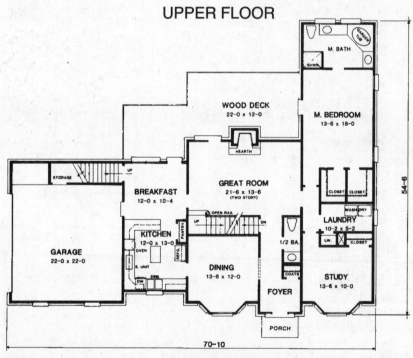

MAIN FLOOR

A Family Tradition

- This traditional design has clean, sharp styling, with family-sized areas for formal and casual gatherings.
- The sidelighted foyer is graced with a beautiful open staircase and a wide coat closet. Flanking the foyer are the spacious formal living areas.
- The everyday living areas include an island kitchen, a bayed dinette and a large family room with a fireplace.
- Just off the entrance from the garage, double doors open to the quiet study, which boasts built-in bookshelves.
- A powder room and a deluxe laundry room with cabinets are convenient to the active areas of the home.
- Upstairs, the master suite features a roomy split bath and a large walk-in closet. Three more bedrooms share another split bath.

Plan A-118-DS

Bedrooms: 4+	Baths: 2½
Living Area:	
Upper floor	1,344 sq. ft.
Main floor	1,556 sq. ft.
Total Living Area:	**2,900 sq. ft.**
Standard basement	1,556 sq. ft.
Garage	576 sq. ft.
Exterior Wall Framing:	2x4

Foundation Options:

Standard basement
(All plans can be built with your choice of foundation and framing. A generic conversion diagram is available. See order form.)

BLUEPRINT PRICE CODE: D

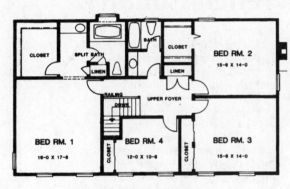

UPPER FLOOR

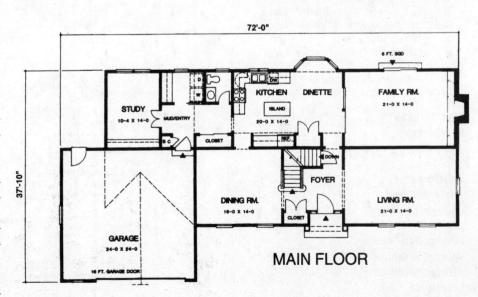

MAIN FLOOR

Sprawling French Country

- A hip roof and gable accents give this sprawling home a country, French look.
- To the left of the entry, the formal dining room is illuminated with a tall arched window arrangement.
- The spectacular living room stretches from the entry of the home to the rear. A vaulted ceiling in this expansive space rises to 19 ft., and windows at both ends offer light and a nice breeze.
- Angled walls add interest to the roomy informal areas, which overlook the covered lanai. The island kitchen opens to the adjoining morning room and the sunny family room.
- The spacious main-floor master suite is highlighted by a 13-ft. vaulted ceiling and a bayed sitting area. The master bath features dual walk-in closets, a large spa tub and a separate shower.
- Three extra bedrooms and two more baths share the upper level.

Plan DD-2889

Bedrooms: 4	Baths: 3½
Living Area:	
Upper floor	819 sq. ft.
Main floor	2,111 sq. ft.
Total Living Area:	**2,930 sq. ft.**
Standard basement	2,111 sq. ft.
Garage	622 sq. ft.
Exterior Wall Framing:	2x4

Foundation Options:

Standard basement

Crawlspace

Slab

(All plans can be built with your choice of foundation and framing. A generic conversion diagram is available. See order form.)

BLUEPRINT PRICE CODE: D

UPPER FLOOR

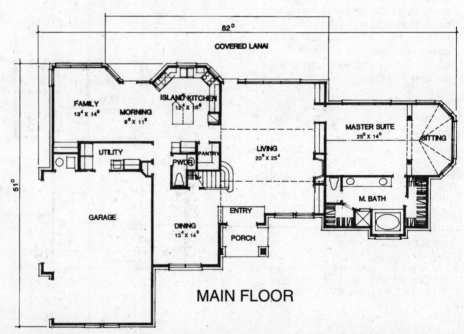

MAIN FLOOR

TO ORDER THIS BLUEPRINT, CALL TOLL-FREE 1-800-547-5570   Plan DD-2889   *PRICES AND DETAILS ON PAGES 12-15*

Super Features!

- Super indoor/outdoor living features are the main ingredients of this sprawling one-story home.
- Beyond the columned entry, the foyer features a 16-ft.-high ceiling and is brightened by a fantail transom. The dining room and the living room enjoy ceilings that vault to nearly 11 feet.
- The family room, with a 15-ft. vaulted ceiling, sits at the center of the floor plan and extends to the outdoor living spaces. A handsome fireplace flanked by built-in shelves adds excitement.
- The adjoining kitchen shares the family room's vaulted ceiling and offers a cooktop island, a large pantry and a breakfast nook that opens to the patio.
- The master suite is intended to offer the ultimate in comfort. A double-door entry, a 10-ft. tray ceiling and private patio access are featured in the bedroom. The master bath shares a see-through fireplace with the bedroom.
- Three secondary bedrooms share two full baths at the other end of the home.

Plan HDS-99-164

Bedrooms: 4	Baths: 3
Living Area:	
Main floor	2,962 sq. ft.
Total Living Area:	**2,962 sq. ft.**
Garage	567 sq. ft.
Exterior Wall Framing:	
2x4 and 8-in. concrete block	
Foundation Options:	
Slab	

(All plans can be built with your choice of foundation and framing. A generic conversion diagram is available. See order form.)

BLUEPRINT PRICE CODE:	D

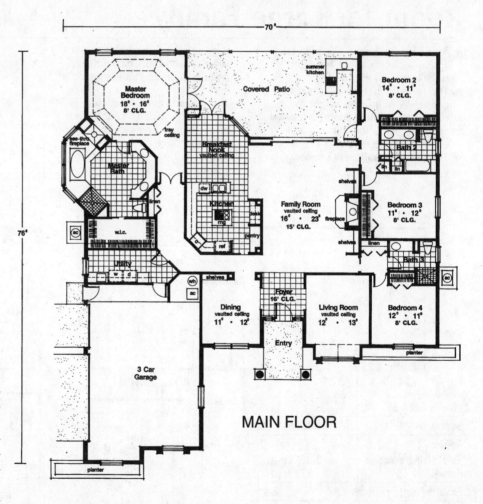

MAIN FLOOR

Room for Large Family

- An expansive home, this plan puts a heap of living space for a big, busy family all on one floor.
- The formal entertaining zone, consisting of a large, bright living room and a dining room, is located at the front, to the left as guests enter the large foyer.
- The more casual areas include a huge family room with a massive fireplace, and wet bar, a huge, open kitchen and sunny breakfast area.
- The magnificent master suite is fit for royalty, with its double-door entry, corner fireplace, incredible bath and large closet.
- Bedroom 2 has a private bath, while bedrooms 3 and 4 share a compartmentalized walk-through bath with private lavatory/dressing areas.
- Note the covered porch and double-doored entry at the front, plus the covered patio at the rear.

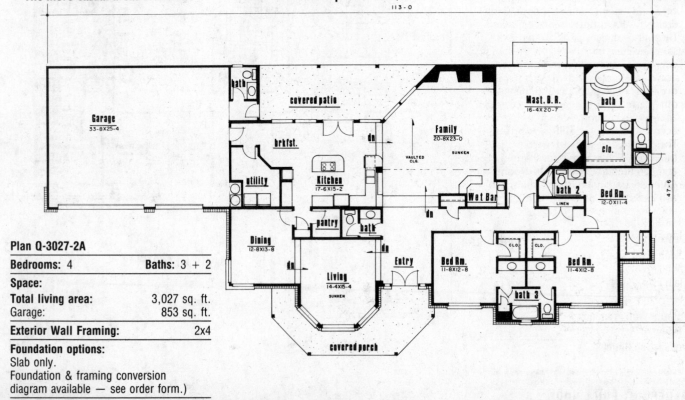

Plan Q-3027-2A

Bedrooms: 4	Baths: 3 + 2
Space:	
Total living area:	3,027 sq. ft.
Garage:	853 sq. ft.
Exterior Wall Framing:	2x4
Foundation options:	
Slab only.	
Foundation & framing conversion diagram available — see order form.)	
Blueprint Price Code:	E

Master Suite
Fit for a King

- This sprawling one-story features an extraordinary master suite that stretches from the front of the home to the back.
- Eye-catching windows and columns introduce the foyer, which flows back to the Grand Room. French doors open to the covered veranda, which offers a fabulous summer kitchen.
- The kitchen and bayed morning room are nestled between the Grand Room and a warm Gathering Room. A striking fireplace, an entertainment center and an ale bar are found here. This exciting core of living spaces also offers dramatic views of the outdoors.
- The isolated master suite features a stunning two-sided fireplace and an octagonal lounge area with veranda access. His-and-hers closets, separate dressing areas and a garden tub are other amenities. Across the home, three additional bedroom suites have private access to one of two more full baths.
- The private dining room at the front of the home has a 13-ft. coffered ceiling and a niche for a china cabinet.
- An oversized laundry room is located across from the kitchen and near the entrance to the three-car garage.

Plan EOF-60

Bedrooms: 4	Baths: 3
Living Area:	
Main floor	3,002 sq. ft.
Total Living Area:	**3,002 sq. ft.**
Garage	660 sq. ft.
Exterior Wall Framing:	2x6

Foundation Options:

Slab
(All plans can be built with your choice of foundation and framing. A generic conversion diagram is available. See order form.)

BLUEPRINT PRICE CODE: E

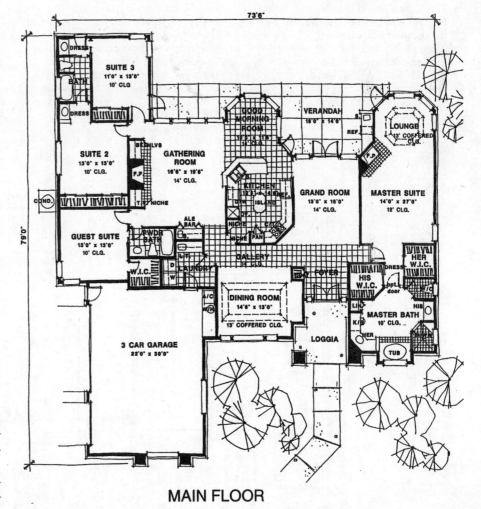

MAIN FLOOR

Country Sophistication

- This sophisticated country-style home features a large front porch and a handsome brick exterior.
- Guests will notice the high ceilings throughout the home. Ceilings are 9 ft. if not otherwise specified.
- The formal living areas consist of a secluded dining room and a spacious living room.
- A two-way fireplace is shared by the living room and the family room, both

of which have access to a large covered rear porch.
- The bayed breakfast room flows into the kitchen, which boasts an island cooktop, a pantry, a unique window and an adjacent utility room.
- The lavish master suite offers a double shower, a huge walk-in wardrobe and a sitting area with porch access.
- Two additional bedrooms share a private, compartmentalized bath. All of the bedrooms feature large, walk-in closets.
- The good-sized study could serve as a fourth bedroom.

Plan KY-3057	
Bedrooms: 3-4	**Baths:** 3
Living Area:	
Main floor	3,057 sq. ft.
Total Living Area:	**3,057 sq. ft.**
Garage	483 sq. ft.
Exterior Wall Framing:	2x4

Foundation Options:
Slab
(Typical foundation & framing conversion diagram available—see order form.)

BLUEPRINT PRICE CODE:	E

MAIN FLOOR

69'—10"

85'—11"

Stately and Roomy

- The exquisite exterior of this two-story home opens to a very roomy interior.
- The magnificent two-story-high foyer shows off a curved, open-railed stairway to the upper floor and opens to a study on the right and the formal living areas on the left.
- The spacious living room flows into a formal dining room that overlooks the outdoors through a lovely bay window.
- A large work island and snack counter sit at the center of the open kitchen and breakfast room. An oversized pantry closet, a powder room and a laundry room are all close at hand.
- Adjoining the breakfast room is the large sunken family room, featuring a 12-ft.-high vaulted ceiling, a cozy fireplace and outdoor access.
- The upper floor includes a stunning master bedroom with an 11-ft. vaulted ceiling and a luxurious private bath.
- Three additional bedrooms share a second full bath.

Plan CH-280-A

Bedrooms: 4+	Baths: 2½
Living Area:	
Upper floor	1,262 sq. ft.
Main floor	1,797 sq. ft.
Total Living Area:	**3,059 sq. ft.**
Basement	1,797 sq. ft.
Garage	462 sq. ft.
Exterior Wall Framing:	2x4

Foundation Options:

Daylight basement

Standard basement

Crawlspace

(All plans can be built with your choice of foundation and framing. A generic conversion diagram is available. See order form.)

BLUEPRINT PRICE CODE: **E**

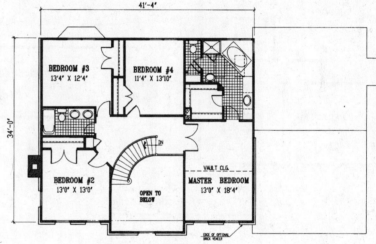

UPPER FLOOR

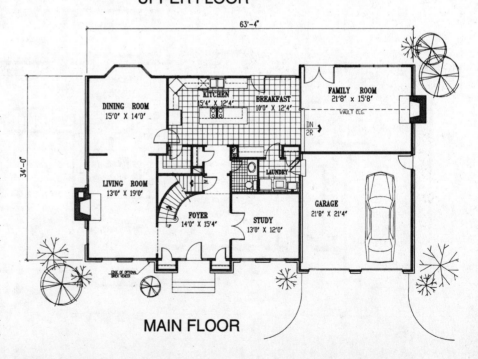

MAIN FLOOR

BEDROOM
12'-0"x17'-6"

DRESS

BATH

CLOSET

RAIL

DN

SITTING
8'-0"x10'-8"

CLOSET

DN

STORAGE
18'-0"x10'-4"

STOR

BEDROOM
13'-0"x11'-10"

BEDROOM
12'-8"x11'-10"

CLOSET

28'-6"

65'-6"

UPPER FLOOR

Bay Windows Enhance a Country Home

A large master bedroom suite includes a deluxe bath with separate shower, garden tub, twin vanities and two large walk-in closets. Kitchen has direct access to both the breakfast nook and the dining room, which features a large bay window. Three bedrooms, a sitting area and storage or bonus room combine to form the second level.

First floor: 2,005 sq. ft.

Second floor: 1,063 sq. ft.

Total living area: 3,068 sq. ft.
(Not counting basement or garage)

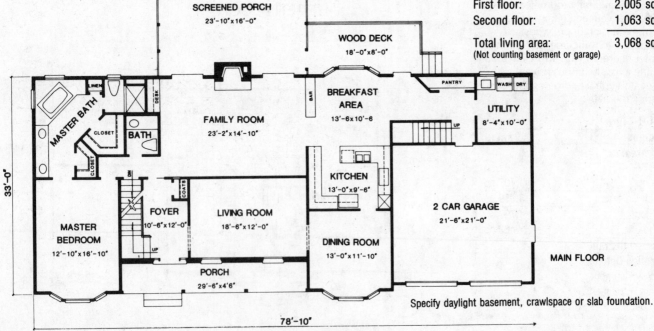

SCREENED PORCH
23'-10"x16'-0"

WOOD DECK
18'-0"x8'-0"

LINEN

DESK

MASTER BATH

CLOSET

BATH

CLOSET

FAMILY ROOM
23'-2"x14'-10"

BAR

BREAKFAST AREA
13'-6"x10'-6

PANTRY

WASH DRY

UTILITY
8'-4"x10'-0"

KITCHEN
13'-0"x9'-6"

UP

2 CAR GARAGE
21'-6"x21'-0"

DN

COATS

FOYER
10'-6"x12'-0"

LIVING ROOM
18'-6"x12'-0"

UP

MASTER BEDROOM
12'-10"x16'-10"

DINING ROOM
13'-0"x11'-10"

PORCH
29'-6"x4'6"

MAIN FLOOR

33'-0"

78'-10"

Specify daylight basement, crawlspace or slab foundation.

Blueprint Price Code E
Plan C-8409

PRICES AND DETAILS
ON PAGES 12-15

Open Floor Plan Enjoys Outdoors

- Luxurious family living begins with a spectacular central Great Room; a fireplace is flanked by double doors that access the large wrapping rear porch.
- Casual dining can take place in the adjoining breakfast nook or island kitchen, with snack bar; access to a convenient laundry room, plus the front porch and rear veranda is also offered in the kitchen.
- Formal dining and living rooms flank the foyer.
- For privacy, you'll find the master suite on the main floor; it features a spacious walk-in closet and large bath with dual vanities, whirlpool tub and separate shower.
- Two extra bedrooms, each with personal dressing areas, share the upper level.

Plan VL-3038

Bedrooms: 3	**Baths:** 2 ½

Space:

Upper floor	836 sq. ft.
Main floor	2,202 sq. ft.
Total Living Area	**3,038 sq. ft.**
Exterior Wall Framing	2 x 4

Foundation options:

Crawlspace

Slab

(Foundation & framing conversion diagram available—see order form.)

Blueprint Price Code	E

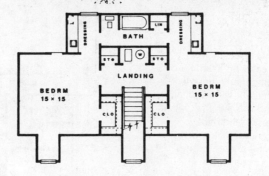

UPPER FLOOR

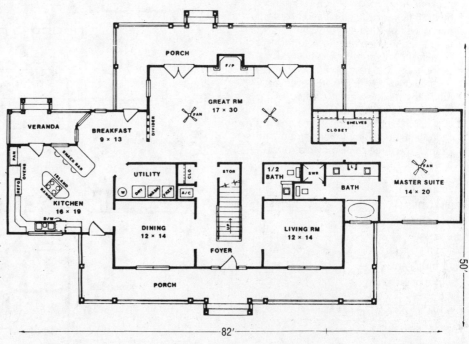

MAIN FLOOR

Large and Luxurious

- This two-story home offers large, luxurious living areas with a variety of options to complement any lifestyle.
- The two-story-high foyer shows off an angled stairway and flows to the elegant formal living spaces on the right.
- The gourmet kitchen boasts a sunny sink, a walk-in pantry and an island cooktop with a serving bar. The adjoining breakfast nook has French doors opening to the backyard.
- Highlighting the main floor is a huge sunken family room, which is expanded by a 17-ft. vaulted ceiling and hosts a handy wet bar and a handsome fireplace. An open rail views to the breakfast room and kitchen beyond.
- Completing the main floor is a den or guest bedroom with private access to a full bath, making a great guest suite.
- Upstairs, the master suite boasts a 10-ft. tray ceiling in the sleeping area and a 15-ft. vaulted ceiling in the garden bath.
- Each of the three remaining bedrooms has private access to a bath.

Plan FB-3071

Bedrooms: 4+	Baths: 4
Living Area:	
Upper floor	1,419 sq. ft.
Main floor	1,652 sq. ft.
Total Living Area:	**3,071 sq. ft.**
Daylight basement	1,652 sq. ft.
Garage	456 sq. ft.
Exterior Wall Framing:	2x4

Foundation Options:

Daylight basement
(All plans can be built with your choice of foundation and framing. A generic conversion diagram is available. See order form.)

BLUEPRINT PRICE CODE:	E

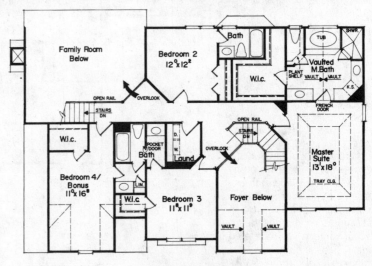

UPPER FLOOR

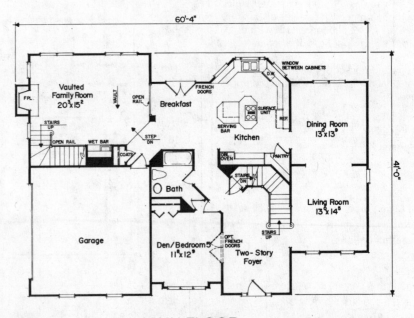

MAIN FLOOR

Plan FB-3071

Striking Stucco

- The facade of this striking stucco home is adorned with elegant window treatments and eye-catching gables.
- Inside, a two-story-high foyer views to an open-railed staircase and is brightened by an arched window.
- To the right of the foyer, an arched opening connects the living room to the formal dining room.
- The casual living areas consist of an open kitchen, a sunny breakfast nook and a family room with a fireplace. The kitchen boasts a island cooktop, while the nook offers a French door leading to the backyard. A second stairway in the family room accesses the upper floor.
- Just off the foyer, a den with access to a full bath may serve as a guest room.
- Ceilings in all main-floor rooms are 9 ft. high unless otherwise specified.
- Upstairs, the master suite features a 9-ft. tray ceiling and a private bath with a 12-ft. vaulted ceiling over a garden tub.
- Three additional bedrooms, one with an 11-ft. vaulted ceiling, share two more full baths. A versatile bonus room is also included.

Plan FB-5081-AVER

Bedrooms: 4+	Baths: 4
Living Area:	
Upper floor	1,325 sq. ft.
Main floor	1,447 sq. ft.
Bonus room	301 sq. ft.
Total Living Area:	**3,073 sq. ft.**
Daylight basement	1,447 sq. ft.
Garage	465 sq. ft.
Exterior Wall Framing:	2x4
Foundation Options:	

Daylight basement

(All plans can be built with your choice of foundation and framing. A generic conversion diagram is available. See order form.)

BLUEPRINT PRICE CODE:	E

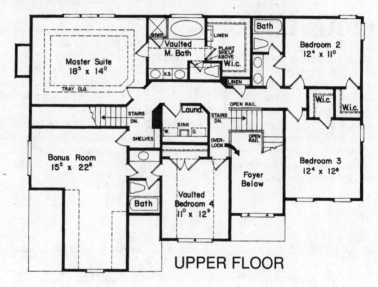

UPPER FLOOR

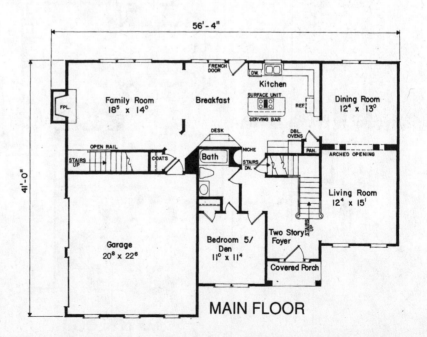

MAIN FLOOR

One-Floor Gracious Living

- An impressive roofscape, stately brick with soldier coursing and an impressive columned entry grace the exterior of this exciting single-story home.
- The entry opens to the the free-flowing interior, where the formal areas merge near the den, or guest room.
- The living room offers a window wall to a wide backyard deck, and the dining room is convenient to the kitchen.

- The octagonal island kitchen area offers a sunny breakfast nook with a large corner pantry.
- The spacious family room adjoins the kitchen and features a handsome fireplace and deck access. Laundry facilities and garage access are nearby.
- The lavish master suite with a fireplace and a state-of-the-art bath is privately situated in the left wing.
- Three secondary bedrooms have abundant closet space and share two baths on the right side of the home.
- The entire home features expansive 9-ft. ceilings.

Plan DD-3076

Bedrooms: 4+	Baths: 3
Living Area:	
Main floor	3,076 sq. ft.
Total Living Area:	**3,076 sq. ft.**
Standard basement	3,076 sq. ft.
Garage	648 sq. ft.
Exterior Wall Framing:	2x4

Foundation Options:

Standard basement
Crawlspace
Slab
(All plans can be built with your choice of foundation and framing. A generic conversion diagram is available. See order form.)

BLUEPRINT PRICE CODE:	E

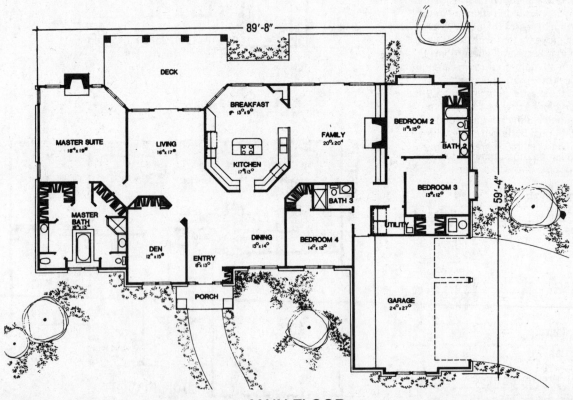

MAIN FLOOR

 Plan DD-3076 *PRICES AND DETAILS ON PAGES 12-15*

Spacious and Striking

- Alluring angles and an open, airy floor plan distinguish this impressive home, designed to take advantage of a sloping lot.
- A gorgeous covered deck and patio give guests a royal welcome.
- Designed for both entertaining and family gatherings, the home's main floor features a bright family room with an 11-ft.-high vaulted ceiling and fabulous windows. A two-way fireplace with a lovely semi-round planter is shared with the adjoining dining room.
- The combination kitchen and breakfast area features a 10-ft. vaulted ceiling, a center island and a high pot shelf.
- The roomy master suite boasts a 10-ft. vaulted ceiling and double doors to a private balcony. The sumptuous master bath includes a beautiful Jacuzzi, a separate shower and a walk-in closet.
- Three more bedrooms and three full baths are located on the lower floor.
- A second family room includes a wet bar and double doors to a large covered patio.

Plan Q-3080-1A

Bedrooms: 4	Baths: 4½
Living Area:	
Main floor	1,575 sq. ft.
Lower floor	1,505 sq. ft.
Total Living Area:	**3,080 sq. ft.**
Garage	702 sq. ft.
Exterior Wall Framing:	2x4

Foundation Options:

Slab

(All plans can be built with your choice of foundation and framing. A generic conversion diagram is available. See order form.)

BLUEPRINT PRICE CODE:	E

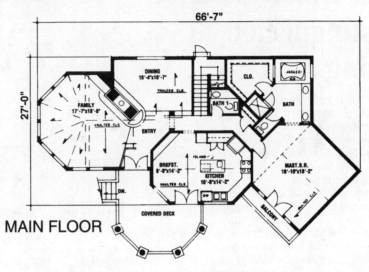

MAIN FLOOR

LOWER FLOOR

Distinguished Living

- Beautiful arches, sweeping rooflines and a dramatic entry court distinguish this one-story from all the rest.
- Elegant columns outline the main foyer. To the right, the dining room has a 13-ft. coffered ceiling and an ale bar with a wine rack.
- The centrally located Grand Room can be viewed from the foyer and gallery. French doors and flanking windows allow a view of the veranda as well.
- A large island kitchen and sunny morning room merge with the casual Gathering Room. The combination offers a big fireplace, a TV niche, bookshelves and a handy snack bar.
- The extraordinary master suite flaunts a 12-ft. ceiling, an exciting three-sided fireplace and a TV niche shared with the private bayed lounge. A luxurious bath, a private library and access to the veranda are also featured.
- The two smaller bedroom suites have private baths and generous closets.

Plan EOF-62

Bedrooms: 3	Baths: 3½
Living Area:	
Main floor	3,090 sq. ft.
Total Living Area:	**3,090 sq. ft.**
Garage	660 sq. ft.
Exterior Wall Framing:	2x6

Foundation Options:

Slab

(All plans can be built with your choice of foundation and framing. A generic conversion diagram is available. See order form.)

BLUEPRINT PRICE CODE: E

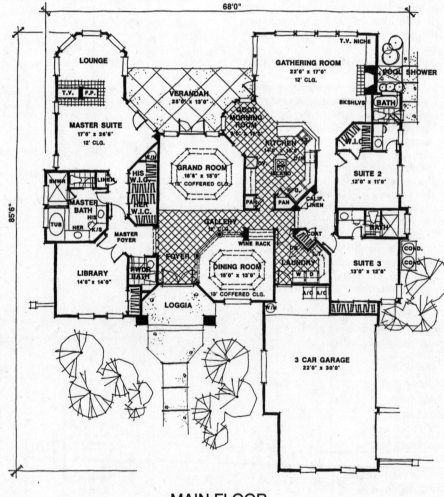

MAIN FLOOR

TO ORDER THIS BLUEPRINT, CALL TOLL-FREE 1-800-547-5570   Plan EOF-62   *PRICES AND DETAILS ON PAGES 12-15*

Spectacular View From Loft

- A soaring foyer and vaulted, step-down parlor with fireplace and decorative brick columns can be seen from an overhead loft in this distinguished two-story.
- Flanking the parlor are a vaulted library with built-in shelves along two walls and a formal dining room with brilliant 12' ceiling.
- Rich-looking brick borders the cooktop in the roomy island kitchen with a handy pantry; an adjoining bayed breakfast room offers a sunny patio.
- The exciting sunken family room off the kitchen features a unique gambrel ceiling, massive fireplace, corner windows and refreshing wet bar.
- Three steps up from the loft is the spacious master suite with private, bayed sitting area and lavish bath with separate vanities and walk-in closets, a garden tub and romantic deck.

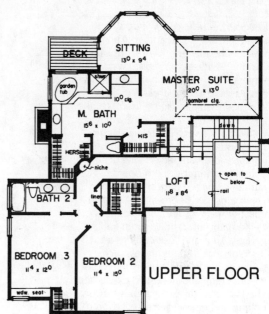

UPPER FLOOR

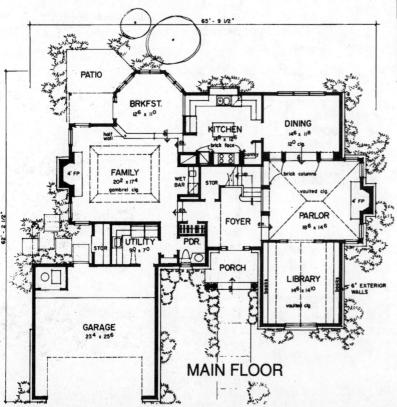

MAIN FLOOR

Plan DW-3108

Plan DW-3108	
Bedrooms: 3	Baths: 2 ½
Space:	
Upper floor	1,324 sq. ft.
Main floor	1,784 sq. ft.
Total Living Area	**3,108 sq. ft.**
Basement	1,784 sq. ft.
Garage	595 sq. ft.
Exterior Wall Framing	2x6
Foundation options:	

Standard Basement
Crawlspace
Slab
(Framing conversion diagram available—see order form.)

Blueprint Price Code	E

Timeless Beauty

- Reflected in its lovely windows and stone and stucco facade, this home has timeless beauty and lasting appeal.
- Past the inviting covered front porch, the two-story-high entry is flanked by the intimate formal areas.
- Warmed by a handsome fireplace, the large family room features a window wall with views to a backyard patio.
- The good-sized kitchen includes a pantry and an angled serving bar. The adjoining morning room opens to the partially covered patio.
- The main-floor bedroom is a perfect guest or in-law suite, with easy access to the bathroom, utility room and garage. All main-floor ceilings are 10 ft. high for added spaciousness.
- Upstairs, a versatile game room boasts a 10-ft. ceiling and access to a nice deck.
- The master bedroom also has a 10-ft. ceiling and enjoys a private covered porch, a roomy walk-in closet and a luxurious bath with a garden tub.
- Three additional upper-floor bedrooms and a full bath all have 9-ft. ceilings.

Plan DD-2952

Bedrooms: 5	Baths: 3
Living Area:	
Upper floor	1,721 sq. ft.
Main floor	1,394 sq. ft.
Total Living Area:	**3,115 sq. ft.**
Standard basement	1,394 sq. ft.
Garage	442 sq. ft.
Exterior Wall Framing:	2x4

Foundation Options:

Standard basement
Crawlspace
Slab

(All plans can be built with your choice of foundation and framing. A generic conversion diagram is available. See order form.)

BLUEPRINT PRICE CODE: E

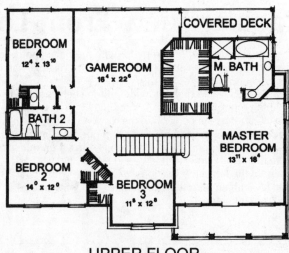

UPPER FLOOR

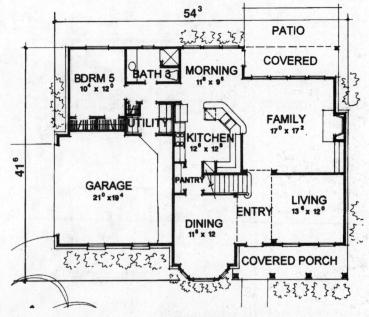

MAIN FLOOR

TO ORDER THIS BLUEPRINT,
CALL TOLL-FREE 1-800-547-5570

Plan DD-2952

PRICES AND DETAILS
ON PAGES 12-15

Tall Two-Story

- This gorgeous two-story is introduced by a barrel-vaulted entry and supporting columns. Inside, a spectacular curved staircase leads to a balcony overlook.
- Off the two-story-high foyer, a library with a 16-ft.-high vaulted ceiling is perfect for reading or study.
- A formal dining room opposite the library opens to the fabulous island kitchen. The kitchen offers an angled serving bar to the bayed breakfast area and adjoining living room.
- The spacious living room, with an 18-ft. vaulted ceiling, opens to a backyard patio. A fireplace flanked by built-in shelving warms the whole family area.
- The master bedroom boasts a 10-ft. gambrel ceiling, a sunny bay window and patio access. The spacious master bath offers his-and-hers walk-in closets, an oval tub and a separate shower.
- A second stairway near the utility room leads to the upper floor, where there are three more bedrooms, two baths and a bonus room above the garage. The bonus room could be finished as a game room, a media center or a hobby area.

Plan DD-3125

Bedrooms: 4+	Baths: 3½
Living Area:	
Upper floor	982 sq. ft.
Main floor	2,147 sq. ft.
Total Living Area:	**3,129 sq. ft.**
Unfinished Bonus	196 sq. ft.
Standard basement	1,996 sq. ft.
Garage	771 sq. ft.
Exterior Wall Framing:	2x4

Foundation Options:
Standard basement
Crawlspace
Slab
(All plans can be built with your choice of foundation and framing. A generic conversion diagram is available. See order form.)

BLUEPRINT PRICE CODE: **E**

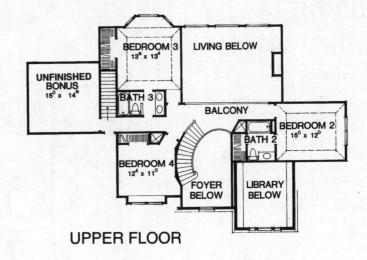

UPPER FLOOR

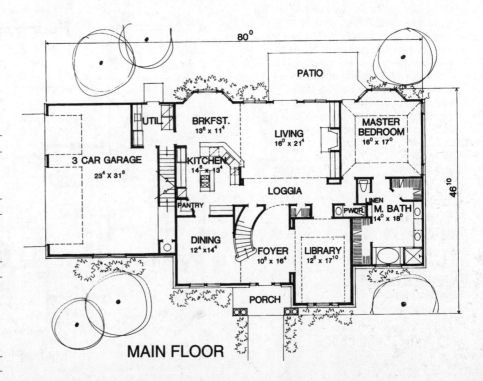

MAIN FLOOR

Stunning Country-Style

- A lovely front porch that encases bay windows provides a friendly welcome to this stunning country-style home.
- Inside, the main living areas revolve around the large country kitchen and dinette, complete with an island worktop, a roomy built-in desk and access to a backyard deck.
- A raised-hearth fireplace, French doors and a 12-ft., 4-in. cathedral ceiling highlight the casual family room.
- The formal dining room is open to the living room and features an inviting window seat and a tray ceiling. A French door in the bay-windowed living room opens to the relaxing porch.
- A quiet den and a large laundry area/mudroom complete the main floor.
- The upper floor showcases a super master suite with a bay window, an 11-ft., 8-in. tray ceiling, two walk-in closets and a private bath with a garden tub and its own dramatic ceiling.
- Three additional bedrooms share a full bath designed for multiple users.

Plan A-538-R

Bedrooms: 4+	Baths: 2½
Living Area:	
Upper floor	1,384 sq. ft.
Main floor	1,755 sq. ft.
Total Living Area:	**3,139 sq. ft.**
Standard basement	1,728 sq. ft.
Garage	576 sq. ft.
Exterior Wall Framing:	2x4

Foundation Options:

Standard basement

(All plans can be built with your choice of foundation and framing. A generic conversion diagram is available. See order form.)

BLUEPRINT PRICE CODE:	E

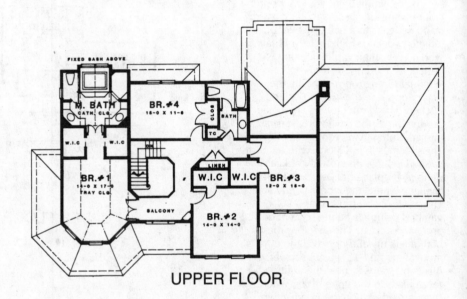

UPPER FLOOR

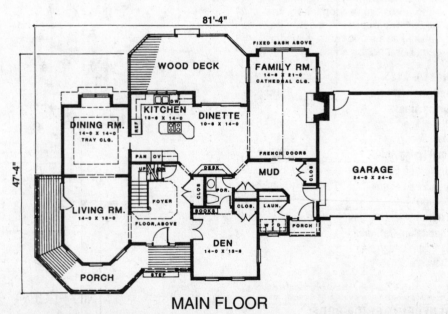

MAIN FLOOR

Traditional Elegance

- This home's stately traditional exterior is enhanced by a stunning two-story entry and brick with quoin corner details.
- The formal living and dining rooms flank the entry foyer.
- The informal living areas face the rear yard and include an island kitchen, a dinette bay and a sunken family room with a fireplace.
- The main floor also includes a handy mudroom that opens to the garage and flows back to a laundry room, a powder room and a sunny den or fifth bedroom.
- The upper floor houses four spacious bedrooms and two full baths, including a lavish master bath with a corner spa tub and a separate shower.

Plan A-2230-DS

Bedrooms: 4+	Baths: 2½
Living Area:	
Upper floor	1,455 sq. ft.
Main floor	1,692 sq. ft.
Total Living Area:	**3,147 sq. ft.**
Standard basement	1,692 sq. ft.
Garage	484 sq. ft.
Exterior Wall Framing:	2x6

Foundation Options:

Standard basement
(All plans can be built with your choice of foundation and framing. A generic conversion diagram is available. See order form.)

BLUEPRINT PRICE CODE:	E

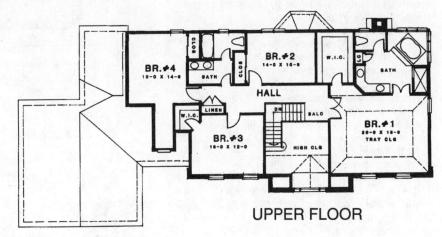

UPPER FLOOR

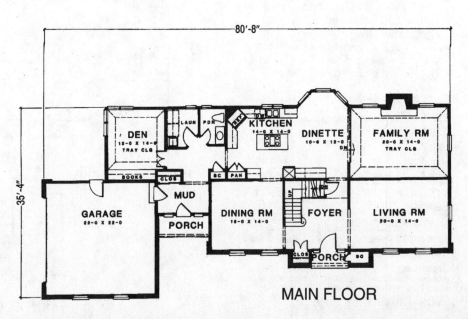

MAIN FLOOR

Creative Spaces

- This expansive home uses vaulted ceilings and multiple levels to create a functional, airy floor plan.
- The broad, vaulted entry foyer leads to the bayed living room, which is warmed by a striking fireplace. A few steps down, the dining room opens to a wide backyard deck.
- The island kitchen features a sunny sink area and a breakfast nook with deck access. A laundry room, a half-bath and a den or extra bedroom are also found on this level.
- Adjacent to the nook, the sunken family room boasts a wet bar, a second fireplace and a bright window wall with sliding glass doors to a lovely patio.
- Upstairs, the master suite includes a sunken bedroom with a private deck. The lavish master bath offers a sunken garden tub, a dual-sink vanity and a skylight near the private shower.
- Three large secondary bedrooms share another skylighted bath. Each bedroom has its own unique design feature.

Plans P-7664-4A & -4D

Bedrooms: 4+	Baths: 2½
Living Area:	
Upper floor	1,301 sq. ft.
Main floor	1,853 sq. ft.
Total Living Area:	**3,154 sq. ft.**
Daylight basement	1,486 sq. ft.
Garage	668 sq. ft.
Exterior Wall Framing:	2x4
Foundation Options:	**Plan #**
Daylight basement	P-7664-4D
Crawlspace	P-7664-4A

(All plans can be built with your choice of foundation and framing. A generic conversion diagram is available. See order form.)

BLUEPRINT PRICE CODE:	E

UPPER FLOOR

BASEMENT STAIRWAY LOCATION

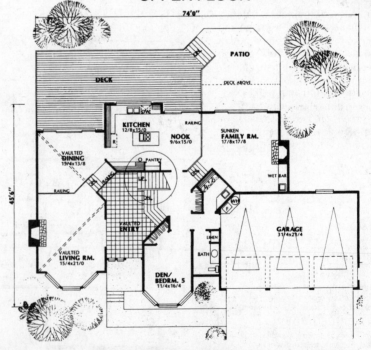

MAIN FLOOR

Plans P-7664-4A & -4D

Ornate Design

- This exciting home is distinguished by an ornate facade with symmetrical windows and a columned entry.
- A beautiful arched window highlights the two-story-high foyer, with its open-railed stairway and high plant shelf. The foyer separates the two formal rooms and flows back to the family room.
- With an 18-ft. ceiling, the family room is brightened by corner windows and warmed by a central fireplace.
- Columns introduce the sunny breakfast area and the gourmet kitchen, which features an angled island/serving bar and a butler's pantry near the dining room. A laundry room and a second stairway to the upper floor are nearby.
- Ceilings in all main-floor rooms are 9 ft. high unless otherwise specified.
- Upstairs, a dramatic balcony overlooks the family room and the foyer.
- The master suite boasts a 10-ft. tray ceiling, a sitting room and an opulent garden bath with a 12-ft. vaulted ceiling. Three more bedrooms, each with a walk-in closet and private bath access, complete the upper floor.

Plan FB-5347-HAST

Bedrooms: 4+	Baths: 4
Living Area:	
Upper floor	1,554 sq. ft.
Main floor	1,665 sq. ft.
Total Living Area:	**3,219 sq. ft.**
Daylight basement	1,665 sq. ft.
Garage	462 sq. ft.
Exterior Wall Framing:	2x4

Foundation Options:

Daylight basement
(All plans can be built with your choice of foundation and framing. A generic conversion diagram is available. See order form.)

BLUEPRINT PRICE CODE:	E

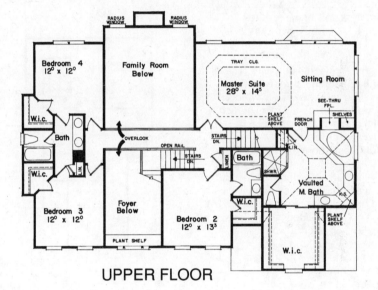

UPPER FLOOR

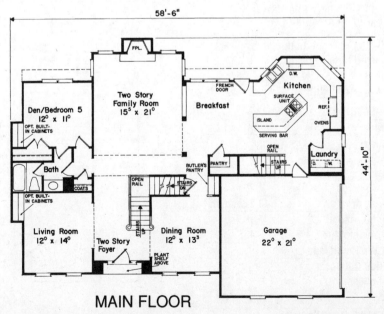

MAIN FLOOR

Set in Stone

- Sure to impress, this home features a stucco finish set off by a two-story entry faced with stone.
- Inside, a stunning 18-ft. vaulted foyer separates the formal living spaces. The secluded living room flaunts a 15-ft. vaulted ceiling and a boxed-out window. Columns outline the dining room, which has French doors to a covered porch.
- The casual spaces begin with a wonderful Great Room that features a two-story-high ceiling and a fireplace flanked by tall arched windows.
- Window walls and a French door to the backyard brighten the breakfast nook, which has a 14-ft. vaulted ceiling. The adjoining kitchen offers a work island, a corner sink and a walk-in pantry.
- The superb master suite includes a 10½-ft. tray ceiling in the angled sleeping area and a 16-ft. vaulted ceiling in the luxurious master bath.
- Ceilings in all main-floor rooms are 9 ft. high unless otherwise specified.
- Upstairs, a balcony hall leads to three nice-sized bedrooms, each with an ample walk-in closet and private access to one of two compartmentalized baths.

Plan FB-5348-BARR

Bedrooms: 4	Baths: 3½
Living Area:	
Upper floor	776 sq. ft.
Main floor	2,165 sq. ft.
Fourth bedroom/bonus room	281 sq. ft.
Total Living Area:	**3,222 sq. ft.**
Daylight basement	2,165 sq. ft.
Garage and storage	456 sq. ft.
Exterior Wall Framing:	2x4

Foundation Options:
Daylight basement
(All plans can be built with your choice of foundation and framing.
A generic conversion diagram is available. See order form.)

BLUEPRINT PRICE CODE: E

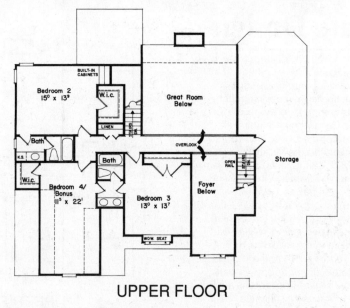

UPPER FLOOR

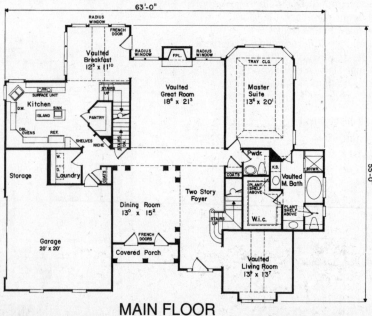

MAIN FLOOR

UPPER FLOOR

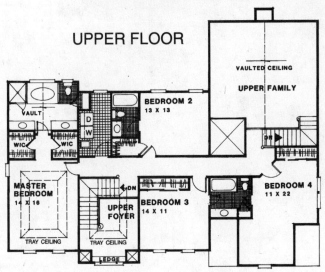

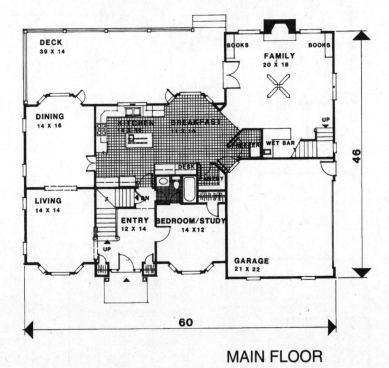

MAIN FLOOR

European Enticement

- This exciting European stucco home exudes elegance with its stunning entry, brick steps, copper-topped bay windows and shuttered windows.
- The dramatic two-story foyer opens to a lovely bayed study or fifth bedroom on one side. Opposite is the formal living room, also with a front bay.
- To the rear is an equally spacious dining room, fitting for formal occasions. Double doors access the spacious kitchen and breakfast room where you'll find a handy work island, a built-in desk, a walk-in pantry and a separate freezer room.
- Access to the huge rear deck is possible from the dining room, breakfast room and family room. The family room also offers a fireplace, an L-shaped wet bar, built-in bookcases and an alternate stairway to the upper floor.
- The upper floor houses four bedrooms, two with private baths. An oversized laundry room is conveniently located on this floor as well.

Plan APS-3203	
Bedrooms: 4-5	**Baths: 4**
Living Area:	
Upper floor	1,525 sq. ft.
Main floor	1,735 sq. ft.
Total Living Area:	**3,260 sq. ft.**
Partial daylight basement	1,170 sq. ft.
Garage	462 sq. ft.
Exterior Wall Framing:	2x4
Foundation Options:	
Partial daylight basement	
(Typical foundation & framing conversion diagram available—see order form.)	
BLUEPRINT PRICE CODE:	E

Anyone for Fun?

- A spectacular sunken game room with a corner window, vaulted ceilings, wet bar and half-wall that separates it from the family room is ideal for the active family or for those who like to entertain.

- The exciting atmosphere continues to the family room, also at a level lower than the rest of the home; here you'll find a fireplace, a rear window wall and a railing that allows a view of the adjoining vaulted nook.

- The spacious kitchen offers an island cooktop, pantry and pass-through to the game room hallway; formal, vaulted living areas are found opposite the entry.

- An upper-level bridge overlooks the game room and joins the two secondary bedrooms with the master suite and luxury, skylit master bath.

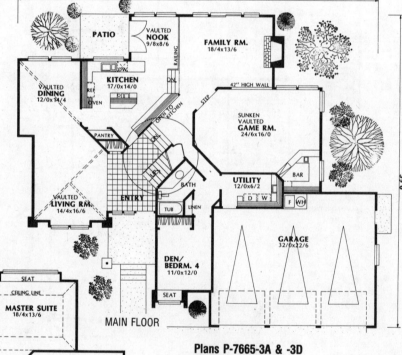

MAIN FLOOR

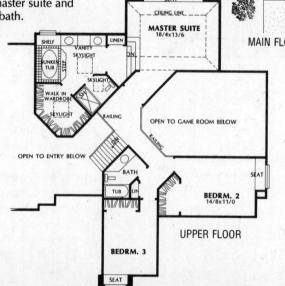

WITH DAYLIGHT BASEMENT

UPPER FLOOR

Plans P-7665-3A & -3D

Bedrooms: 3-4	Baths: 3
Space:	
Upper floor	1,160 sq. ft.
Main floor	2,124 sq. ft.
Total Living Area	**3,284 sq. ft.**
Basement	2,104 sq. ft.
Garage	720 sq. ft.
Exterior Wall Framing	2x4
Foundation options:	Plan #
Daylight Basement	P-7665-3D
Crawlspace	P-7665-3A
(Foundation & framing conversion diagram available—see order form.)	
Blueprint Price Code	E

Smart Two-Story

- This simple yet classically designed two-story is functional and spacious.
- The recessed entry opens to a wide reception foyer that offers dual closets and access to each of the living areas.
- The enormous sunken living room with an optional fireplace stretches from the front of the house all the way to the back! Charming French doors open to the backyard.
- The big family room also provides easy outdoor access. A fireplace would look nice between the corner windows.
- The efficient kitchen features an island range, a work desk and a handy pantry. The adjoining breakfast area is enhanced by a lovely bay window that opens to the backyard.
- Four big bedrooms and two baths are housed on the upper floor.
- The master bedroom boasts a private sitting area and the option of a fireplace. Two walk-in closets and an elegant skylighted bath with a cathedral ceiling are also included.

Plan AX-87105

Bedrooms: 4	Baths: 2½
Living Area:	
Upper floor	1,552 sq. ft.
Main floor	1,734 sq. ft.
Total Living Area:	**3,286 sq. ft.**
Standard basement	1,734 sq. ft.
Garage	434 sq. ft.
Exterior Wall Framing:	2x4

Foundation Options:

Standard basement

(All plans can be built with your choice of foundation and framing. A generic conversion diagram is available. See order form.)

BLUEPRINT PRICE CODE: E

UPPER FLOOR

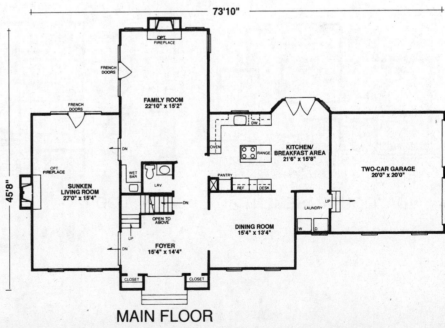

MAIN FLOOR

Tremendous Tri-Level Living

- Perfect for a scenic or sloping lot, this stunning home offers three levels of living space for maximum privacy and flexibility.
- At the heart of the main floor is the sunken living room, which boasts a cozy woodstove, skylights and French doors to a deluxe library.
- Just off the formal dining room is a gourmet kitchen, complete with a pantry closet, a boxed-out window and an angled snack bar overlooking the nook. The glassed-in nook includes a built-in desk and access to the huge, wraparound backyard deck.
- Located near the garage entrance is an oversized utility room with space for a freezer, an ironing center and a laundry tub. A half-bath is nearby.
- An open stairway leads up to the very private master suite. Featured here are a raised sleeping area, a walk-in closet, a private deck and a luxurious bath with a step-up spa tub and a corner shower.
- Two more bedrooms are housed in the daylight basement, which also offers a game room, a wine cellar and a central family room with a woodstove and access to a ground-level patio.

Plan NW-855	
Bedrooms: 3	**Baths:** 2½
Living Area:	
Upper floor	549 sq. ft.
Main floor	1,388 sq. ft.
Daylight basement	1,371 sq. ft.
Total Living Area:	**3,308 sq. ft.**
Garage	573 sq. ft.
Exterior Wall Framing:	2x6

Foundation Options:

Daylight basement
(All plans can be built with your choice of foundation and framing. A generic conversion diagram is available. See order form.)

BLUEPRINT PRICE CODE: E

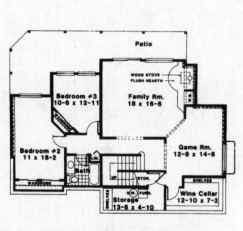

DAYLIGHT BASEMENT

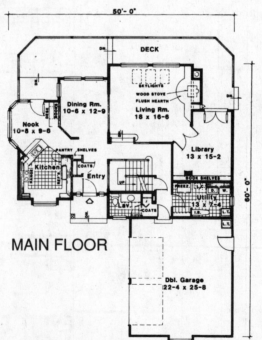

MAIN FLOOR

UPPER FLOOR

Attractive European Look

- Arched windows with keystones, the stucco finish with corner quoins and many other fine flourishes give this European-style home its good looks.
- The two-story foyer flaunts a handsome open stairway to the upper floor. A second stairway is offered in the family room.
- Columns act as dividers between the formal living spaces to the left of the foyer. Double doors in the dining room close off the kitchen, which features a center island, a walk-in pantry and a handy freezer room.
- A bright, bayed breakfast area is nestled between the kitchen and the family room and offers access to the deck.
- The vaulted family room also opens to the deck and has a fireplace and two built-in bookcases.
- A bonus room or fourth bedroom shares the upper floor with three other bedrooms, three full baths and a convenient laundry room.

Plan APS-3302

Bedrooms: 4+	Baths: 4
Living Area:	
Upper floor	1,276 sq. ft.
Main floor	1,716 sq. ft.
Bonus room	382 sq. ft.
Total Living Area:	**3,374 sq. ft.**
Standard basement	1,716 sq. ft.
Garage	693 sq. ft.
Exterior Wall Framing:	2x4

Foundation Options:

Standard basement
(Typical foundation & framing conversion diagram available—see order form.)

BLUEPRINT PRICE CODE: E

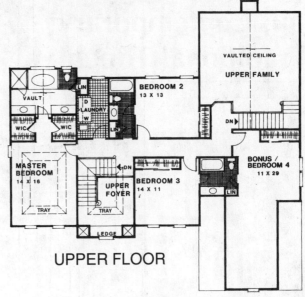

UPPER FLOOR

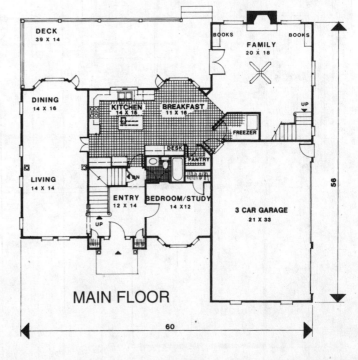

MAIN FLOOR

Spacious Contemporary with Traditional Touch

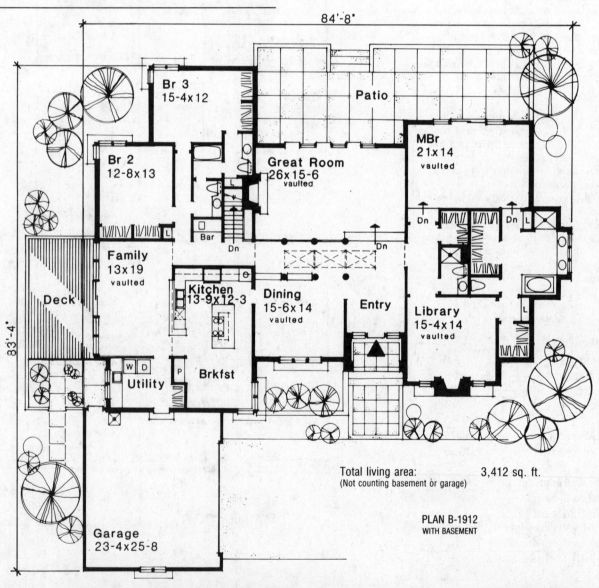

84'-8"

83'-4"

Br 3
15-4x12

Patio

Br 2
12-8x13

MBr
21x14
vaulted

Great Room
26x15-6
vaulted

Family
13x19
vaulted

Bar

Dn

Dn

Deck

Kitchen
13-9x12-3

Dining
15-6x14
vaulted

Entry

Library
15-4x14
vaulted

W D

P

Utility

Brkfst

Garage
23-4x25-8

Total living area: 3,412 sq. ft.
(Not counting basement or garage)

PLAN B-1912
WITH BASEMENT

Design Excellence

- This stunning one-story home features dramatic detailing and an exceptionally functional floor plan.
- The brick exterior and exciting window treatments beautifully hint at the spectacular interior design.
- High ceilings, a host of built-ins and angled window walls are just some of the highlights.
- The family room showcases a curved wall of windows and a three-way fireplace that can be enjoyed from the adjoining kitchen and breakfast room.
- The octagonal breakfast room offers access to a lovely porch and a handy half-bath. The large island kitchen boasts a snack bar and a unique butler's pantry that connects with the dining room. The sunken living room includes a second fireplace and a window wall.
- The master suite sports a coffered ceiling, a private sitting area and a luxurious bath with a gambrel ceiling.
- Each of the four possible bedrooms has private access to a bath.

Plan KLF-922

Bedrooms: 3+	**Baths:** 3½

Living Area:	
Main floor	3,450 sq. ft.
Total Living Area:	**3,450 sq. ft.**
Garage	698 sq. ft.
Exterior Wall Framing:	2x4

Foundation Options:

Slab
(All plans can be built with your choice of foundation and framing. A generic conversion diagram is available. See order form.)

BLUEPRINT PRICE CODE:	E

MAIN FLOOR

Elegant Arches

- Gracious arched windows and an entry portico create rhythm and style for this home's brick-clad exterior.
- An elegant curved staircase lends interest to the raised, two-story foyer.
- Two steps down to the left of the foyer lies the living room, with its dramatic 14-ft. cathedral ceiling. Lovely columns define the adjoining dining room. A cozy fireplace warms the entire area.
- The island kitchen overlooks the bayed breakfast room and offers a handy pass-through to the adjoining family room.
- The two-story-high family room boasts a second fireplace and a wall of windows topped by large transoms.
- The quiet master bedroom features a bay window and an 11-ft. sloped ceiling. The master bath shows off a garden tub and a separate shower.
- A sizable deck is accessible from both the breakfast room and the master suite.
- Three more bedrooms and two baths share the upper floor. A balcony bridge overlooks the foyer and family room.

Plan DD-3639

Bedrooms: 4+	Baths: 3½
Living Area:	
Upper floor	868 sq. ft.
Main floor	2,771 sq. ft.
Total Living Area:	**3,639 sq. ft.**
Standard basement	2,771 sq. ft.
Garage	790 sq. ft.
Exterior Wall Framing:	2x4

Foundation Options:

Standard basement
Crawlspace
Slab

(All plans can be built with your choice of foundation and framing. A generic conversion diagram is available. See order form.)

BLUEPRINT PRICE CODE: F

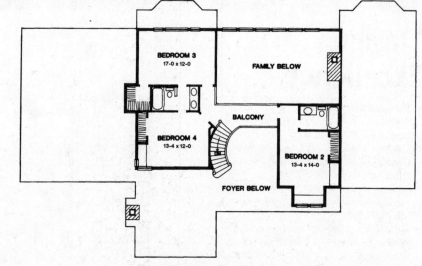

UPPER FLOOR

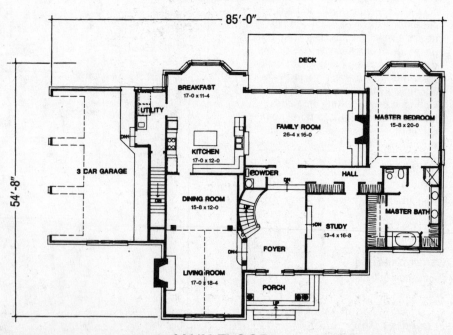

MAIN FLOOR

Plan DD-3639

PRICES AND DETAILS ON PAGES 12-15

Luxury Suite

- A distinctive roofline, a pair of porches and a wonderful exterior of stone and stucco give this elegant home an inviting European look.
- The two-story-high foyer is flanked by the living room and the formal dining room, which are defined by columns.
- The bright and airy island kitchen adjoins a two-story-high breakfast area. A laundry room, a powder room and a versatile butler's pantry are nearby.
- The bay-windowed family room is enhanced by a 20-ft., 9-in. vaulted ceiling and a handsome fireplace.
- Double doors lead into the spectacular master suite, which has an 11-ft. tray ceiling and boasts a morning kitchen and a private porch.
- The bedroom's see-through fireplace adds warmth to the master bath, which features a 17½-ft. vaulted ceiling, a spa tub, a designer shower, dual vanities with knee space and a walk-in closet.
- Upstairs, a balcony bridge overlooks the foyer and the breakfast area below. Four bedrooms offer private access to the two additional full baths.

Plan FB-3676

Bedrooms: 5	Baths: 3½
Living Area:	
Upper floor	1,405 sq. ft.
Main floor	2,271 sq. ft.
Total Living Area:	**3,676 sq. ft.**
Daylight basement	2,271 sq. ft.
Garage and storage	528 sq. ft.
Exterior Wall Framing:	2x4

Foundation Options:
Daylight basement
(All plans can be built with your choice of foundation and framing. A generic conversion diagram is available. See order form.)

BLUEPRINT PRICE CODE: F

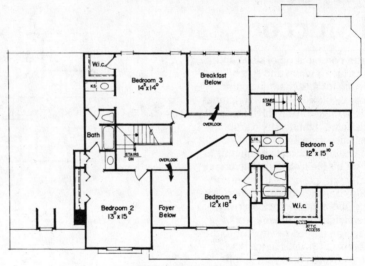

UPPER FLOOR

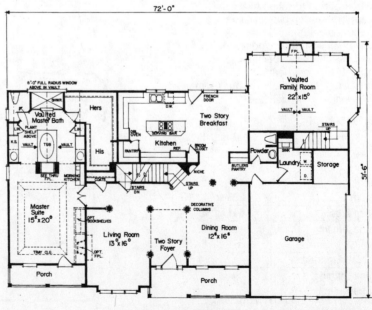

MAIN FLOOR

Stately Stone and Stucco

- A graceful combination of stone and stucco creates a warm and stately appearance for this charming home.
- The ornate, columned porch welcomes guests into the two-story-high foyer. Flowing to the right, the living room features a fireplace and a 15½-ft. vaulted ceiling. Decorative columns to the left set off the formal dining room.
- More columns introduce the two-story Great Room, which offers another fireplace and a handy back stairway.
- The open kitchen includes a work island and an angled serving bar to the bayed breakfast nook. French doors open to a covered backyard porch.
- The private master suite boasts a three-sided fireplace and a 10½-ft. tray ceiling in the bedroom; the sitting room and the luxurious garden bath each have a 16-ft. vaulted ceiling.
- Ceilings in all main-floor rooms are 9 ft. high unless otherwise specified.
- Upstairs, three more bedrooms share two full baths. The optional bonus room is a nice extra.

Plan FB-5345-JERN

Bedrooms: 4+	Baths: 3½
Living Area:	
Upper floor	928 sq. ft.
Main floor	2,467 sq. ft.
Bonus room	296 sq. ft.
Total Living Area:	**3,691 sq. ft.**
Daylight basement	2,467 sq. ft.
Garage	531 sq. ft.
Exterior Wall Framing:	2x4

Foundation Options:

Daylight basement

(All plans can be built with your choice of foundation and framing. A generic conversion diagram is available. See order form.)

BLUEPRINT PRICE CODE: **F**

UPPER FLOOR

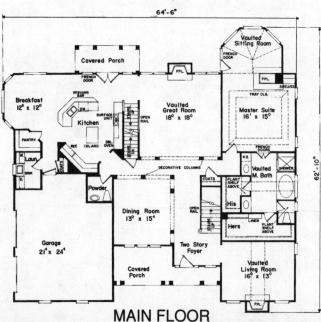

MAIN FLOOR

TO ORDER THIS BLUEPRINT, CALL TOLL-FREE 1-800-547-5570   Plan FB-5345-JERN   *PRICES AND DETAILS ON PAGES 12-15*

Bright Design

- Sweeping rooflines, arched transom windows and a stucco exterior give this exciting design a special flair.
- Inside the high, dramatic entry, guests are greeted with a stunning view of the living room, which is expanded by a 12-ft. volume ceiling. This formal expanse is augmented by an oversized bay that looks out onto a covered patio and possible pool area.
- To the left of the foyer is the formal dining room, accented by columns and a 14-ft. receding tray ceiling.
- The island kitchen overlooks a sunny breakfast nook and a large family room, each with 12-ft.-high ceilings. A handy pass-through transports food to the patio, which offers a summer kitchen.
- The master wing includes a large bedroom with a 10-ft.-high coffered ceiling, a sitting area with patio access, a massive walk-in closet and a sun-drenched garden bath.
- The private den/study could also serve as an extra bedroom.
- Two to three more bedrooms share two full baths. The front bedrooms boast 12-ft. ceilings and the rear bedroom is accented by a 10-ft. ceiling.

Plan HDS-90-814

Bedrooms: 3+	**Baths:** 3½

Living Area:

Main floor	3,743 sq. ft.
Total Living Area:	**3,743 sq. ft.**
Garage	725 sq. ft.

Exterior Wall Framing:

2x4 and 8-in. concrete block

Foundation Options:

Slab
(All plans can be built with your choice of foundation and framing. A generic conversion diagram is available. See order form.)

BLUEPRINT PRICE CODE: F

◄86'8"►

◄93'4"►

Bedroom 2
15'8" x 12'4"

Patio

Family Room
20' x 20'

Breakfast Nook

Kitchen

Living Room
21'2" x 20'0"

Master Bedroom
21'0" x 17'8"

Bedroom 4/Media
15'0" x 13'4"

Bath

w.i.c.

Bath

Dining
14' x 13'

Foyer

Bedroom 3
13'4" x 12'8"

Entry

Den/Study
12'0" x 10'8"

Private Garden

planter

3 Car Garage

planter

MAIN FLOOR

Luxuries Galore

- Ideally suited for a scenic site, this deluxe walk-out design offers panoramic views of the outdoors and a long list of luxuries.
- Warm brick accents highlight the exterior, where a covered porch leads to a large entry. Straight ahead, the sunken living room and the spacious family room feature window walls overlooking a huge covered deck.
- The strategically placed woodstove warms the family room as well as the adjoining kitchen and nook. The island kitchen boasts deck access, a large walk-in pantry, a glass-filled nook and a top-notch laundry room.
- The formal dining room is just across the hall and features a charming window seat.
- The master bedroom features private deck access, a roomy walk-in closet and a superb bath that offers a bayed step-up spa tub, a separate shower and a built-in desk or makeup table.
- Another bedroom and an innovative hall bath complete the main floor.
- Downstairs, you'll find two more bedrooms, a large bath, two storage areas and a recreation room with a woodstove and a full-service wet bar. The storage areas are not included in the basement square footage.

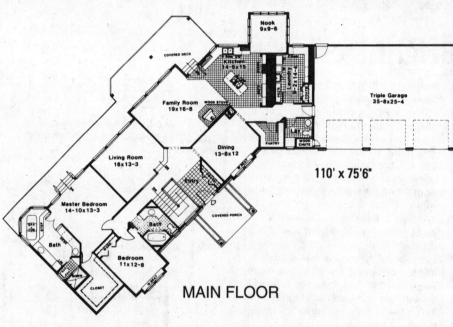

110' x 75'6"

MAIN FLOOR

DAYLIGHT BASEMENT

Plan NW-744

Bedrooms: 4	Baths: 3½
Living Area:	
Main floor	2,539 sq. ft.
Daylight basement	1,461 sq. ft.
Total Living Area:	**4,000 sq. ft.**
Garage	904 sq. ft.
Storage	948 sq. ft.
Exterior Wall Framing:	2x6

Foundation Options:

Daylight basement

(All plans can be built with your choice of foundation and framing. A generic conversion diagram is available. See order form.)

BLUEPRINT PRICE CODE: G

TO ORDER THIS BLUEPRINT,
CALL TOLL-FREE 1-800-547-5570

Plan NW-744

PRICES AND DETAILS
ON PAGES 12-15

Luscious and Luxurious

- This stately home's appealing exterior gives way to a luxurious and impressive interior.
- The step-down parlour is the centerpiece of the home, and boasts a 13-ft.-high flat ceiling and a full-wall fireplace and entertainment center.
- The master suite features a step-down sitting room and a corner fireplace. The opulent master bath has a linen island, a morning kitchen and a bidet.
- The library offers private access to the main hall bath.
- Graceful arches and a high, coffered ceiling adorn the formal dining room.
- The spacious kitchen includes a cooktop island, a walk-in pantry, a menu desk, a vegetable sink and a bright 'good morning' room.
- Each of the three secondary suites has a large closet and direct access to a bath.
- The huge gathering room boasts wraparound glass and a full fireplace and entertainment wall.

Plan EOF-58

Bedrooms: 4-5	**Baths:** 4

Living Area:

Main floor	4,021 sq. ft.
Total Living Area:	**4,021 sq. ft.**
Garage	879 sq. ft.
Exterior Wall Framing:	2x4

Foundation Options:

Slab

(Typical foundation & framing conversion diagram available—see order form.)

BLUEPRINT PRICE CODE:	**G**

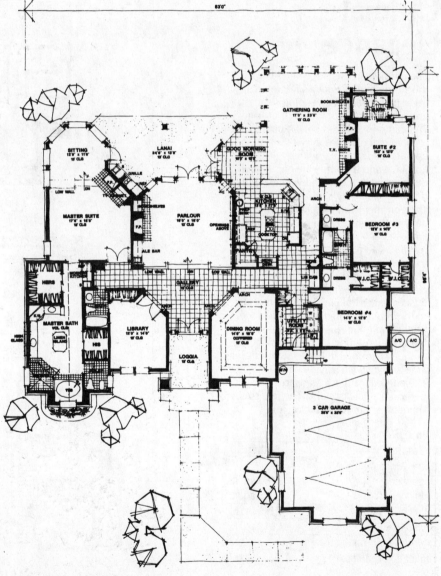

MAIN FLOOR

Ultimate Elegance

- The ultimate in elegance and luxury, this home begins with an impressive foyer that reveals a sweeping staircase and a direct view of the backyard.
- The centrally located parlor, perfect for receiving guests, has a two-story-high ceiling, a spectacular wall of glass, a fireplace and a unique ale bar. French doors open to a covered veranda with a relaxing spa and a summer kitchen.
- The gourmet island kitchen boasts an airy 10-ft. ceiling, a menu desk and a walk-in pantry. The octagonal morning room has a vaulted ceiling and access to a second stairway to the upper level.
- A pass-through snack bar in the kitchen overlooks the gathering room, which hosts a cathedral ceiling, French doors to the veranda and a second fireplace.
- Bright and luxurious, the master suite has a 10-ft. ceiling and features a unique morning kitchen, a sunny sitting area and a lavish private bath.
- The curved staircase leads to three bedroom suites upstairs. The rear suites share an enchanting deck.

Plan EOF-3

Bedrooms: 4+	Baths: 5½
Living Area:	
Upper floor	1,150 sq. ft.
Main floor	3,045 sq. ft.
Total Living Area:	**4,195 sq. ft.**
Garage	814 sq. ft.
Exterior Wall Framing:	2x6

Foundation Options:

Slab
(All plans can be built with your choice of foundation and framing. A generic conversion diagram is available. See order form.)

BLUEPRINT PRICE CODE: **G**

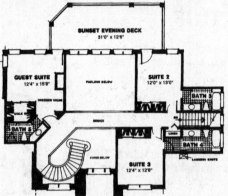

UPPER FLOOR

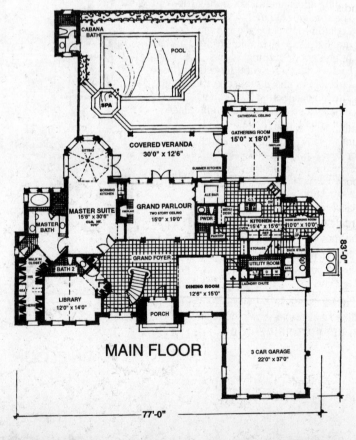

MAIN FLOOR

Plan EOF-3

Design Leaves Out Nothing

- This design has it all, from the elegant detailing of the exterior to the exciting, luxurious spaces of the interior.
- High ceilings, large, open rooms and lots of glass are found throughout the home. Nearly all of the main living areas, as well as the master suite, overlook the veranda.
- Unusual features include a built-in ale bar in the formal dining room, an art niche in the Grand Room and a TV niche in the Gathering Room. The Gathering Room also features a fireplace framed by window seats, a wall of windows facing the backyard and a half-wall open to the morning room. The cooktop-island kitchen is conveniently accessible from all of the living areas.
- The delicious master suite includes a raised lounge, a three-sided fireplace and French doors that open to the veranda. The spiral stairs nearby lead to the "evening deck" above. The master bath boasts two walk-in closets, a sunken shower and a Roman tub.
- The upper floor hosts two complete suites and a loft, plus a vaulted bonus room reached via a separate stairway.

Plan EOF-61

Bedrooms: 3+	Baths: 4½
Living Area:	
Upper floor	877 sq. ft.
Main floor	3,094 sq. ft.
Bonus room	280 sq. ft.
Total Living Area:	**4,251 sq. ft.**
Garage	774 sq. ft.
Exterior Wall Framing:	2x6

Foundation Options:

Slab

(All plans can be built with your choice of foundation and framing. A generic conversion diagram is available. See order form.)

BLUEPRINT PRICE CODE: **G**

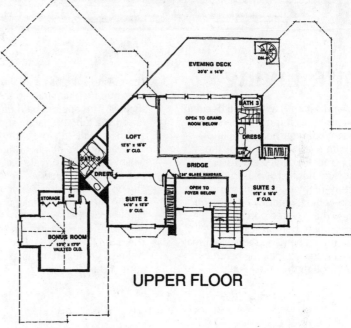

UPPER FLOOR

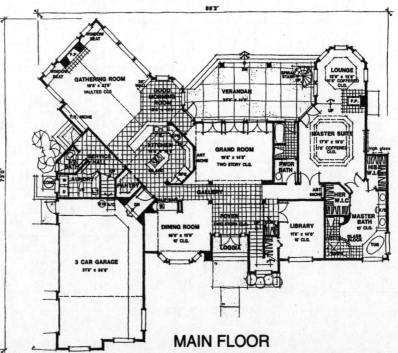

MAIN FLOOR

Estate Living

- This grand estate is as big and beautiful on the inside as it is on the outside.
- The formal dining room and parlor, each with a tall window, flank the entry's graceful curved staircase.
- The sunken family room is topped by a two-story-high ceiling and wrapped in floor-to-ceiling windows. A patio door opens to the covered porch, which features a nifty built-in barbecue.
- The island kitchen and the bright breakfast area also overlook the porch, with access through the deluxe utility room.

- The master suite has it all, including a romantic fireplace framed by bookshelves. The opulent bath offers a raised spa tub, a separate shower, his-and-hers walk-in closets and a dual-sink vanity. The neighboring bedroom, which also has a private bath, would make an ideal nursery.
- The upper floor hosts a balcony hall that provides a breathtaking view of the family room below. Each of the two bedrooms here has its own bath.
- The main floor is expanded by 10-ft. ceilings, while 9-ft. ceilings grace the upper floor.

Plan DD-4300-B	
Bedrooms: 4	**Baths:** 4½
Living Area:	
Upper floor	868 sq. ft.
Main floor	3,416 sq. ft.
Total Living Area:	**4,284 sq. ft.**
Standard basement	3,416 sq. ft.
Garage and storage	633 sq. ft.
Exterior Wall Framing:	2x4 or 2x6
Foundation Options:	
Standard basement	
Crawlspace	
Slab	

(All plans can be built with your choice of foundation and framing. A generic conversion diagram is available. See order form.)

BLUEPRINT PRICE CODE: G

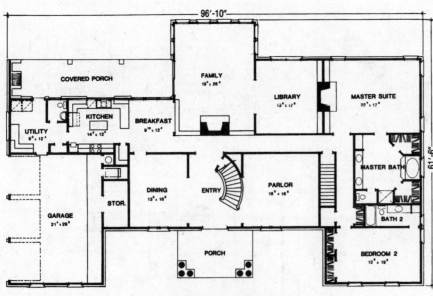

MAIN FLOOR

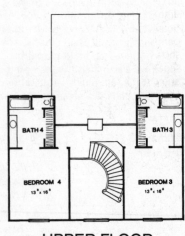

UPPER FLOOR

Plan DD-4300-B

PRICES AND DETAILS ON PAGES 12-15

Extraordinary!

- For a home that is truly outstanding in style and size, this design is hard to beat! From the entry's spectacular curved stairways and 19-ft. ceiling, to the master suite's luxurious skylighted bath, elegance is found throughout.
- The spacious central living room is set off with decorative entry columns and boasts a dramatic fireplace, a 14-ft. vaulted ceiling and outdoor access.
- The gourmet kitchen is concealed behind double doors. The kitchen offers a great windowed sink area, a cooktop island, a walk-in pantry and a snack bar. The octagonal breakfast nook has a patio door to the backyard and adjoins a sunken family room with a 12-ft. ceiling and another cozy fireplace.
- Up one flight of stairs is a quiet den and an extravagant master suite. Behind dramatic double doors, the master bedroom has a romantic sitting bay and panoramic views. The skylighted bath shows off an exciting garden tub, a separate shower, a huge walk-in closet and a toilet room with a bidet.
- Up one more flight are two secondary bedrooms, each with a private bath.

Plan R-4029

Bedrooms: 3+	Baths: 4½
Living Area:	
Upper floor	972 sq. ft.
Main floor	3,346 sq. ft.
Total Living Area:	**4,318 sq. ft.**
Partial basement	233 sq. ft.
Garage	825 sq. ft.
Exterior Wall Framing:	2x6

Foundation Options:

Partial basement
(All plans can be built with your choice of foundation and framing. A generic conversion diagram is available. See order form.)

BLUEPRINT PRICE CODE: G

UPPER FLOOR

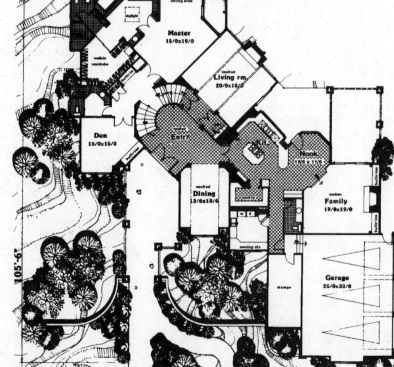

MAIN FLOOR

Elegance Perfected

- The grand style of this luxurious home brings elegance and grace to perfection.
- The contemporary architecture exudes an aura of grandeur, drawing the eye to its stately 2½-story entry portico.
- The interior is equally stunning with open, flowing spaces, high ceilings and decorative, room-defining columns.
- The formal zone is impressive, with a vast foyer and a sunken living room highlighted by dramatic window walls and a 20½-ft. ceiling. Round columns set off a stunning octagonal dining room with a 19-ft., 4-in. ceiling. A curved wet bar completes the effect!
- The informal areas consist of an island kitchen, a breakfast nook, a large family room and an octagonal media room. Activities can be extended to the covered back patio through doors in the breakfast nook and the family room.
- The fabulous master suite shows off a romantic fireplace, a 12-ft. ceiling, an enormous walk-in closet and a garden bath with a circular shower!
- Two more main-floor bedrooms, an upper-floor bedroom and loft area, plus two more baths complete the plan.

Plan HDS-90-819

Bedrooms: 4+	Baths: 3½
Living Area:	
Upper floor	765 sq. ft.
Main floor	3,770 sq. ft.
Total Living Area:	**4,535 sq. ft.**
Garage	750 sq. ft.
Exterior Wall Framing:	2x4

Foundation Options:
Slab
(All plans can be built with your choice of foundation and framing. A generic conversion diagram is available. See order form.)

BLUEPRINT PRICE CODE: G

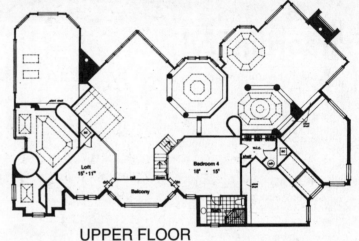

UPPER FLOOR

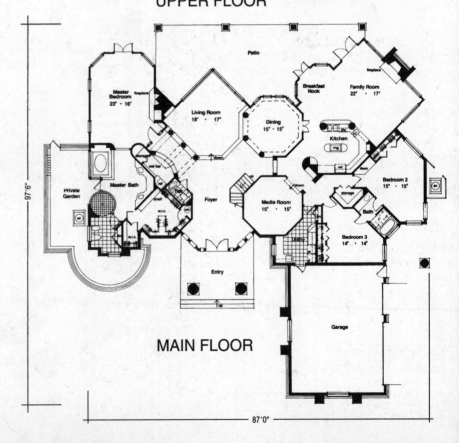

MAIN FLOOR

87'0"

97'6"

  Plan HDS-90-819 *PRICES AND DETAILS ON PAGES 12-15*

Superbly Done!

- A durable tile roof, magnificent concrete columns and extravagant fixed glass are a prelude to the many amenities found in this sensational contemporary home.
- The raised foyer offers a breathtaking view of the spectacular lanai and pool area through French doors.
- The fascinating living room has a high ceiling with exposed rafters and a dramatic curved wall of glass!
- The full-sized kitchen is equipped with a cooktop island and a serving counter that faces the gallery and family room. A walk-in pantry and a beautiful morning room are other features.
- An inviting fireplace, a TV center and a refreshing ale bar beckon guests into the spacious family room, which has dual access to the pool deck. The bar's handy pass-through window provides easy beverage service to the pool area.
- Three secondary bedrooms and two full baths complete this wing of the home. Each bedroom has a walk-in closet and private access to one of the baths.
- The isolated master suite is exquisitely furnished with a private sitting area, a three-way fireplace, his-and-hers closets and dressing areas, a glass-enclosed tub and a personal exercise room, plus a raised deck and spa.

Plan EOF-70

Bedrooms: 4	Baths: 3½
Living Area:	
Main floor	5,013 sq. ft.
Total Living Area:	**5,013 sq. ft.**
Garage	902 sq. ft.
Exterior Wall Framing:	concrete block

Foundation Options:

Slab

(All plans can be built with your choice of foundation and framing. A generic conversion diagram is available. See order form.)

BLUEPRINT PRICE CODE: G

MAIN FLOOR

Spectacular Executive Estate

- The unique angular design of this executive home focuses attention on the spectacular entrance, which is enhanced by two balconies above.
- Beyond the vestibule, a 19-ft. ceiling presides over the columned Great Room and the sunny dining room. A two-story window wall overlooks the expansive backyard pool area.
- The gourmet island kitchen and breakfast nook open to a side deck and offer easy service to both the dining room and the family room.
- A nice-sized media room or library boasts two walls of built-ins.
- The master suite is a masterpiece, with its 15-ft. vaulted ceiling, romantic fireplace and sliding glass doors to a secluded sun deck and hot tub. The luxurious bath offers a whirlpool tub, a separate shower and two vanities.
- A classy, curved staircase accesses the upper floor, where three more bedrooms each have a private bath. A lounge with a window seat and a central area with outdoor balconies are other special appointments found here.

REAR VIEW

Plan B-05-85

Bedrooms: 4+	Baths: 4 full, 2 half
Living Area:	
Upper floor	1,720 sq. ft.
Main floor	3,900 sq. ft.
Total Living Area:	**5,620 sq. ft.**
Standard basement	3,900 sq. ft.
Garage	836 sq. ft.
Exterior Wall Framing:	2x6

Foundation Options:

Standard basement

(All plans can be built with your choice of foundation and framing. A generic conversion diagram is available. See order form.)

BLUEPRINT PRICE CODE:	G

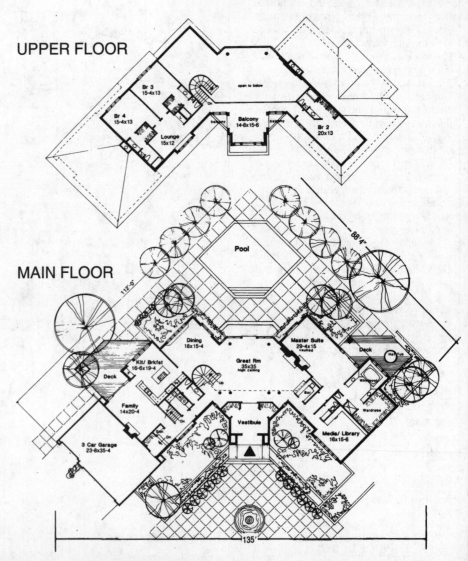

UPPER FLOOR

MAIN FLOOR

Plan B-05-85

PRICES AND DETAILS
ON PAGES 12-15

Spacious and Stately

- This popular home design boasts a classic Creole exterior and a symmetrical layout, with 9-ft.-high ceilings on the main floor.
- French doors lead from the formal living and dining rooms to the large family room. The central fireplace is flanked by French doors that open to a covered rear porch and an open-air deck.
- The kitchen is reached easily from the family room, the dining room and the rear entrance. An island cooktop and a window-framed eating area are other features found here.
- The real seller, though, is the main-floor master suite with its spectacular bath. Among its many extras are a built-in vanity, a spa tub and a 16-ft. sloped ceiling with a skylight.
- Three upstairs bedrooms, each with double closets and private bath access, make this the perfect family-sized home.

Plan E-3000

Bedrooms: 4	Baths: 3½
Living Area:	
Upper floor	1,027 sq. ft.
Main floor	2,008 sq. ft.
Total Living Area:	**3,035 sq. ft.**
Standard basement	2,008 sq. ft.
Garage	484 sq. ft.
Storage	96 sq. ft.
Exterior Wall Framing:	2x6

Foundation Options:

Standard basement

Crawlspace

Slab

(All plans can be built with your choice of foundation and framing. A generic conversion diagram is available. See order form.)

BLUEPRINT PRICE CODE: E

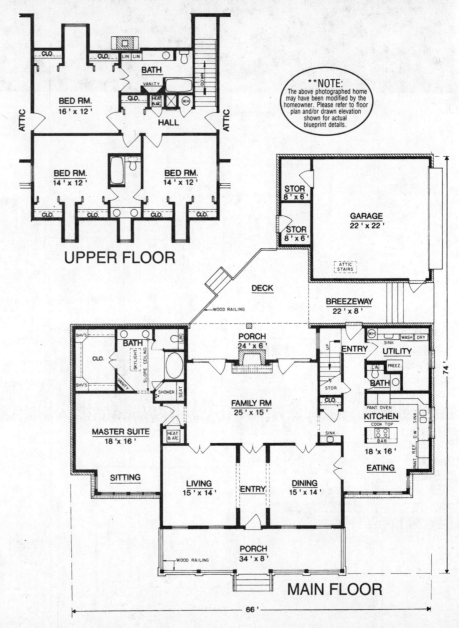

NOTE:
The above photographed home may have been modified by the homeowner. Please refer to floor plan and/or drawn elevation shown for actual blueprint details.

UPPER FLOOR

MAIN FLOOR

Photo courtesy of Barclay Home Designs.

Tudor-Inspired Hillside Design

- The vaulted entry opens to a stunning living room with a high ceiling and massive fireplace.
- The dining room, five steps higher, overlooks the living room for a dramatic effect.
- Double doors lead into the informal family area, which consists of a beautifully integrated kitchen, nook and family room.
- The magnificent master suite, isolated downstairs, includes a sumptuous bath, enormous wardrobe and double-door entry.
- The upstairs consists of three more bedrooms, a bath and balcony hallway open to the entry below.
- Three-car garage is tucked under the family room/dining room area.

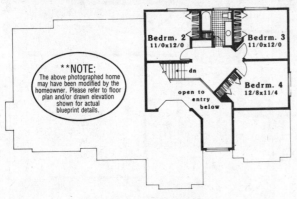

NOTE: The above photographed home may have been modified by the homeowner. Please refer to floor plan and/or drawn elevation shown for actual blueprint details.

UPPER FLOOR

MAIN FLOOR

Plan R-4001	
Bedrooms: 4	**Baths:** 2½
Living Area:	
Upper floor	709 sq. ft.
Main floor	2,388 sq. ft.
Total Living Area:	**3,097 sq. ft.**
Garage	906 sq. ft.
Exterior Wall Framing:	2x6

Foundation Options:

Crawlspace
(Typical foundation & framing conversion diagram available—see order form.)

BLUEPRINT PRICE CODE: E

Photo by Mark Englund/HomeStyles

Master Suite with Fireplace, Deck

- This brick-accented two-story has front stacked bay windows, a three-car garage and staggered rooflines.
- Inside you'll find large, open living areas oriented to the rear and fireplaces in the living room, sunken family room and master bedroom.
- Both the family room and study open out to a rear patio; the island kitchen and bayed nook join the family room, which also offers a wet bar.
- Room for two to three bedrooms plus the master suite with private deck and lavish, skylit spa bath is found on the upper level.

Plan P-7751-3A and P-7751-3D

Bedrooms: 3-4	Baths: 2 ½
Space:	
Upper floor	1,411 sq. ft.
Main floor	1,737 sq. ft.
Total Living Area	**3,148 sq. ft.**
Basement	1,737 sq. ft.
Garage	677 sq. ft.
Exterior Wall Framing	2x6
Foundation options:	**Plan #**
Daylight Basement	P-7751-3D
Crawlspace	P-7751-3A
(Foundation & framing conversion diagram available—see order form.)	
Blueprint Price Code	E

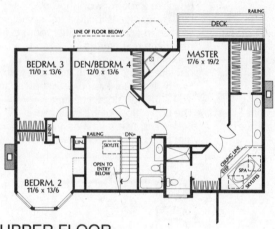

UPPER FLOOR

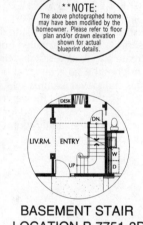

BASEMENT STAIR
LOCATION-P-7751-3D

NOTE:
The above photographed home may have been modified by the homeowner. Please refer to floor plan and/or drawn elevation shown for actual blueprint details.

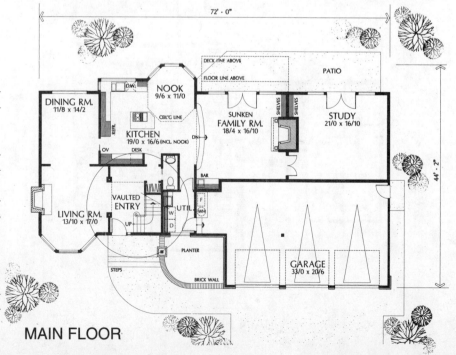

MAIN FLOOR

Victorian Farmhouse

- Fish-scale shingles and horizontal siding team up with the detailed front porch to create a look of yesterday. Brickwork enriches the sides and rear of the home.
- The main level features 10-ft.-high ceilings throughout the central living space. The front-oriented formal areas merge with the family room via three sets of French doors.

- The island kitchen and skylighted eating area have 16-ft. sloped ceilings.
- A breezeway off the deck connects the house to a roomy workshop. A two-car garage is located under the workshop and a large utility room is just inside the rear entrance.
- The main-floor master suite offers an opulent skylighted bath with a garden vanity, a spa tub, a separate shower and an 18-ft.-high sloped ceiling.
- The upper floor offers three more bedrooms, two full baths and a balcony that looks to the backyard.

Plan E-3103

Bedrooms: 4	**Baths:** 3½

Living Area:	
Upper floor	1,113 sq. ft.
Main floor	2,040 sq. ft.
Total Living Area:	**3,153 sq. ft.**
Daylight basement	2,040 sq. ft.
Tuck-under garage and storage	580 sq. ft.
Workshop and storage	580 sq. ft.
Exterior Wall Framing:	2x6

Foundation Options:

Daylight basement
Crawlspace
Slab
(All plans can be built with your choice of foundation and framing. A generic conversion diagram is available. See order form.)

BLUEPRINT PRICE CODE:	E

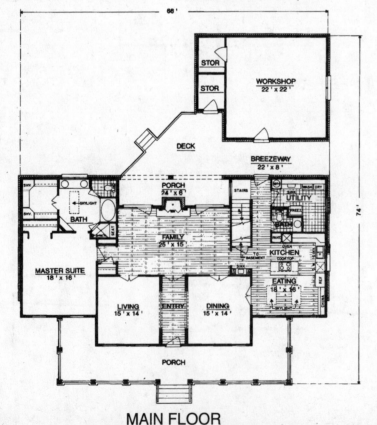

MAIN FLOOR

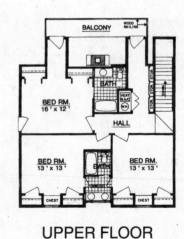

UPPER FLOOR

TO ORDER THIS BLUEPRINT, CALL TOLL-FREE 1-800-547-5570   Plan E-3103   *PRICES AND DETAILS ON PAGES 12-15*

Photo by Mark Englund/HomeStyles

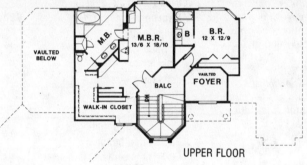

UPPER FLOOR

VAULTED BELOW

M.B.

M.B.R.
13/6 X 18/10

B

B.R.
12 X 12/9

BALC

VAULTED FOYER

DN

WALK-IN CLOSET

**NOTE:
The above photographed home may have been modified by the homeowner. Please refer to floor plan and/or drawn elevation shown for actual blueprint details.

89'-9"

57'-0"

VIEW DECK

VAULTED FAMILY
14/0 X 19/0+

KIT

DINE
12/4 X 16/9

VAULTED LIVING
17/5 X 14/7

B.R. 4/ DEN
15/4 X 13/7

BUFFET

PANTRY

P

3 CAR GARAGE
35/6 x 24/0

UTIL

GALLERY

VAULTED FOYER

G

B.R. 3
12/0 X 13/6

ENT

MAIN FLOOR

Designed with Elegance in Mind

- This expansive home boasts 3,220 sq. ft. of living space designed with elegance in mind.
- The front of the home is finished in stucco, with the rest in lap siding for economy.
- The vaulted foyer leads directly into an impressive sunken and vaulted living room, guarded by columns that echo the exterior treatment.
- The formal dining room is visually joined to the living room to make an impressive space for entertaining.
- An unusually fine kitchen opens to a large family room, which boasts a vaulted ceiling, a corner fireplace and access to a sizable rear deck.
- In the front, the extra-wide staircase is a primary attraction, with its dramatic feature window.
- A terrific master suite includes a splendid master bath with double sinks and a huge walk-through closet.
- A second upstairs bedroom also includes a private bath.

Plan LRD-11388

Bedrooms: 3-4	Baths: 3

Living Area:

Upper floor:	1,095 sq. ft.
Main floor	2,125 sq. ft.
Total Living Area:	**3,220 sq. ft.**
Standard basement	2,125 sq. ft.
Garage	802 sq. ft.

Exterior Wall Framing:	2x6

Foundation Options:
Standard basement
Crawlspace
Slab
(Typical foundation & framing conversion diagram available—see order form.)

BLUEPRINT PRICE CODE: E

Photo by Jon Soeck

Luxuries Abound

- This design is filled with luxuries, beginning with the dramatic columned entrance. Sidelights and a large transom window flood the vaulted, raised entry with light.
- Straight ahead, French doors and windows in the living room provide a stunning view of the backyard.
- The formal dining room is elegantly accented with an arched ceiling.

- Vaulted ceilings further expand the combination kitchen, eating nook and family room. This entire area opens to a four-season porch, which gives way to a deck for even more entertainment space outdoors.
- The fabulous main-floor master suite showcases a bath with a tray ceiling, a luxurious whirlpool tub and double-door access to the backyard.
- Upstairs, a versatile loft and a balcony hall lead to three more bedrooms and a versatile compartmentalized bath.
- Ceilings in all main-floor rooms are at least 9 ft. high for added spaciousness.

Plan AH-3230	
Bedrooms: 4	**Baths:** 2½
Living Area:	
Upper floor	890 sq. ft.
Main floor	2,340 sq. ft.
Total Living Area:	**3,230 sq. ft.**
Daylight basement	2,214 sq. ft.
Garage	693 sq. ft.
Exterior Wall Framing:	2x6
Foundation Options:	

Daylight basement
(All plans can be built with your choice of foundation and framing. A generic conversion diagram is available. See order form.)

BLUEPRINT PRICE CODE: E

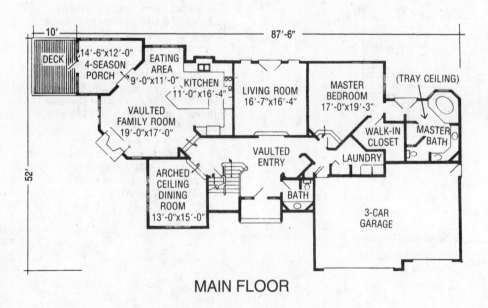

MAIN FLOOR

UPPER FLOOR

NOTE:
The above photographed home may have been modified by the homeowner. Please refer to floor plan and/or drawn elevation shown for actual blueprint details.

Oriented for Scenic Rear View

- That elegant look of the past is found in this expansive post-modern design.
- A two-story vaulted entry leads to spacious formal entertaining areas.
- A dining room with built-in China closet is to the left.
- To the right is a formal living room with a strikingly elegant bow window.
- The family room and living room share an interesting corner fireplace.
- A convenient powder room is tucked away behind the sweeping curved staircase.
- A see-through wine rack is an eye-catcher in the kitchen, along with its green-house window, island chopping block and abundant counter space.
- The living and family rooms are defined by decorative columns and arches and are a step-down from the foyer/hallway.
- Upstairs, a luxurious master suite boasts a sunny bow window, deluxe bath and enormous closet.
- Three other bedrooms, a full bath and a large unfinished "bonus space" complete the second floor.

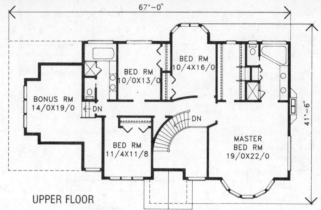

UPPER FLOOR

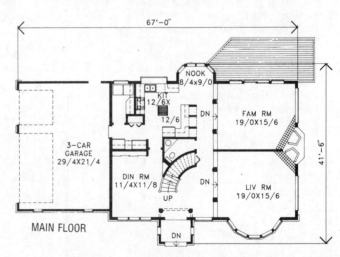

MAIN FLOOR

Plan SD-8819

Bedrooms: 4-5	Baths: 2½

Space:

Upper floor:	1,500 sq. ft.
Main floor:	1,476 sq. ft.
Total living area:	**2,976 sq. ft.**
Bonus area:	266 sq. ft.
Basement:	approx. 1,476 sq. ft.
Garage:	626 sq. ft.

Exterior Wall Framing: 2x6

Foundation options:
Standard basement.
Crawlspace.
(Foundation & framing conversion diagram available — see order form.)

Blueprint Price Code: D

Truly Nostalgic

- Designed after "Monteigne," an Italianate home near Natchez, Mississippi, this reproduction utilizes modern stucco finishes for the exterior.
- Columns and arched windows give way to a two-story-high foyer, which is accented by a striking, curved stairwell.
- The foyer connects the living room and the study, each boasting a 14-ft. ceiling and a cozy fireplace or woodstove.
- Adjacent to the formal dining room, the kitchen offers a snack bar and a bayed eating room. A unique entertainment center is centrally located to serve the main activity rooms of the home.
- A gorgeous sun room stretches across the rear of the main floor and overlooks a grand terrace.
- The plush master suite and bath boast his-and-hers vanities, large walk-in closets and a glassed-in garden tub.
- A main-floor guest bedroom features a walk-in closet and private access to another full main-floor bath.
- Two more bedrooms with private baths are located on the upper level. They share a sitting area and a veranda.

Plan E-3200

Bedrooms: 4	Baths: 4
Living Area:	
Upper floor	629 sq. ft.
Main floor	2,655 sq. ft.
Total Living Area:	**3,284 sq. ft.**
Standard basement	2,655 sq. ft.
Garage	667 sq. ft.
Exterior Wall Framing:	2x6

Foundation Options:

Standard basement
Crawlspace
Slab
(All plans can be built with your choice of foundation and framing. A generic conversion diagram is available. See order form.)

BLUEPRINT PRICE CODE: E

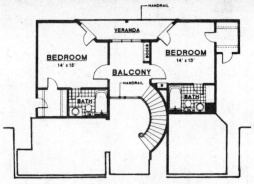

UPPER FLOOR

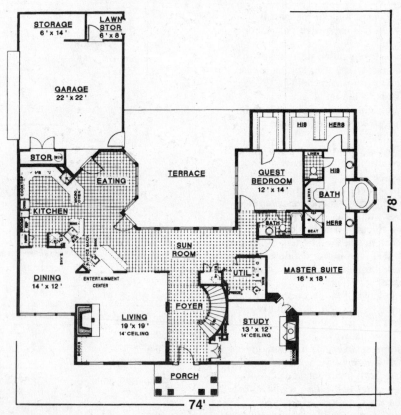

MAIN FLOOR

TO ORDER THIS BLUEPRINT, CALL TOLL-FREE 1-800-547-5570   Plan E-3200   *PRICES AND DETAILS ON PAGES 12-15*

Deluxe Master Suite

- This traditional home has an enticing style all its own, with a deluxe main-floor master suite.
- In from the covered porch, the front entry flows into the main living areas.
- Straight ahead, the family room features a handsome fireplace flanked by doors to a screened back porch.
- The kitchen easily services the formal dining room and offers a snack bar to the bayed breakfast nook. A nice utility room with a pantry and a half-bath is just off the nook and the garage entry.
- The secluded master suite boasts a 9-ft. tray ceiling and a luxurious bath with a garden tub, a separate shower and two vanities, one with knee space.
- Upstairs, each of the two additional bedrooms has a walk-in closet and a private bath. The optional bonus room can be finished as a large game room, a bedroom or an office.

Plan C-8915

Bedrooms: 3+	Baths: 3½
Living Area:	
Upper floor	832 sq. ft.
Main floor	1,927 sq. ft.
Bonus room	624 sq. ft.
Total Living Area:	**3,383 sq. ft.**
Daylight basement	1,674 sq. ft.
Garage	484 sq. ft.
Exterior Wall Framing:	2x4

Foundation Options:
Daylight basement
Crawlspace
(All plans can be built with your choice of foundation and framing. A generic conversion diagram is available. See order form.)

BLUEPRINT PRICE CODE: E

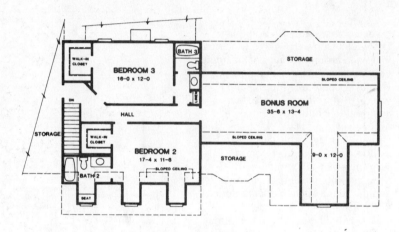

UPPER FLOOR

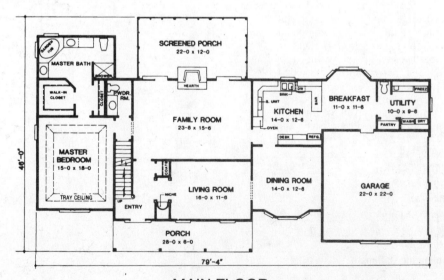

MAIN FLOOR

Spectacular Design

- The spectacular brick facade of this home conceals a stylish floor plan. Endless transoms crown the windows that wrap around the rear of the home, flooding the interior with natural light.
- The foyer opens to a huge Grand Room with a 14-ft. ceiling. French doors access a delightful covered porch.
- A three-sided fireplace warms the three casual rooms, which share a high 12-ft. ceiling. The Gathering Room is surrounded by tall windows; the Good Morning Room features porch access; and the island kitchen offers a double oven, a pantry and a snack bar.
- Guests will dine in style in the formal dining room, with its 13-ft. tray ceiling and trio of tall, arched windows.
- Curl up with a good book in the quiet library, which has an airy 10-ft. ceiling.
- A 12-ft. ceiling enhances the fantastic master suite, which is wrapped in windows. The superb master bath boasts a step-up garden tub, a separate shower, two vanities, a makeup table and a bidet.
- Two sleeping suites on the other side of the home have 10-ft. ceilings and share a unique bath with private vanities.

Plan EOF-8

Bedrooms: 3+	Baths: 3½
Living Area:	
Main floor	3,392 sq. ft.
Total Living Area:	**3,392 sq. ft.**
Garage	871 sq. ft.
Exterior Wall Framing:	2x6

Foundation Options:

Slab

(All plans can be built with your choice of foundation and framing. A generic conversion diagram is available. See order form.)

BLUEPRINT PRICE CODE: E

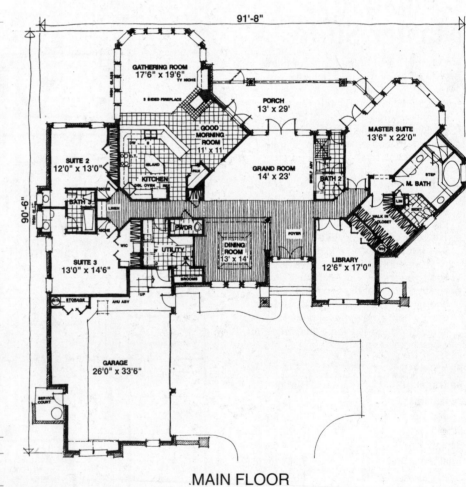

.MAIN FLOOR

TO ORDER THIS BLUEPRINT, CALL TOLL-FREE 1-800-547-5570

Plan EOF-8

PRICES AND DETAILS ON PAGES 12-15

Luxurious, Open Contemporary

This contemporary "open concept" plan is great for the established family and couples who enjoy entertaining. The vaulted "Great Room" features an overhead balcony. Breakfast, kitchen and dining areas feature standard ceilings, which emphasize the height of the vaulted Great Room.

A centrally located stone fireplace is the home's focal point, offering visual privacy to first floor areas. Major areas of the home are oriented to a view toward the rear.

This home is 81'6" wide by 52' deep, excluding your custom deck configuration. Total square footage of home is 3,425 sq. ft., not including the oversized garage.

First floor:	2,016 sq. ft.
Second floor:	1,409 sq. ft.
Total living area:	3,425 sq. ft.

(Not counting garage or basement)
Please specify crawlspace or standard basement.

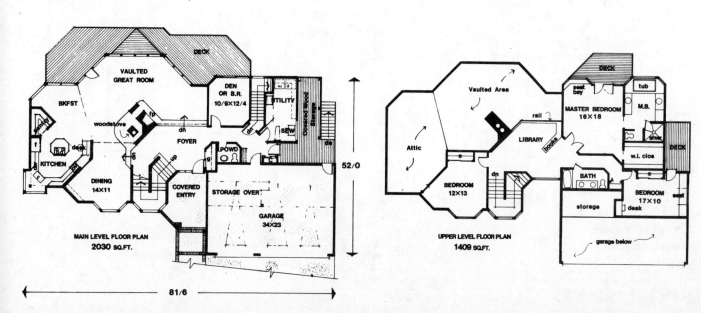

MAIN LEVEL FLOOR PLAN
2030 SQ.FT.

81/6

52/0

UPPER LEVEL FLOOR PLAN
1409 SQ.FT.

Photo Courtesy Northwest Home Design

Superb Views

- This superb multi-level home is designed to take full advantage of spectacular surrounding views.
- The two-story-high entry welcomes guests in from the covered front porch. An open-railed stairway and a 23-ft. domed ceiling are highlights here.
- The sunken living and dining rooms are defined by archways and face out to a large wraparound deck. The living room has a 13-ft. cathedral ceiling and a nice fireplace. The dining room offers a 9½-ft. domed ceiling and a wet bar.
- The octagonal island kitchen hosts a Jenn-Aire range, a sunny sink and a bayed breakfast nook. Nearby, the utility room reveals a walk-in pantry, laundry facilities and garage access.
- The quiet den boasts a second fireplace, a cozy window seat and deck access.
- The entire upper floor is occupied by the master bedroom suite, which has a spacious bayed sleeping room with a 12½-ft. cathedral ceiling. Other features include a huge walk-in closet, separate dressing areas and a private bath with a curved shower and a Jacuzzi tub.
- The exciting daylight basement has a recreation room, an exercise room and another bedroom, plus a sauna and a hot tub surrounded by windows!

Plan NW-229

Bedrooms: 2+	Baths: 2½
Living Area:	
Upper floor	815 sq. ft.
Main floor	1,446 sq. ft.
Daylight basement	1,330 sq. ft.
Total Living Area:	**3,591 sq. ft.**
Garage	720 sq. ft.
Exterior Wall Framing:	2x6

Foundation Options:

Daylight basement

(All plans can be built with your choice of foundation and framing. A generic conversion diagram is available. See order form.)

BLUEPRINT PRICE CODE: **F**

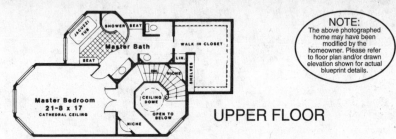

NOTE:
The above photographed home may have been modified by the homeowner. Please refer to floor plan and/or drawn elevation shown for actual blueprint details.

UPPER FLOOR

MAIN FLOOR

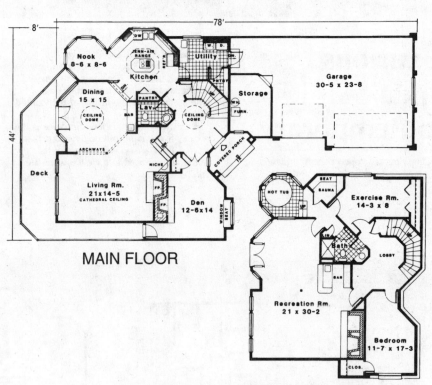

DAYLIGHT BASEMENT

REAR VIEW

Spacious Western Ranch

- A three-bedroom sleeping wing is separated from the balance of the home, with the master suite featuring a raised tub below skylights and a walk-in dressing room.
- Sunken living room is enhanced by a vaulted ceiling and fireplace with raised hearth.
- Family room is entered from the central hall through double doors; a wet bar and a second fireplace grace this gathering spot.
- Kitchen has functional L-shaped arrangement, attached nook, and pantry.

Plan H-3701-1A

Bedrooms: 4	Baths: 3½
Total living area:	3,735 sq. ft.
Garage:	830 sq. ft.
Exterior Wall Framing:	2x4

Foundation options:
Crawlspace only.
(Foundation & framing conversion diagram available — see order form.)

Blueprint Price Code:	F

110'-0"

DECK

BEDROOM 16'-6"×20'-0"

wdw. seat

BATH 12'-7"×12'-2" skylights

WC

Shower

SUNKEN LIVING ROOM 30'-0"×20'-0"

DINING 15'-9"×14'-0"

steps down

vaulted ceiling

clerestory window

WET BAR

KITCHEN 15'-4"×11'-6"

ref.

linen dresser

raised tub

WALK-IN DRESSING ROOM 11'-3"×7'-6"

furnace

raised hearth

PANTRY

dw

CLOSET

LINEN

STOR

POWDER ROOM

ENTRY 15'-3"×15'-3"

BEDROOM 12'-0"×14'-6"

BATH

LAV

BEDROOM 12'-0"×14'-6"

CLOSET

CLOSET

NOOK 11'-6"×10'-0"

DECK

wdw. seat

wdw. seat

FAMILY ROOM 15'-0"×24'-0"

LAUNDRY skylight

D W

Shower

BATH

furnace

THREE CAR GARAGE 31'-10"×23'-8"

BEDROOM 19'-0"×13'-0"

CLOSET

STORAGE

wdw. seat

64'-0"

Stately Colonial

- A magnificent columned portico and numerous windows adorn the exterior of this classic American home.
- The formal foyer is flanked by the dining and living rooms, both with ample living space and tall windows.
- For more casual occasions, the family will enjoy the spacious sunken den accented with exposed beams, a fireplace, built-in bookshelves and access to the screened backyard porch.
- Open railings distinguish the den from the adjoining breakfast room. Sliding glass doors allow dining to be extended to the porch.
- The U-shaped kitchen has a windowed sink and a handy pantry.
- The luxurious master suite boasts a recessed ceiling, two walk-in closets and a skylighted private bath with a tiled garden tub.
- The second floor holds four bedrooms, two with their own baths. Another bath services the two front-facing bedrooms.

Plan C-8334

Bedrooms: 5	Baths: 4 full, 2 half
Living Area:	
Upper floor	1,403 sq. ft.
Main floor	2,334 sq. ft.
Total Living Area:	**3,737 sq. ft.**
Daylight basement	1,460 sq. ft.
Garage and storage	578 sq. ft.
Exterior Wall Framing:	2x4

Foundation Options:

Daylight basement

Crawlspace

(All plans can be built with your choice of foundation and framing. A generic conversion diagram is available. See order form.)

BLUEPRINT PRICE CODE:	F

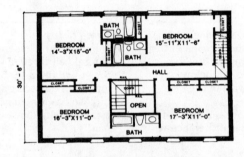

UPPER FLOOR

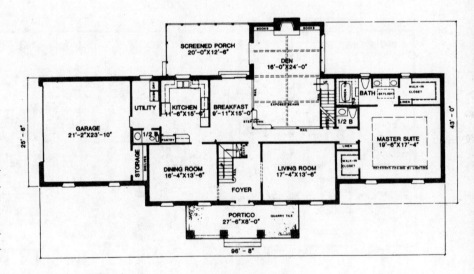

MAIN FLOOR

Plan C-8334

PRICES AND DETAILS ON PAGES 12-15

Photo by Mark Englund/HomeStyles

Exquisitely Done

- The circular front steps, the stately two-story entryway and the three-car side garage give an indication of the exquisite interior features you'll find.
- The foyer with sweeping stairway opens to flanking formal living areas and a massive family room to the rear with a vaulted ceiling and a masonry fireplace.
- The roomy gourmet kitchen and bayed breakfast room feature a nearby wet bar and pantry; attached is a skylighted screened porch with built-in barbecue.
- A library sits next to the beautiful master suite with a coffered ceiling and a spacious bath with a huge garden tub and a curved shower.
- Three additional bedrooms share the upper level with a balcony that overlooks the foyer below.

Plan DD-4458

Bedrooms: 4	Baths: 3½
Living Area:	
Upper floor	1,067 sq. ft.
Main floor	3,391 sq. ft.
Total Living Area:	**4,458 sq. ft.**
Standard basement	3,391 sq. ft.
Garage	774 sq. ft.
Exterior Wall Framing:	2x4

Foundation Options:
Standard basement
Crawlspace
Slab
(Typical foundation & framing conversion diagram available—see order form.)

BLUEPRINT PRICE CODE: G

NOTE:
The above photographed home may have been modified by the homeowner. Please refer to floor plan and/or drawn elevation shown for actual blueprint details.

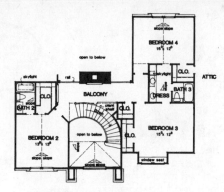

UPPER FLOOR

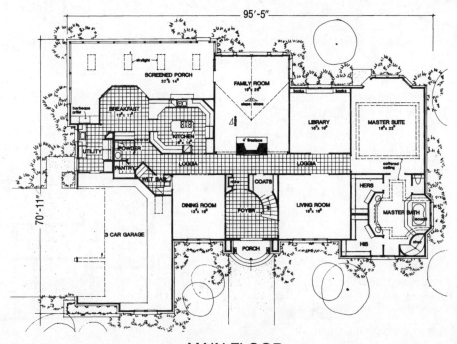

MAIN FLOOR

Photo by Mark Englund/HomeStyles

Beauty and Balance

- A beautiful front porch topped by a trio of dormers gives this plan its striking beauty and balance.
- A spacious foyer bisects the formal living areas, which feature built-in shelves and views of the porch.
- At the center of the home is a spacious Great Room with an inviting fireplace and three French doors that open to a covered back porch.
- A handy butler's pantry with a wet bar and a pantry closet lies between the Great Room and the Keeping Room.
- A snack bar unites the island kitchen with the sunny breakfast room and the Keeping Room, which offers a warm fireplace flanked by built-in shelves.
- The spectacular master suite boasts his-and-hers baths, two walk-in closets and a spiral staircase that leads to an upper-floor study.
- A versatile sitting room rests at the center of the upper floor, surrounded by three bedrooms, two baths and the study or optional fifth bedroom.

Plan V-4566

Bedrooms: 4+	Baths: 4½
Living Area:	
Upper floor	1,847 sq. ft.
Main floor	2,719 sq. ft.
Total Living Area:	**4,566 sq. ft.**
Exterior Wall Framing:	2x6

Foundation Options:

Crawlspace

(All plans can be built with your choice of foundation and framing. A generic conversion diagram is available. See order form.)

BLUEPRINT PRICE CODE:	**G**

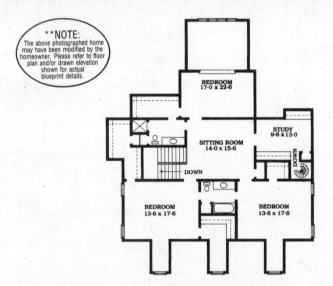

NOTE:
The above photographed home may have been modified by the homeowner. Please refer to floor plan and/or drawn elevation shown for actual blueprint details.

UPPER FLOOR

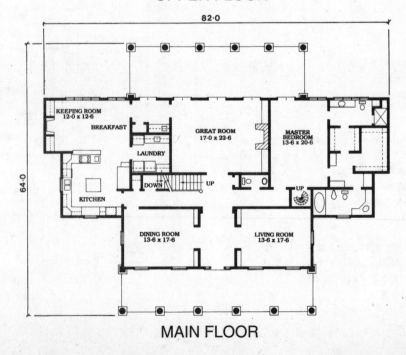

MAIN FLOOR

TO ORDER THIS BLUEPRINT, CALL TOLL-FREE 1-800-547-5570   Plan V-4566   *PRICES AND DETAILS ON PAGES 12-15*